REACHING FOR THE STARS

MELVYN EARLE

This gay lives in Waddingham!

LANTHANUM PRESS

First published in Great Britain in 2021 by Lanthanum Press.

Designed by Leigh Brown Design
Cover photograph: Olena Earle
Colour plates: Melvyn Earle

First impression printed in Spain by Gráficas Zamudio Printek

ISBN 978-1-8383695-0-7

LANTHANUM PRESS

www.lanthanum-press.co.uk

To my mother and father,
Marie,
Christina and Catherine,
Olena and Yuliya
and all my wonderful friends,
without whom this book would not have been possible.
And with special thanks to Jock,
without whose encouragement I would never have thought to write it.

Contents

Chapter One
My Way

When it was suggested I ought to write my autobiography, I didn't expect it would be easy but no sooner had I put pen-to-paper than I was confronted by so many conflicts and hard choices that it nearly didn't happen.

Begin with one of the darkest moments of your life, advised a writer friend: *the sudden death of your elder daughter in March 2018. She was 31, at the height of her career as a senior journalist on The Sun and married for little more than eight months. That's a compelling starting point.*

It is.

It *was* distressing. It *was* heart-rending. But that one black moment in our family's history doesn't define my life. It certainly didn't define hers. So to start there would be to set aside 31 years of her life and everything that went before – all the fun times we shared, the comical moments, the good times and the achievements that preceded that terrible day – and it would be to see her out of context and misunderstand her as much as me.

I know Christina would not want to be the centre of attention and I can almost hear her urging me: *Dad, ignore him. Tell the little stories we used to laugh about. Let others laugh along with them. Don't write my story. I'll be in it but in all the right places. Write your story.*

I didn't take her advice often enough. This time I will.

So, this is my story. Christina will be in it...in all the right places.

As much as I'm writing it for you, I'm also writing it for her and for those close to me who knew us both.

My life has been good, very good. There have been a few dramatic ups and downs but overall it's been fun. I've enjoyed it and I'm still enjoying it.

If I can pinch the words of my writer friend...this is not so much an autobiography, more the diary of a reporter-of-things, eye-witness reflections on events...while I've had a hand in a few, there are many more in which I haven't. Things of interest – sometimes even fascination – have happened around me.

But at least *I was there!*

I've always thought of biographies as the preserve of the rich and famous or those accredited with the title of celebrity, either for reason of talent or because of some rather tawdry episode that catapulted them out of the shadows and into the hands of scandal-hungry media.

I don't belong to the super-rich clan, though my life has been filled with enriching and entertaining experiences, so without any tawdry episodes to spice the pages of a book and no real claim to fame either, you can quite imagine my reaction when that writer friend, a biographer, journalist and broadcaster with a string of books to his name – someone who should know what makes a good read – asked *When are you going to write your autobiography?*

I've spent most of my working life as a writer and editor, though I started out as a musician and even won minor accolades as a composer before rising through the teaching ranks to Head of Music in a high school. I left teaching to establish a furniture-design business that later morphed into a publishing company with Furniture Journal at its core.

Alongside that, photography has been a lifelong passion. I started my own business when I was 11 years of age, mostly taking portraits of kids and animals for doting mothers, plus the occasional wedding. I've put on a few solo photographic exhibitions in later life and will do more when time allows.

There's scarcely a day passes when I'm not in my studio shooting products for magazines, in a factory photographing the captains of industry, or poking my lens inside some new design of machine. I travel the length and breadth of Europe to get the images I need.

I particularly enjoy special-effect photography and most of my commercial photographs have been published either as backdrops to articles or in advertisements. Even in leisure time, I'm seldom seen without a camera in my hand. I've put together a series of themed coffee-table photo collections on diverse topics and have recently learned to case-bind.

Business etiquette accords me the title Managing Director and although I'm nobody's idea of a Dragon's Den star, in a modest way I've enjoyed successes and ridden the roller-coaster of business for over 30 years.

I'm immensely proud and grateful that so many global manufacturers – the best in their field – have put their trust in me, taken me into their confidence and allowed me to write about their ground-breaking technologies, often in intimate detail and before any hint of their entrance to the market has been made public.

It has been a privilege and at times, a humbling experience to work with such talented people.

Along the way, I have also enjoyed the role of philanthropist whenever the opportunity has presented itself and always go the extra mile to support new businesses and novel ideas in the articles I write and edit.

There have been times when the winds of political change have decimated plans and I've found myself moving two steps back for every one I've moved forwards – many times, in fact – but weathering the storms and establishing straight and level when turbulence passes are all part of life in business.

There's nothing here to make me stand out from anyone else.

I'm better known as Editor than Managing Director – both are positions I've occupied since 1990 – but en route to the black leather chair, as well as calling myself a photographer, I've been

an organist and choirmaster,
first euphonium in a brass band,
a trombonist (not a very good one),
a pianist,
a composer,
a kitchen slave in an Asian restaurant,
a teacher (of music and photography),
a furniture designer,
a salesman (advertising),
a publisher,
a pilot (aeroplanes),
the financial backer and partner in an aviation business,
an amateur scuba diver,
an artist (of sorts),
the principal investor and MD of a car-wash business,
father to two beautiful daughters,
step-father to a third,
and husband to two lovely ladies (not both at the same time, of course).

I love all things creative and thrive on blue-sky thinking. I'm a prolific letter-writer and thoroughly enjoy getting to grips with a good article.

My CV doesn't demonstrate a straight-line career to stardom, nothing like and recounting my school days in any detail would be a very bad example for any youngster who might get to read this.

That's your cue to look away if you haven't already chosen a career route.

Aside from music, art and pottery, in which I always excelled because I enjoyed them, my school reports usually read, 'Melvyn has ability but could do better with more effort'. It was a euphemism to disguise a reality my teachers understood well: 'Melvyn thinks the subject is irrelevant, doesn't like the teacher and sees no point in wasting his life on either.'

What they couldn't understand was why someone who once came out of an IQ test with a score that, had the teacher in charge known anything about it, would have pushed him well into Mensa territory – a student who had led the school chess team from the age of 12 – couldn't do algebra.

They hadn't figured out, it wasn't *couldn't*, it was *didn't want to*.

I didn't see how it had any relevance to me, so, as with many supposedly 'academic' school subjects that held little or no interest, I made negligible effort.

I considered myself immensely lucky when, during a detention for passing notes in a chemistry lesson, a handful of friends and I created a firework while our sixth-form minder was otherwise occupied and accidentally demolished the glass cabinet when our third attempt at a rocket went out of control.

I was the tallest so I took the blame and was immediately banished from chemistry lessons. That was fine because it meant I had more free time to play the school organ and practise for piano lessons.

In fact, it was doubly fine: the chemistry teacher was also the physics teacher and thus ended any prospect of me pursuing a career in physics.

At least the biology teacher had nice legs. I enjoyed her lessons.

French and German I fared badly at, too, though I'm told I converse tolerably well in both nowadays. I seem to remember spending more French lessons stood in a corner with my hands on my head than I ever spent reading the adventures of Monsieur et Madame Thibaut or conjugating être in every variant of past, present and future.

Geography – well, I may be of good Yorkshire stock but there was only so much I was prepared to absorb about limestone regions and sheep-farming.

History... I lost interest shortly after cave man.

Ironically, perhaps, I'm now fascinated by ancient civilisations, archaeology enthrals me and I love nothing better than to visit far-off places and absorb myself in the geography and culture of different countries whenever the opportunity presents itself.

My first wife, Marie, had French ancestors; my second wife, Olena, is Ukrainian. We have five languages in our house. Some of my closest friends are French, Spanish, German, Italian, Russian or American and I am an ardent Francophile.

Everything was in there from a young age. Six years of Grammar School education just didn't bring it out.

You might think I would have been good at English – in fact, I was. At least the writing part.

Creative writing, letter-writing, précis...they came easily to me. Literature never really lit my candle, so I never made it past O-Level. I am woefully unfamiliar with the classics and I'm not a reader of fiction or horror. There's more than enough fiction and horror on TV for me. Normally, I switch over to something factual, historical, philosophical, cultural or a current affairs programme, though I'm never sure whether The News fits better into fiction or horror these days, so more often than not, I don't even watch that with much enthusiasm.

The only book I've ever read from cover-to-cover that wasn't either a photography book or a necessary academic tome for university was the 1968 paperback, Chariots of the Gods by Erich von Däniken. I found it so absorbing I read it twice to make sure I hadn't missed anything.

Oh, and Keith Floyd's cookery books. He's my idol in the kitchen – and the best TV chef ever! His *quick slurp* and *don't watch* asides to cameraman Clive always made me laugh and I loved the spontaneity in his programmes as much as the impromptu style of his cheffery.

I left school with three high-grade A-levels in the subjects I *did* like and a handful of the umpteen diplomas and degrees I went on to collect in music but a despicably low grade in maths – pretty close to the bottom of the pile, as I recall.

I'd spent most of the O-level maths exam composing the first movement of a string quartet in my head and just wanted to get out of the exam room to put it down on paper. The maths exam simply got in the way of a creative moment. Did that mean I was rubbish at maths? That's what I was told. That's what my father was told.

But when I took up flying, I never needed a calculator to work out wind speeds and headings, fuel endurance or any of the calculations for which most pilots use special calculators.

Things that were relevant to me I enjoyed, so I was good at them. I enjoyed flying and collected ratings as enthusiastically as I'd once collected diplomas in music. The maths had relevance and it came easily to me.

I did the cash-flows for business on the back of a three-metre sheet of wallpaper taped to my office wall. While the maths graduate we employed in our accounts department constructed incomprehensibly-elaborate spreadsheets to prove God-knows-what, my predictions were always closer to the mark.

If you take where I am now to be the measure of my success, the lesson in it for recruiters might be not to place so much store in exam results and look instead at potential. It's more difficult to measure but considerably more worthwhile, as I've found out many times while recruiting others to my own modest venture.

So now you know I was more of a maverick than a model student and any career teacher would regard my career path as the stuff of nightmares, what can I bring to the party?

My encouragement lies in a passage from the opening chapter of a book by Jock Gallagher, the writer who inspired me to embark on this quest:

This is not an autobiography although it is of necessity autobiographical, he writes. *It's not about me although it does tabulate something of what I've been doing while on this mortal coil and it's perhaps a hopeful assertion that my life has not been wasted. I hope I will have left some faint tracks along the way.*

Chapter Two
Meet the Family

Every good biography needs at least a few facts, right? Even those that don't aspire to be biographies in the purest sense. Let's get a few out of the way to put things in perspective:

I was born on a freezing November evening in an outlying district of Leeds, West Yorkshire, the only son of Doreen, a dressmaker and Dennis, a commercial artist. In those days, home births were commonplace and I was one of them.

I have it on good authority that the midwife, who arrived in the middle of a snowstorm, hadn't taken kindly to Father's presence during my début. Her opinion didn't improve when, on seeing me emerge, he apparently proclaimed, *Oh God, isn't it awful? Put it back!*

I'm rather glad she took no heed.

For the next fifty-seven years, I enjoyed the most incredible relationship with both my father and my mother. They were model parents, model grandparents, inspirational mentors to two generations and constant friends to the whole clan.

I owe them a debt of gratitude, not only for the immensely-creative genes they passed down but also for their continual support and encouragement, the confidence they inspired and an underlying ethos they shared that both empowered and motivated the whole family to give their all to any and every undertaking.

I'm also grateful for the fun times, the humour, the experiences and for sharing their view of the world, a view that inspired me to explore new angles and find things of interest, even in the most mundane of corners.

My earliest recollection is knocking seven bells out of a tulip in the garden at the age of about two, an event Father captured on the 35mm Voigtländer Vito B camera that seldom left his side. The image became a family classic.

More often, he was to be seen pointing his lens at odd things few would consider worth committing to film...arrangements of seaweed and pebbles in the sand, relics from old boats, fragments of sun-bleached timber, patterns in mud. It was not so much what they were, nor even what they appeared to be that interested him, though he'd effervesce enthusiastically over their colour, texture, shape and form.

He photographed them for their potential to inspire and become something entirely different; for what he could turn them into when he returned to his art studio.

From the most unlikely subject matter, he developed designs for curtains, upholstery fabrics and carpets that would outsell the best-sellers on the market time and time again. The way his mind worked was fascinating and six decades on, I still find myself following his lead, looking at things, situations, people, products – life – from outside the box.

Mother and Father were like two pieces from the same jigsaw: they were a perfect fit, devoted, in unison, always together. They didn't always see eye-to-eye but there was seldom a cross word between them, even though she affectionately nicknamed him Head Grumbly in later life.

She was kind, patient, attentive – his equal but in her own way.

In her prime, she designed and made elaborate wedding dresses with richly-embroidered trains (including her own), formal and informal outfits, blouses, skirts, coats, jackets... There seemed to be nothing she couldn't create out of material and thread.

For the family, she made trousers, shirts, even tailored jackets. I can clearly recall the shirts she made for Father and me out of old parachutes and the buckets of Dylon she'd mix in the kitchen sink to colour them.

She was just as resourceful and creative in the kitchen as she was skilled with the old Singer sewing machine I used to play under with my toy cars and aeroplanes while she worked.

Those were pre-school times; the days of 'Watch with Mother' and the black-and-white test card that appeared when there were no programmes on the box.

Later, in my early teenage years, when we first started to venture abroad for holidays, she'd research for hours, scouring the pages of borrowed travel books in search of things to see and do – and restaurants we could visit to sample the local cuisine.

On arrival at one of her chosen restaurants, she'd order some exotic delicacy we'd never heard of and while we all enjoyed it, she would make detailed notes of the ingredients so the dish could be recreated when we returned home.

It's a habit I've adopted from time to time.

I remember very clearly one of our first holidays on the Costa del Sol. In one of her library books, she'd found a harbour-side restaurant in the fishing village of Blanes, famed for its Zarzuela de Pescado, an elaborate fish stew. It was a train ride from the hotel but we found it.

Our Zarzuela arrived in a vast paella pan that overflowed with freshly-caught fish, clams, mussels and a choir of giant crevettes that hung over the sides. They'd been cooked to perfection in a delicious tomato and garlic sauce. Perched high on the top was a lobster of gargantuan proportions. With crusty white bread and a crisp white wine that Mother had identified as the perfect companion, it was nothing short of divine.

Zarzuela de Pescado became a firm family favourite, one she recreated many times in her own kitchen.

I inherited her love of cooking and in much the same way, I've added countless dishes to the family repertoire from Spain, Portugal, Italy, Germany, France, Morocco, America, Thailand, Pakistan and India – pretty much everywhere I've visited since and one or two places I haven't.

While the friends I made in early school years took turns to leap off the coal bunker with toy guns and pursue imaginary Red Indians around the garden astride imaginary horses, I was often to be found in my grandfather's workshop. He was a cabinet-maker, though he seemed able to turn his hand to anything practical.

His workshop was fascinating: shafts of light penetrated the sawdust-engrained net curtains Grandma had insisted on hanging to obscure row upon row of sharpened chisels from prying eyes; the smell of freshly-sawn oak mingled with the oil from a well-used sharpening stone; the neatly laid out workbench with shelves of screws, all meticulously arranged by size; the sheets of elaborately-figured veneer he kept in racks; and the cramps that hung from the wall.

It wasn't a big workshop. It was a very cosy place, a haven from the pounding of pretend hooves and shouts of *Geronimo!* from the garden outside.

From him, I learned to cut joints, book-match veneers, cut marquetry, add stringing lines – even lay stone for ornamental gardens.

The day he died, I thought I would, too. I was just 11 and he had been my rock.

Grandma – his wife and my maternal grandmother – was of altogether different character. Granddad's passing heralded a major upheaval, both for her and for our small family. She couldn't countenance being on her own so her house was sold, our house was sold and the whole family upped sticks and moved in together.

Grandma was a tiny little lady, quite portly but as best I can recall, no more than five feet tall in bare feet. Not that you ever wanted to see her in bare feet. She had bunions like golf balls and yellow toenails that turned up like crinkle-cut chips at the edges.

But she was a real sweetie. There was nothing she wouldn't do for anyone who needed help and she had earned something of a name for her charitable endeavours. In middle age, she was apparently very active, always knitting for people, crocheting, arranging coffee mornings for the WI and inviting folks around to her house.

She was a prolific and talented baker of all manner of cakes and buns and she enjoyed fund-raising and getting involved with charity work and the local community. Granddad never quite knew what he was coming home to. There were frequent stories of furniture being rearranged, even whole rooms being stripped of wallpaper and redecorated in his absence.

After his death, her confidence and zest for life gradually ebbed away. She reverted to the post-Victorian values of her childhood, developed curious habits and a general timidity and fear of life that manifested in odd ways. Oh, and a problem – a *waterworks* problem.

Grandma loved Scotland so every year after Granddad died, we took her on an annual pilgrimage to the Lowlands. We never ventured to the Highlands. Grandma would start her *I'm going to die* routine every time Father drove anywhere near hills. She hated the thought of having to look down over precipices.

Apart from screams of fear, tears and feigned angina attacks, it brought on the dreaded *urgency*. We always knew what she meant when she said she had the *urgency*. It came on at the most inconvenient times but Mother was always well-prepared.

On one holiday in particular, the summer after Granddad's death, we were heading up the A1 towards Scotland – our normal convoluted route to the northwest along a road that tracks broadly northeast – when one of Grandma's *urgencies* struck.

Normally, it would be mentioned discreetly in whispers. If the call was not heard, the volume and frequency would increase until Father, whose deafness was the result of wartime experience adjusting guns under the wings of aeroplanes while someone else fired them, finally noticed.

On this particular occasion, Grandma's *urgency* must have gone unnoticed for a while and by the time news had reached the front seats, she was all but ready to pop her cork.

Father applied the brakes heavily, slung the car into the first available stopping point and left a ten-yard skid mark on the tarmac. Everyone piled out, except Grandma. Father opened the boot, Mother rummaged dutifully amid the sandwiches, flasks of tea and coffee, suitcases and toys and after some minutes, during which the *urgency* from within the car had reached red alert and heart attacks had been threatened, Mother emerged triumphantly bearing a small, pink, plastic potty.

It has to be said, while potties could no doubt have been purchased in more inconspicuous colours, Grandma liked pink. Bright pink. Screaming bright pink. Discreet it was not. It all but glowed in the dark.

Dutifully, Mother presented the objet d'art to Grandma who was waiting as patiently as the *urgency* would allow but nevertheless seemed to be corkscrewing on the back seat of the Wolseley. Next, rugs and blankets were hastily ushered from the boot and like the ceremonious unveiling of some historic monument in reverse, the car was draped until all the windows were obscured. A call from within confirmed all trace of daylight had been eradicated and Grandma commenced the matinée performance.

Eventually, Mother received the signal from behind a rug and re-entered the mummified Wolseley to extract the potty, now swathed neatly in a matching-pink tea towel that had been purchased for the task of hiding the goods.

The Wolseley, affectionately known as 'The Mrs' because of its now highly-desirable number plate, MRS 86, was one of Father's better cars and it was one of the few he ever managed to keep more or less in one piece.

Its immediate predecessor, an Austin A70, hadn't fared so well and spent much of the short time we had it mounting kerbs and challenging stone walls. As a result, it was more fibreglass than metal, more rust than chrome and more patchwork than paintwork.

Religiously, before every journey, we'd be underneath it together, applying cans of resin mixed with powder to fibreglass sheet in a futile attempt to reattach bits that had separated during its off-road adventures and fill holes in the floor pan in case it rained.

The Mrs was at least whole and functioning when he bought it. And it didn't leak. All the same, I clearly remember bequeathing two new leather footballs, given to me as birthday presents, to bolster the sagging leaf suspension at the rear when The Mrs developed bottom crunch after getting airborne, fully-laden and at high speed, from a hump-backed bridge.

Such things never fazed Father. He had no feeling for the limitations of engineering. A car was just a car; *a box on wheels*, he'd call it. If it made hideous grinding noises when the gears were changed or kangarooed to a halt when he forgot to depress the clutch, clearly it wasn't a good car and we needed to look for another.

It had taken him 13 attempts to pass his driving test and the pass was probably a fluke – that or Father had scared the examiner so badly that a pass certificate had been issued hurriedly in order to expedite the examiner's escape.

Even at the ripe old age of 87, he was still frightening rabbits in the lanes, mounting the verges as he passed at breakneck speed and tearing along in second gear because he couldn't hear the engine was pleading for third.

By that time, we'd bought him a new BMW, a little three-series in dark blue with a whole bunch of extras he never managed to figure out. It was easily the best car he'd had but still he couldn't resist remodelling it occasionally on a fence, a wall or some other inconsiderate object that had apparently leapt out from the hedgerow at an inopportune moment.

Mother was quite content to sit at the side and admire the view, whatever scraped down the side. She never learned to drive and seldom criticised.

It was most probably from my paternal grandmother, or her line, that I inherited my musical ability. It can only have been a genetic inheritance. There was never any hint of encouragement from her. She was an entirely different kettle of fish to the rest of the family. She lived in a little cottage in a remote corner of Old Farnley, near Leeds – it's long since been demolished – and to the end of her life, she remained aloof from most of those around her except the folks who lived opposite.

They had a very high-sounding name – Delahunty I think it was – and she loved it. She used to relish every opportunity to enunciate it, rolling it around with great pleasure before releasing it from her lips with exaggerated theatrical diction. I believe the origins of the name are Irish (there's what's described as a contemporary Irish restaurant with a similar name in Dublin), much like her own maiden name, Maher.

But I digress.

Father's father, who died some years before I was born, was brought up to be a country gentleman but somewhere along the line, the mansion and the inheritance due to him had been lost. It's rumoured someone drank it away.

My paternal grandmother was his second wife and she was determined to continue the image of aristocracy that came with marrying an Earl – even if grandfather was an Earle with an extra 'e'.

Unapproachable, arrogant, indifferent to opinion and always on stage when in company, she enjoyed the spotlight and played the part well.

In her day, she was reputed to have played the piano reasonably, though my only recollection of her at the keyboard was being subjected to after-dinner renditions from the musical Chu Chin Chow. She'd vamp out a chord and howl a few notes at high volume that didn't seem to fit with anything her hands were doing on the keyboard before turning the page and mercilessly annihilating the first few bars of some other piece from early 20th century music-hall repertoire.

I don't remember her ever finishing a piece but her performance over, she'd smile condescendingly to her audience and lower the lid to mark the end of the concert. That was my cue to play for a while. Aged three or four, I hadn't yet learned how to add tunes to chords, let alone read music but it was fun. Until the lid was lowered again.

Children should be seen and not heard, she'd say.

She was intensely intolerant, especially of me or so it seemed.

The only other thing I can remember about her was that she had one functioning eye. The other was glass. I saw it once when it fell in the salad bowl.

My earliest recollection is knocking seven bells out of a tulip in the garden at the age of about two but it's clear the indifference I felt for gardening started much earlier.

1946 – before my time. Mother and Father were like two pieces from the same jigsaw: they were a perfect fit, devoted, in unison, always together.

I enjoyed the most incredible relationship with both my mother and my father.

My maternal grandparents lived next door.
From my grandfather I learned cabinet-making.
Grandma was a great baker and there seemed to
be nothing she couldn't knit or crochet too.

From a very early age, I wanted to learn to play the piano.
This was an early concert performance on Grandma's piano
– before the lid was lowered.

Father's mother was an entirely different kettle
of fish to the rest of the family. She was intensely
intolerant, especially of me or so it seemed.

Father's father, who died some years before I was born,
was brought up to be a country gentleman but somewhere
along the line, the mansion and the inheritance due to him
had been lost.

Chapter Three
Schooldays, Music and Photography

From a very early age, I wanted to learn to play the piano. Both my parents had been obliged to learn from childhood and had not enjoyed the experience. They never progressed far and didn't want me to go through what they'd been obliged to endure. Ergo, it wasn't until the whole family moved and I started a new school that the opportunity presented itself to learn an instrument.

But it wasn't the piano I started with.

What I brought home to practise on was something far more entertaining. It was big. It was loud. And until I'd mastered control of embouchure and diaphragm, it was vulgar – like some large animal with excruciatingly-bad flatulence.

I loved it.

It was my kind of instrument.

It was a euphonium, the harmonious tenor of the brass band and it wasn't long before I'd progressed sufficiently to join a local band.

Brass-band contests followed, along with concerts in the park, marches through the streets on auspicious occasions, even the odd solo opportunity. My party piece was always the 'Grandfather's Clock' theme and variations, though the finale with the long high note at the end gave the odd anxious moment.

At much the same time, realising music was not just a passing phase – or, perhaps, realising school reports weren't showing an obvious track to stardom in other subjects – Mother and Father succumbed, took me to piano lessons and bought a second-hand piano on which I could practise.

I progressed rapidly and was soon taking organ lessons as well. Music became my preoccupation, my passion, my escape – and the perfect excuse to avoid rugby.

Rugby was *the* game at my school. Anyone who didn't take part was immediately labelled soft – or less complimentary words to that effect – and ostracised by the popular clan, at the head of which was the sports teacher himself.

It wasn't the sport I found distasteful, though I've never been one to engage willingly in mud-baths and mayhem. It wasn't even the steamy-communal-showering session sporty types seem to relish that switched me off to the idea of rugby. At the root of my dislike for the game was the sports teacher himself and wherever possible I avoided him and his derogatory comments about 'arty-farty' people like he had the plague.

Anyone who didn't join in or was lucky enough to have a sick note and could sit out the match on a bench knew they'd be on the receiving end of one of his high-volume, ego-boosting attacks at some point.

What he lacked in stature, he made up for in noise and he used volume to mask an almost-contralto speaking voice that was at odds with the he-man image and the bulging muscles he paraded in front of the mirrors in the changing room when he thought no one was looking.

He would make a point of entering the field with a stern look on his face, eyebrows lowered in an aggressive frown, neck chickening in and out and an odd gait that involved flinging his feet out at an awkward angle and strutting with legs wide apart, as if to imply the presence of something enormous between them that interfered with normal walking.

I suppose one has to resort to such things if one has a speaking voice like a virgin chorister and most of one's mid-teenage charges are significantly taller.

At six feet something, I wasn't just significantly taller, I towered above him.

That made me an instant target for abuse and he never failed to wheel it out in front of an audience. The fact I also wore thick glasses, well…they were the red rag to the bull. I always ended up as tight-head prop in the scrum.

Half a term in and three pairs of glasses down, Father, who could be quite firm when he wanted to be and didn't waste words unnecessarily, paid the sports teacher a visit. I'm given to understand the options presented were either find something else for me to do or pay for all future breakages. The latter option evidently didn't appeal so from then on I was given cross-country routes to run.

That suited me perfectly.

If I ran around the edge of the field, dodged behind the back of the sports hut and hoofed it down the alleyway, I could be in the music suite in under ten minutes.

I always enjoyed a great relationship with the music teacher and although he never said so in as many words, it was clear to all that he was no great fan of the sports teacher either.

For the best part of two years, I used the opportunity to work up piano sonatas and études on my favourite Bechstein grand and practise my closing organ voluntary for the Sunday service at the local church where, by the time I was in the fifth form, I'd managed to secure myself a position as organist and choirmaster.

Just before closure of the rugby session, which usually took most of the afternoon, I'd hop off the piano stool, still wearing my pristine white shorts and running shirt, and, with the music teacher hooting in amusement from the other side of the window, I'd find a muddy puddle to roll in before running back to the rugby field. Carefully timing my arrival until the sports teacher was preoccupied by some event at the opposite end of the field, I'd make my entry, panting and grubby.

In two years, he never noticed I always arrived from the wrong end of the cross-country route.

With O-levels out of the way, a flourishing photographic business already established, and pin-money coming in from playing the organ at funerals, weddings and Sunday services, providing any kind of careers advice for me – at least as far as the careers teacher was concerned – was a waste of time. I was either going to be a musician or a photographer and there was nothing further to be discussed.

Me, I was undecided. I enjoyed both but I also harboured a desire to be a pilot.

Flying, my teacher assured me, wasn't for musicians nor photographers, so eager to find a way of shortening his diary on parents' evening, any potential in the idea was quickly dismissed on the grounds of eyesight. Pilots, he told my Father, don't wear glasses, and that was an end to it.

Every summer holiday, I'd find myself a job in photography and gradually advanced both my ability and my kit bag. It was one such holiday job that provided quite possibly one of the luckiest breaks I've ever had.

I'd just finished a Friday afternoon shift at the local photo-processors where I was working for the summer of '74 and emerged from my darkroom, one of several in a horseshoe around the processing machine, to hear raised voices from the print-delivery area. One of the professional photographers who used the lab – I later discovered he was called Ken – was furious.

My immediate boss, a quiet and unassuming chap who'd innocently found himself in the wrong place at the wrong time, was witnessing the unleashing of fire and brimstone and seemed unable to placate the source.

It transpired Ken's assistant had quit without notice, leaving him in the lurch for an important shoot he'd organised for the weekend.

The studio was ready, everything was in place, he was in a hole and at this late hour, *where was he supposed to find a replacement?*

That seemed to be my cue.

My assistant organist was playing for both Sunday services and there was no wedding on the Saturday, so I wasn't busy that weekend.

What did he need?

Someone to move lights and load cameras.

I can do that.

Can you load Hasselblad backs?

I guess so.

Keen to encourage my interest in photography, Father bought me a Russian-built Lomo Lubitel camera when I was about four years old. This photograph of my maternal grandfather was one of the first portraits I ever took with it.

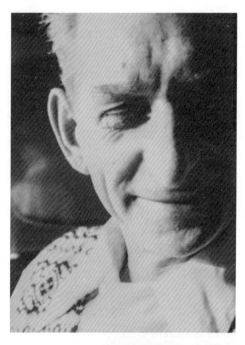

A portrait of my mother, taken when I was about eight years of age on the new 35mm FED 3 rangefinder camera Father bought me for my birthday.

I started my own photography business when I was about 11 years of age, mostly taking portraits of kids and animals for doting mothers, plus the occasional wedding.

I need someone for the whole weekend.

I can be free.

Fine. I'll pick you up tomorrow morning, four o'clock. What's your address?

It's not hard to imagine my father's reaction when I told him over dinner that evening. Questions shot across the table like bullets from a machine gun: *who is this guy? Where are you going? Where are you staying? When will you be back?* There wasn't much I could tell.

It wasn't easy to persuade him but eventually he relented on condition I would telephone.

Four o'clock arrived and Ken pulled up outside in a scruffy, pale-blue Ford Anglia estate that would have been quite at home in Father's scrapbook of old wrecks. Closing the passenger door pressed us together, shoulder to shoulder and I could feel the springs in the base of the seat.

It was noisy, draughty, the heater didn't work, it seemed to be completely divest of suspension and it rattled continuously, even over smooth surfaces. To all intents and purposes, it was little better than a sardine tin on wheels.

It would be our sardine tin for the next five hours: we were heading to London.

Not since I was in my pushchair feeding pigeons in Trafalgar Square had I been to London and as we approached the outskirts, dark, unkempt buildings, tired from centuries of overwork, crowded in from both sides. Claustrophobic, overbearing, oppressive and completely devoid of trees and fields, it was like nowhere I'd ever seen before.

Even the studio was unlike any studio I'd worked in. There was nothing cosy about it. It was vast, warehouse-like and had huge sliding metal doors and few windows. Inside, the lights were dingy and came to life reluctantly but as Ken closed the door behind us, I could see sets with backdrops emerging in two of the corners.

One seemed to consist of nothing more than an elegant bottle sitting on dark velvet. More or less overhead hung a single, dreary lightbulb without a reflector and in front was an old plate camera. *Perfume,* Ken confirmed, noticing my curiosity. *French – for an advert. But we're over here.*

The second set was much more complicated: a fake wall decorated with striped wallpaper stood on stands and in its centre was a glassless Georgian window frame that had been painted white and draped with curtains. In front, a chaise longue had been positioned at an angle. A plain red rug partly obscured wooden flooring that had been laid, polished and left unfinished where the edges went out of shot.

Lights, some on boom arms, were pointing in odd directions, not so much arranged as pushed aside hastily after some previous event.

This one needed to be here, that one needed to be there, *swap that for a Fresnel,* another needed to go behind the window frame. It needed barn doors so the light didn't fall here...

The backs are in that case.

Load six to begin with.

We'll need more later.

Kodachrome is in the fridge over there.

What are we shooting? I asked between instructions that arrived without pause. I could see nothing particularly worth pointing a lens at.

You'll see.

Six backs loaded, I clipped the first to the Hasselblad and pulled out the blind while Ken disappeared through a doorway right of set that had been obscured by a black curtain.

When he returned, he was accompanied by a young lady, a very pretty young lady. She was quite unlike any of the girls I'd ever seen at school: tall, slim, with long, dark, curly hair, she moved as if she was on a cushion of air, almost drifting towards the set in slow motion.

Momentarily, she paused, then she smiled. Ken was behind her. It can only have been at me. There was no one else. Had I died and gone to Heaven? Things like this never happened to me, the tall, long-haired, slightly awkward lad in the baggy jeans and the thick-rimmed bottle-bottoms.

She couldn't have been much older than me but her makeup, her bright red lipstick, the bright red scarf around her neck, that captivating smile... she could have come straight out of the pages of a magazine.

All the same, I remember thinking how strange it was that she should be wearing a trench coat that she'd wrapped around herself and was holding together at the front – and shiny red shoes with the tallest and narrowest of heels that clicked on the concrete at the side of the set as she walked towards it.

I'd never seen anyone wear anything like them before.

As she moved into the lights on the set, she turned towards me, smiled again, slipped the coat off her shoulders and draped herself elegantly on the chaise, one leg in front of the other.

The idea had not crossed my mind, not the slightest hint of an idea, not even in my wildest teenage dreams, that we'd be shooting for men's magazines.

Off and on for the next year-and-a-half, I worked for Ken as his assistant. Sometimes it was once a month, sometimes two or three weekends on the trot. The rattle down to London in the old Ford Anglia seemed to get better and better with each trip and I looked forward to our four o'clock Saturday morning starts eagerly. Even the City seemed less uninviting.

We worked long hours, often late into the evening and it was intensive, non-stop shooting with barely time to grab a sandwich between set and lighting changes. Sometimes we'd shoot jewellery, perfumes, watches, even fashion and accessories.

Fashion shoots were really fast-paced. I enjoyed them most of all. Other times it was models with and without attire. Always, it was for magazines, advertisements or posters.

I learned about softboxes, reflectors, barn doors, honeycombs and gels; about portrait and figure lighting – Holywood lighting, Rembrandt lighting and more.

I learned about quality of light, lighting ratio and the throw and pattern of each reflector; how to use colour, light and shadow to set a mood; colour psychology; how to control shadow density and contrast; exposure, apertures, lenses and, long before the term first appeared in Photo Techniques magazine, how to create an appealing *bokeh*.

Ken was a mine of information and experience. He was always coming up with neat little tricks to enhance his images, many of which I still use in different forms today. But most importantly – and this, I believe, is the essential ingredient many photographers forget – he taught me to look in detail and take the time to understand my subjects so I could bring out something of their character in the photographs I took.

That, for me, was and still is the key to a good portrait. It's far more important than having the latest camera, the newest lenses, or the fanciest lighting equipment because understanding the character of a subject and taking the time to figure out how to bring that out in a picture is the real key to levitating it beyond a sterile recording.

Products also have character and need to be understood to emphasise key facets of their nature. Applying the same guiding principal to the product photography I've been shooting for magazines every day for the last few decades has never failed to get me the shot I needed.

At the end of every weekend, as he dropped me back at home, Ken would hand me an envelope: £100 for a weekend's 'work'.

This was 1974.

Wages were a tenth of what they are today.

Petrol was 50 pence a gallon (4.5 litres).

My first car was a six-year-old Hillman Hunter with 70,000 miles on the clock and it cost me £140.

Ken's £100 was like winning the lottery every week.

By the time I was an undergrad, I'd already worked my way up to an Audi 100 – and a top model Bronica camera with a bunch of Zenzanon lenses that cost a lot more than the car.

Not long after my last A-level exam, with the longest holiday ahead and high hopes of working full-time before starting at the School of Music, Ken died. His Ford Anglia failed to negotiate a bend as he made his way back from London in the rain and he hit a tree. He was only in his late fifties.

Ken's was the last funeral I ever played the organ for. I had to improvise the exit piece because I couldn't read the music for tears. Such a talented guy and an amazing mentor...so tragic.

Good fortune may not have been on Ken's side but being out of work that summer proved not to be my destiny.

I'd exhausted all my usual possibilities when a classmate by the name of Parvez came up with an intriguing suggestion: his father had a small restaurant in the back streets of Bradford – *nothing very special,* he said – and he was going to be working there before heading off to university in the autumn.

If I was willing to be a kitchen slave, wash dishes, clean surfaces and help prepare vegetables, there could be a job for me as well. The pay was poor, the hours were dreadful but while I'd been working for Ken, I'd stopped looking for wedding and portrait work and had handed back the keys to the church.

For the first time since I turned 11, I had no work.

I've never been one for idleness, so I arranged to meet with Parvez and together we drove over to Bradford to meet his father.

I'd always got on well with Parvez. He was studious, clever, never got into trouble but he had asthma. That made him another of the sports teacher's favourite targets because his family had forbidden him to play rugby, so we had something in common. He was also rejected by the popular clan, who didn't take kindly to anyone not visibly testosterone-charged and brimming with bravado. It seemed inevitable we'd end up as friends.

Parvez's family was from Pakistan, though he'd never lived there. They were farmers, quite wealthy farmers, who'd run a successful business in Uganda but they'd been obliged to leave the country when Idi Amin's henchmen drove them out of their house, took their lands and their Mercedes and left them with nothing. Having taken refuge in England, they were starting again.

Parvez had summed the restaurant up pretty well: it was small, desperately in need of painting and from the outside, it was nothing very special to look at but it served the local Pakistani community and they flocked there in droves to fill their three-tier metal lunch boxes.

Inside, there were half a dozen scruffy tables clad in flecked yellow laminate, each with four or five plastic-covered, metal-framed chairs, few of which seemed to match. Four guys, all dressed in unfamiliar garb, had occupied the window seat and were heavily engrossed in conversation when we arrived.

As we made our way towards the glass display cabinet in the corner, the soles of my shoes stuck to the lino flooring, peeling noisily with each step.

Behind the glass and to one side was a large tray of something made with carrot, while at the back were two smaller trays, one with sticky, goo-coated, orange-coloured balls and the other, a deeper tray, contained a mixture I took to be rice pudding. They all looked very exotic.

To one side of the cabinet was a tall fridge, half-full with fizzy drinks – orange, Coca Cola and several with interesting labels I couldn't make out – while at the other was an open doorway that led to the kitchen.

Separated from the seating area only by a dangling fly screen, it was easy to hear the frenetic activity, the chopping and beating and the excited chatter from beyond, though I had no clue what was being said.

I'd entered a foreign country, one I'd never visited before. Just being there made me feel intrepid.

Moments later, the fly-screen parted and a short, stocky, heavily-bearded man – I guessed in his early to mid forties – made his way to the front of the cabinet. This was Chef Hassan, Parvez's father and the bear hug he gave Parvez lifted him momentarily from the sticky lino.

Turning to me, he smiled a big broad smile, placed a hand on his heart and bowed his head. *We will be working in there,* he said in a strongly-accented voice, looking at me from beneath a raised eyebrow that hinted towards an impish sense of humour.

It looked as if I'd already got the job.

When Chef Hassan smiled, it was as if the whole world had no option but to smile with him. His boyish face would crease into deep furrows, he'd throw his head back and burst into the loudest laugh imaginable. He smiled a lot and he laughed a lot, and it was infectious laughter that incited frenetic energy in his kitchen.

Even elbow-deep in soapy water with dirty pans and a small mountain of karahi to chisel the remnants of food from, it was impossible not to feel his enthusiasm, his zest for life, his love for the craft of cooking. This wasn't just a job to him, it had become his life, his passion.

The more he laughed, the faster Parvez and I would work. And always, at the end of service, when the last customer had departed and all the surfaces had been scrubbed, there was something to look forward to.

Father's National Service with the RAF during the war years had left him with an insatiable appetite for spicy food that Mother, who had no experience of the Far Eastern cuisine he'd talk about with such affection, had done her best to satisfy. Her stews with shop-bought curry powder and sultanas added for exotic effect couldn't compete with the fragrance of roasted spices, cardamom, freshly chopped coriander and the multitude of brightly coloured seasonings Chef Hassan would add to his incredible late-night treats.

There was nothing quite like the home-style Seekh Kebab he'd serve with freshly made Raita, the Daig Biriyani – his personal favourite – or the magical Murghi Karahi he'd bring over with hot Naan breads peeled from the inside of his Tandoor.

Fragrant, exotic, magical, they were a window to another world and I wanted to explore it.

As the days and weeks passed by and Parvez and I perfected our teamwork, we'd ask if there were other jobs we could do between dish-washing. Little by little, he'd entrust more to us.

At first it was peeling, scrubbing and preparing vegetables. Sometimes, he'd let us watch as he prepared his Garam Masala. Later, we'd get to grind the cardamoms, cinnamon, peppercorns, cloves and dried bay leaves with a mortar and pestle and on occasions, we were allowed to stir the Gajar ka Halwar (the sweet dessert made from carrot I'd seen when I first came to the restaurant), fry the Gulab Jaman balls in preparation for evening service or prepare sweet Mango Lassi.

Chef Hassan had his own special recipe for that. He seemed to have his own special recipe for everything and without exception, they were all delicious and exciting.

Although the entire extended summer break I spent working in Chef Hassan's kitchen netted me the equivalent of three day's work with Ken, it was an experience that fired my interest in all things culinary and enhanced my enthusiasm for exotic cuisine and the art of cooking.

In later years, the kitchen became my domain and to this day, most hallowed are my spice drawers.

Whenever we had guests at home, preparing dinner would fall to me. Dinner parties, curry evenings with Mother and Father, Christmas feasts, birthday celebrations, anniversary dinners, whatever the occasion I was always to be found in the kitchen.

My experience under the watchful eye of Chef Hassan combined readily with the traditions Mother established when we used to travel as a family, melding into an appreciation of cuisine that spanned continents – and never do we enjoy it more than when friends from far-flung nations come to stay.

Whenever business takes me up north, I still return to Bradford to buy ingredients at the supermarket on Woodhead Road.

Chapter Four
The University Years

Turned down by six universities for having taken 'non-academic' exam subjects, it fell to the School of Music in Huddersfield, in those days part of the Polytechnic, to see if they could make anything of me.

As best I can recall, the interview went modestly well. I'd prepared my piano piece and executed my performance deftly; I'd blown enough right notes on the French horn my school music teacher had convinced my Father to buy; and I'd impressed sufficiently with the test piece I'd been asked to compose. I'd earned my place on the degree course. If my A-level exams included an A in Music, I would be accepted.

When results day arrived, an A in Music was among them and so for the next 12 years, with an illuminated tunnel in front of me pointing at music to the exclusion of all else, I enthusiastically pursued ...completely the wrong career path.

September '75 arrived and the School of Music flung open its doors to another clutch of Freshers. I remember my first day well: everybody milling around in the foyer; Dotty – the School of Music secretary – screeching names from the doorway of her office; second and third years checking notice-boards while the rest of us waited for instructions.

Gradually, order evolved from chaos and the crowd dissipated to leave two smaller groups, diploma students at one side and degree students at the other.

Stood on the boundary, I couldn't help but notice one of the students in the diploma group laughing loudly. It didn't seem to be at me but he'd clearly noticed I'd picked up on his amusement and made his way over. *My name's Dave,* he announced with gusto, slapping me on the back and extending a hand to shake. *What's yours?*

It was to be the start of a lifelong friendship that, in the fullness of time, would see us visiting cathedrals and churches together, playing organs, turning pages for each other during performances, recording each other, recording recitals, comparing notes on the interpretation of Bach and others and devouring bowel-burning Phall curries served with red-hot minted gram beans at Chiefy's curry parlour until the early hours.

David was a larger than life character who could always see the funny side of a situation. Tall, with a mop of curly blond hair atop a round, beaming face, everyone knew when he was around, especially the girls and he was popular with most of them – much more so than I'd ever considered myself to be.

I'd had friends who were girls, several in fact but only one I'd ever considered a proper girlfriend and that had ended as spectacularly as it began a few months earlier.

David, as I learned in the months and years that followed, always had a ready supply of charm and jokes – I could never tell jokes – and wheeled them out whenever the opportunity arose. He never seemed to be without a girlfriend for long before another would arrive on the scene. We hit it off from the first meeting, so when he suggested we should go to the Freshers' evening together, it sounded like a good idea.

Freshers' evening was an opportunity for all the first-year music students to get to know each other socially, meet a few second and third years, chat – and in those days, smoke, drink and get as drunk as possible for minimal cost. Subsidised by the Students' Union, it was hosted in the students' common room, a large but hardly salubrious sanctuary from practice and work tucked away down a corridor to the side of the entrance foyer.

Inside, nicotine-browned pale-yellow walls rose behind a line of grey steel lockers along one side that merged seamlessly into a more-brown-than-white ceiling, while along two other walls were well-used, cigarette-burnt easy chairs that been pushed together for the event to form an irregular line in front of the common room windows. At the centre was a makeshift dance floor. Just the sight of it made me shudder.

It's impossible to play the organ without good coordination. There's a pedal board to be played with the feet, several keyboards, dozens of stops, thumb pistons, toe pistons, swell pedals and music to read with pages that need turning. I never struggled. But my dancing… it was closer to a walrus performing on an iceberg than anything Bruce Forsyth and the 'Strictly Come Dancing' judges might ever have applauded.

However, this was Freshers' evening, there were girls, I was unattached and with a little Dutch courage, I vowed to give it a go if the opportunity presented itself.

On the far wall, a makeshift bar had taken the place of the snack bar behind a serving hatch and either side of it were two enormous speakers. A sound-system with an impressive array of sliders, switches and flashing lights was perched precariously on a stand at the edge of the bar, dangerously close to the flight path of beers passing between bartenders and boozers.

It was noisy – deafeningly noisy – as my new-found friend, David and I arrived. The music was about as far removed from the subtleties of the Monteverdi 'Vespro della Beata Vergine' I'd been studying most of the afternoon as could be imagined but there was atmosphere in spades, not to mention a thick fog of cigarette smoke.

The beat was heavy and regular and in the hushed lighting, the peeling paint and cigarette-burnt chairs were forgotten as we made our way carefully beneath layers of bunting that had come adrift from the ceiling and negotiated a passage through the gyrating mass of lithe, scantily-clad sirens on the dance floor and towards the bar.

David signalled towards a pair of vacant seats and I headed off to claim them, leaving him to bring the drinks.

That was the last I saw of him all evening.

The springs in the base of the chair poked annoyingly into the squashed foam making it less than comfortable and there was a distinct sag to the cushion from years of abuse but at least I'd found a seat.

Around the room everyone was occupied, involved. Some were dancing, some were chatting, others had moved off to pair bond in dark, smoke-filled recesses. One pair had become entangled beneath a table that had been pushed against the adjacent wall. I assumed one or other of them must have mislaid something, though they were clearly having trouble finding out which layer of clothing it had become lodged in and were hastily removing as many as possible.

My moment of voyeurism was interrupted with a gentle tap on the knee.

Beer had arrived – but without David.

In his place was a tall, dark-haired, long-legged, short-skirted young lady. *From David*, she shouted, projecting her voice above the music. *Is this spot free?*

Her smile was beguiling: cute but at the same time cheeky. It took me back to London with Ken and the girl with the trench coat. The hair, the makeup... there was definitely more than a passing resemblance.

As she took up residence on my right knee, the chair gave gently, becoming more comfortable with the extra weight and the reason for the sag in the cushion became apparent.

As she wiggled herself into a comfortable position, I took a swig of the beer, then another. It wasn't especially good and had a curious bitterness.

My right hand was on her waist, without which, I reasoned, she'd be on the floor. It was a slim waist, an enjoyable waist.

It's so loud in here! she yelled. The chair gave again.

My hand slipped lower as the cushion gasped. She seemed to enjoy it, raising an eyebrow cheekily, so I left it there.

My name's Sophie. I haven't seen you around. Is this your first year?

Yes. And you? I responded, taking another gulp. It hadn't improved. Probably I wasn't used to it.

I'm a second year. I'm on the diploma course. You must be doing the degree course, right?

What's your instrument?

I'm an organ student.

Wow! I love big organs. I fiddle a bit, she added cheekily. *Mine's a big one. I grip it between my legs!*

That was a euphemism for cellist.

I'd hardly got into the idiom of the repartee when another long-legged beauty arrived. *Do you know Cathy? She's on your course. Come and sit down... he's got two knees.*

The cushion beneath us gasped again and sank further as Cathy found her perch. The seats either side had been occupied leaving little room for three on one. It was getting cosier with each sag.

Hi! What do you play? she asked, somewhat exhausted from a stint on the dance floor. I assumed it was the dancing that had left her out of breath. It could have been the dense fog of cigarette smoke. I hated cigarettes.

Big organs! Sophie answered on my behalf.

I like things to bang and jingle myself.

A percussionist?

Eyes rolled heavenwards.

You <u>must</u> be a first year!

I took another swig of the beer. Noticing my aversion to the taste, Cathy took the glass and sipped. *Fresher's cocktail,* she announced, grimacing in distaste and sticking a tongue out but I'd already finished three quarters of it and no longer cared what it tasted like. With one final gulp, I downed the remainder and planted the glass carelessly with a pile of its friends on the windowsill behind.

There was a crash as a stack of spent glasses tumbled but nothing broke.

The heavy beat of the music was becoming distant; surreal, like the situation. The girls were conversing: hair, makeup, clothes, who was with whom, who was about to get dumped. I'd become little more than a convenient perch.

Dim though it was, the lighting seemed to have shifted up a gear. It was contrasty now; a myriad of pinpoints that would grow and shrink as I looked in their direction then explode in a wild flourish as I glanced away. I was happy. Intensely happy. Smoke swirled around creating patterns that shrouded the faces of dancers. I couldn't tell one from the other but it didn't matter. I glanced toward the table under which the bonding pair had been hard at work disrobing but the spot was vacant. David was nowhere to be seen.

What was the time?

My watch was wedged beneath a shapely buttock on my left knee. I tugged but it wouldn't free... once, twice, three times.

Hey! You're keen! Cathy leaned over, her right elbow now on my shoulder for balance.

I could feel her breath on my face and for a moment we lingered. Whatever my imagination thought we might have been on the verge of, it never happened. Smoke poured down her nose. She'd lit up and I hadn't noticed.

Suddenly I needed the boys' room. Urgently.

Outside the common room the cold air hit me like a wall of ice after the intense heat and smoke of the dance floor. With each step forward the corridor swung like a rope bridge over a ravine. Ducking to avoid swinging strip lights, I made an uneasy track towards the boys' room. I'd almost made it when another vision of loveliness appeared at the foot of the stairs.

She seemed content away from the noise and the smoke. Did I really need the boys' room? The necessity evaporated as I drew closer.

She smiled and cocked her head on one side inquisitively. I asked her name but the words came out strangely. She smiled again. Maybe she was shy.

I remember being very taken with her fiery red hair, intoxicatingly green eyes and long eyelashes. She was quite charming and a world away from the who-had-been-dumped-and-who-was-going-to-be-dumped conversation I'd left in the common room.

Conversation flowed easily between us, dipping in and out of dreams and aspirations, places and people. The hours slipped by, melting from evening into morning, but still she wouldn't tell me her name.

It was a sad parting when Harold the caretaker arrived with the keys to lock up but we vowed to meet the following day.

Nine in the morning is an ungodly hour for a lecture when sleep doesn't arrive until five but on this course, arrive late and it was guaranteed you'd be spending the next week catching up. It was fast-paced, relentless and unforgiving and the lecturers had reputations for being the hardest of taskmasters.

Many were seasoned professionals, accustomed to the demands of a professional musician's life and their expectations were high.

Between lectures, hours of daily practice were mandatory. There were compositions to write, pieces to orchestrate, choir practices, orchestra practices, wind groups, chamber groups, improvisation and keyboard harmony classes to attend, dissertations to write and conducting lessons.

History was an intensive set of lectures with no let up that flowed seamlessly from the Chori Spezati of the Renaissance to the heady counterpoint of the Baroque period, through the great works of the Classical and Romantic periods and onwards to the 20th Century with its dissonances, serialism and aleatoricism. And after most came an intensive stylistic recognition test. Miss the pointers in history, or lose concentration for a moment and you were sure to fail.

Keyboard harmony sessions were taken to extremes: break wind in class and you'd be expected to improvise a fugue in the style of Bach on the notes you'd blown.

Even Harold, the caretaker, was an ardent student of intensive listening who had developed the impeccable timing expected of all students at the School of Music. And he was as devoted to his calling as any lecturer.

Harold was a strange and exceptionally mischievous character; likeably odd, if you were on his right side but with a devilish streak that often caught unwitting students on the back foot.

Tall, thin and in his early sixties, he had a mop of greying pan scrub for hair and the brightest, most piercing blue eyes. His features were pointy and angular and he had unnaturally-high cheekbones under almost translucent skin that sank into deep chasms either side of his mouth. It was rumoured that Harold's nose had been used as the model for an Olympic ski slope.

His secret weapon was a wicked sense of humour and it was guaranteed that when he unleashed it, someone, somewhere would feel pain. He chose his victims carefully and when they least expected it, he'd strike with venom, binding them with evidence gathered over days, weeks even, and devour them with great relish. The end would be painful, public and never swift.

That particular morning it was my turn.

I was hardly on form. The single beer I'd downed the night before was still pounding between my ears but when Harold started, public humiliation followed and there was no escape, no mitigation, whatever the circumstances.

How's the head? he yelled unsympathetically from the doorway of his cupboard beneath the stairs. I'd just entered the foyer and must have been a good 50 feet away. Little Bob, his assistant, chortled.

Did you make out with that lass you were chatting up?

I could remember nothing. My head hurt. I had a history lecture to get to and it was upstairs. I tried ignoring him but it was futile.

Come on Casanova, this is no time to be shy! he yelled to the amusement of a curious crowd that had paused by the notice-board. *You were hard at it last night. You wouldn't let the poor lass get to bed. I had to throw you out!*

Still I could remember nothing.

I'd just about made it to the foot of the stairs when he unleashed another volley: *Better get your act together, lad! She's right behind you!*

I turned.

Slowly, the beer allowed my brain to catch up but it floated on and parked up somewhere beyond the point I was facing. There were girls everywhere but recognising none of them I turned back in the vain hope of continuing up the stairs.

Harold couldn't contain himself – and now he had an audience. *No, no, over there,* he laughed, smacking his thigh and pointing agitatedly. I tried to follow the line of his scrawny finger, my head still spinning from the last turn but recognised no one I might have spent the evening with. I had some fleeting recollection of time spent with Sophie and Cathy but no one else.

Harold's laughter – I'd liken it to Basil Brush – was infectious. Others were joining in. Giggles were turning into guffaws. Guffaws were turning into full-blown belly laughs.

Harold! I pleaded, *I have a lecture to go to. Quit this!* But Harold was having none of it.

She's right there! Right there on the corner.

I turned again.

There were two Freshers on the corner but neither were girls. Both made a swift exit for fear of being implicated.

There! he yelled. *She's waiting for you! Come here!*

Roughly, he took my arm and steered me in the direction of the boys' room. *There!* His scrawny finger came to rest inches away from my date of the evening before.

Random flickers of the evening's encounter started to appear behind bleary morning-after eyes and slowly, very slowly, realisation dawned: red hair, bright green eyes...

The crowd was hysterical now.

I suddenly felt the need to evaporate – permanently, completely, immediately.

Does she look as good this morning as she did last night? he yelled, working his audience like a pantomime pro.

On the wall, no more than four feet from floor level and sporting two green stickers on which someone had drawn pupils and Betty Boop eyelashes was a large, red fire extinguisher, its black hose bent in a semicircular smile. I'd spent the whole evening chatting her up.

My French horn tutor was another character who never took prisoners and didn't mince words. I remember my first lesson well. He took one look at me, one look at the instrument and yelled across the room, *What are you going to do with that, lad? Play it or eat it?*

In the last year of high school, my music teacher – who I'd always held in some regard – managed to convince my father that the euphonium I so enjoyed playing and had become quite proficient on was not an orchestral instrument and without an orchestral instrument as a second study, no music college or university would accept me. The instrument I'd borrowed from the school to learn on was now needed by someone else but there would still be a spot for me in the school orchestra if I switched to the French horn. But there was a snag: the school didn't have a French horn.

Unlike the plethora of motley cornets, tenor horns, baritones, euphoniums, trombones and tubas that had been donated by disbanded brass ensembles or handed down when they'd become too tired for regular use, the school had never had a French horn. Would Father buy one for me?

Either my music teacher didn't know or, more likely, his desire for a French horn among the disparate bunch of blowers, bangers and scrapers he referred to as an orchestra led him not to reveal that the euphonium was otherwise known as the tenor tuba in orchestral circles. It had been used to great effect in orchestral works by Gustav Mahler and in Gustav Holst's renowned Planets Suite – a work he often played during first and second year class listening sessions.

The act of taking it away under false pretences felt like treachery but within days my beloved euphonium had been repossessed, a shiny new French horn had been bought, free lessons had been arranged through the school and at the most critically-important time just ahead of making applications to universities, any chance of me progressing as a brass player had been brutally immobilised.

It fell to my tutor at the School of Music to break the news.

Play it or eat it pretty much summed up the problem. The French horn has a tiny mouthpiece that sits in the middle of the embouchure and playing it requires a concentration of controlled muscle power where I didn't have it.

French horn players are generally endowed with thin lips. Mine were big smackers. They were perfectly suited to a large mouthpiece that all but covers the embouchure, like that of the euphonium. Ergo, I had more chance of swallowing the mouthpiece than playing the French horn.

Almost as swiftly as the French horn had arrived, it was whisked away, replaced this time by a tenor trombone. The mouthpiece problem had been eradicated but now I had a slide to master instead of valves – and weeks rather than years in which to reach degree level second study expectations.

Being able to drive a car doesn't mean you can jump in an aeroplane and expect to fly it first pop off. Switching from valves to a slide… they're chalk and cheese. It was just never going to happen.

I narrowly made it through the first-year exams, fared better in the second year but attempting the second movement of Paul Hindemith's infamous first trombone sonata as one of my second study final-year exam pieces was a bridge too far. The piano accompaniment is a wild thrash-about that seems almost devoid of connection with the solo part when it kicks off. Hesitate at the start or allow yourself a moment's lapse in concentration and you may as well go home. It's not a piece to recover from.

My accompanist for the exam, one of the lecturers who was best known for his exceptional sight-reading abilities, had played it many times and not appreciating I didn't possess the same level of virtuosity, didn't see the need to make himself available for more than a cursory half-hour rehearsal. Inevitably, in the exam performance, with three professional musicians in front of me who all knew the piece inside out, he set off like a ball from a musket – without me.

We got it right the second time but false starts do not go down well with adjudicators. I'd already lost my chance of achieving the Bachelor of Arts (Honours) First Class that had been predicted.

Composition was something I enjoyed much more than performance and I excelled at it. Song cycles, piano sonatas, string quartets, quintets, orchestral pieces, orchestrated arrangements – whatever I was given to write flowed easily onto manuscript paper and I consistently took top marks. By the third year, I'd already netted a gong for a piece I'd written for the Radio France Concours Internationale de Gitare and been elected a Member of the Composers' Guild of Great Britain, a Fellow of the Royal Society of Arts and a few other things.

My 'Ancient Mariner', a contemporary piece of musical theatre for voice, clarinet, flute and percussion based on the poem by Samuel Taylor Coleridge, received a standing ovation when it was performed. It's not a piece that's to everyone's taste. It certainly wasn't to mine but it achieved the result I needed and that was what mattered.

On arrival at the School of Music, I'd been assigned to an organ tutor who had a reputation for accepting nothing short of perfection. While David's organ tutor had him pounding through the organ repertoire at breakneck speed, mine let no detail slip. Time and time again I was hauled back to the beginning. *Don't practice until you get it right,* he'd say, *practice until it can't go wrong.* Accuracy, interpretation, perfection, those were his hallmarks and his expectations and until I'd delivered all of them consistently I wasn't moving onto the next piece.

I must have spent a whole term on J S Bach's 'Prelude and Fugue in F minor' (it's known as BWV 534 among organists), ensuring every occurrence of the fugue subject was identical to the first, measuring the trills, changing stops and manuals seamlessly. Only then was I allowed to progress to Hindemith, Messian and the wider recital repertoire.

But what I took away from that first term – that first piece – was an obsession with detail that permeated everything else I did and set me up for life.

By the time I'd progressed to the third year, I'd worked up one of Bach's most challenging organ works to perfection - the 'Fantasia and Fugue in G Minor' (BWV 542) - and delivered it with confidence and panache as part of my final exam recital.

It was in the October of my first year at the School of Music that David introduced me to a talented young violinist called Marie. They'd both arrived at the School of Music a year or so before me and had known each other for some time. Though even in later years he never admitted to it, I have a notion David might have harboured a desire for a date at one point but Marie had quashed any prospect of that long before he had chance to develop the idea.

She was far too dedicated to her violin to be interested in lads, he told me after our first introduction in the foyer, she didn't like organists and I had no chance. But it was already too late. I'd brushed aside his boyish cautions and taken my chance.

Marie was bright, sparkly and cute – very cute. She had a mane of long, dark, flowing hair, big blue eyes, a captivating smile and talent in spades. There seemed to be nothing from the orchestral repertoire she couldn't play and she'd performed with a good many professional orchestras before we met and was on first name terms with the leaders of several. At 17 years of age, that was a rare achievement.

Our first meeting knocked me sideways. I don't recall which of us asked the other out but towards the end of the October we started dating.

We were on different courses with timetables that seldom saw us in the same place at the same time but every opportunity we could find we were together, working, playing music, visiting concerts, rehearsing for concerts, eating pots of black cherry yoghurt in the car at lunchtime while the rain hammered on the roof. We became inseparable.

By the end of the third year, I was a graduate. With Marie already working full-time as a violin teacher, I became preoccupied to the point of obsession with paper collection. Blindly, I continued to follow the obvious track through a year of teacher training to yet more diplomas and degrees.

Did I pause to question whether it was the right direction?

Yes, I did. Many times, in fact.

But with little else on the horizon, what were the options?

I knew I wasn't fast enough at learning pieces to earn a living as a professional musician and in any case, there were plenty better than me.

Composition didn't seem to be a way I could make much either. The options were narrowing. Everything pointed towards a career as a high school teacher but that wasn't a direction I wanted to take.

Music had totally swamped photography; my cameras had been relegated to

David sneaked this picture as I was rehearsing on one of the many cathedral organs we played during our time together at the School of Music.

David was a larger than life character with a mop of curly blond hair atop a round, beaming face.

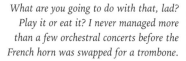

What are you going to do with that, lad? Play it or eat it? I never managed more than a few orchestral concerts before the French horn was swapped for a trombone.

It was in the October of my first year at the School of Music that David introduced me to a talented young violinist called Marie.

Marie, pictured near the Mull of Galloway in Scotland with one of a string of cars I bought while I was a student. The Capri took almost as long to get to 60mph as it took to fill the fuel tank but it looked good.

hobby status. I managed to delay entry to the teaching profession by taking a post-grad degree in music composition – and in an ironic twist, found myself on the receiving end of bursary offers to study at three of the universities that had turned down my undergrad application on the grounds I was 'non-academic'.

With great pleasure, I waved two fingers at them all and went to Southampton University.

It was while I was in Southampton that I wrote 'The Hamburg Suite', an intensely-organised four-movement string quartet that later won recognition in the Dresden Music Festival.

I remember the first time I presented the manuscript to my professor. I was so proud. It was the most academic work I'd ever written; the Earle equivalent of Brahms' 'Academic Festival Overture' but in a wildly different genre.

It was intense – beyond intense – in its arithmetical construction and the meticulous structure of chords and the order of the notes used in each melody. I figured even Luigi Dallapiccola, whose 'Quaderno Musicale di Annalibera' I'd analysed in detail that year for my thesis and taken some inspiration from, would have been proud of me.

Even for professional string players, it was a difficult work to perform and I had that on good authority from Marie, who'd helped by adding bowing marks. But with me turning the pages, my professor sight-read it faultlessly at the piano from one end to the other.

I was stunned. That was skill. I couldn't come close to his level.

If there were such virtuosi around, what chance did I have?

At the end, he paused for a moment, turned to me and without the slightest ignominious intent, quietly announced he'd found a mistake in the 12-tone series on which it had been constructed, right here in the second movement.

One note – just one note in the entire 30-minute work – had been enharmonically transposed and while sight-reading it from the four staves of a hand-written manuscript, he'd spotted it.

He was a genius. He was the reason I chose Southampton. It was humbling just to breathe the same air.

Chapter Five
The World of Work

Eventually, I succumbed to Father's pleas to find a job and applied for a teaching post in the market town of Thirsk. I don't recall the interview being one of my more sparkling performances but the paperwork I'd amassed must have impressed. I was offered the position to start in September.

I may not have chosen teaching any more intentionally than I'd chosen music – it just seemed to be a track I'd been pointed down that I hadn't made any attempt to change – *but I did choose Thirsk*. If nothing else, I was determined to swap concrete and crowds for fields and fresh air. More than anything, I wanted to live in the country.

Thirsk is a delightful market town in the heart of North Yorkshire. I considered myself especially fortunate to have found a nice place to lodge that was quite close to the town but far enough away not to be central and only a short walk from the school.

My landlady, Flora, who was probably in her early 70s when we first met, was a charming lady and all she was missing in her life was someone to fuss over. She'd lost her husband some years earlier and didn't have children, so regarded a lodger more as a companion than a means to an income. She certainly didn't need the pin money it brought her but she enjoyed having someone to cook for and talk to in an evening as much as I enjoyed being there.

It suited us both perfectly that I would leave for school on a Friday morning with my weekend case packed, head home after work, spend time with Mother and Father and of course, Marie and return on the Sunday evening, leaving Flora with the weekend to herself.

During the week, Flora and I would have dinner together in an evening and while I marked books or prepared the next day's lessons, she'd flit around the house, dusting, singing away, occasionally stopping to have an in-depth discussion about something and nothing with Freddie, the yellow canary she kept in a cage by the fireplace.

Flora was a kind soul, one of the kindest I've ever met but she was also an eccentric. Her heart was in the right place but she had her own way of doing things, her own way to get through life's ups and downs and her own version of logic.

I remember finding a bicycle in the outhouse once and seeing it hadn't been used for a while, asked if she'd ever ridden it. *Not recently,* she admitted sheepishly. Her husband had forbidden her to ride bicycles. He used to have a shop in the town and had caught her riding it around the S-bend with her eyes closed one lunchtime.

When he asked what she was doing, she was quite sincere when she told him she didn't want to see if she fell off.

I was still in my first year of teaching when I arrived for breakfast one morning to find Flora in floods of tears. She'd discovered her beloved canary with its legs up in the bottom of the cage. She was beside herself and begged me to call Jimmy, the vet.

Jimmy was none other than James Wight, sometimes known as Alf Wight – James Herriot to millions of 'All Creatures Great and Small' fans – and Jimmy had a reputation for performing miracles.

Hastily, I found his name in the phone book and called, arranging to meet him outside the house when he arrived.

There was nothing he could do for the bird, I knew that but Flora adored it and she worshipped Jimmy. I had to find out where I could get a replacement. Inside, Jimmy carefully wrapped the bird in the tea towel Flora covered the cage with each night and took it away, promising to do everything he could.

As soon as school was over, I headed over to the pet shop Jimmy had recommended, my mission to find a yellow canary. As luck would have it, they had one that looked almost identical to Flora's, so I bought it and delivered it to the surgery.

The next day, I arrived back from school to find Flora singing happily again and flicking around with her feather duster. Jimmy had been. It was a miracle! He'd cured little Freddie, who was chirping noisily from his perch and Flora was overjoyed. *Wasn't Jimmy wonderful? Only Jimmy could have cured Freddie!* He'd made her day.

I think it was about six months later, Freddie did the unthinkable: he laid an egg.

We put it down to another of Jimmy's miracles.

By the end of my first year in teaching, I'd exchanged the tired Volvo that had stood up well to the commute between home and Southampton for a new car and I was eager to run it in properly.

Why don't we take a trip to Scotland this year? Marie ventured, leafing her way through the flimsy pages of a rather tattered tourist board brochure. *We've never been to the islands.*

I liked that idea so we set about making arrangements.

Our study years had been intensive, so whenever work allowed we would take time out. Sometimes it was just a short hop to the other side of the Pennines for a concert or up to the Yorkshire Dales for an orchestral weekend.

This summer, however, we would head north to Scotland, taking a Tilley stove, a gas bottle and a small mountain of food that we'd cook whenever the mood took us.

It was the best part of a decade before Keith Floyd would arrive on the TV screen with his 'Floyd on Food' series but I'd already got the al fresco bug and was no stranger to impromptu cookery in a lay-by with a view.

The first time we ventured over the border, I remember Marie being particularly impressed with my ability to navigate the Lowlands by the toilets – a throwback from family holidays with Grandma and her *urgency*. But now we were planning a trip to the Highlands and islands. I'd never ventured that far north and the chance to take my brand new, pristine, black Renault 18 Turbo – one of the first of its kind to be imported to the UK – for a proper spin held a lot of appeal.

It was early August when we set off. Scotland at that time of year was a sight to behold. The trees had just begun to turn, their rich, warm tones offsetting the purple hues of the heather adorning moorlands that rolled effortlessly from peaked hills to wide glens below.

We'd chosen a long route that took us through the Trossachs to Cairndow at the tip of Loch Fyne, south-west for a while to explore its shores, then north again through Fort William and Inverness towards ever-wilder and more rocky regions.

The smell of beached bladder-wrack, kelp and brackish water mingled evocatively with the oak fires of tiny smoking-houses and burning peat as we reached Loch Fyne and we pulled in to savour its intoxicating effect.

Outside, the silence was deafening.

Every now and then, the supreme tranquillity of a perfect evening would be punctuated by the scream of a solitary bird, anxious to make its mark on an otherwise pristine canvas.

It was a rare moment. Scotland at its best. This was my Scotland, the Scotland I'd grown to love as a boy.

That evening we slept by the side of the loch. As the sun dipped below the horizon, the calm water receded from its pebbly edge and the fish stopped rising. For a while, we sat, admiring the perfection, listening to the earth tick.

It proved to be a long and eventful trip from the Western Highlands to the Isle of Lewis. The rolling green fir forests adorning shallow hills and wide glens gave way to craggy, barren and often inhospitable terrain dotted with spiky yellow gorse bushes and hardy grasses as we ventured north towards the ferry port of Ullapool for the crossing to the Outer Hebrides.

The weather had been unexpectedly kind en route: by night it had been balmy with a gentle south-westerly breeze; by day an intense sun had picked out the boulder-strewn features of mountain after mountain in high relief to delight us as we journeyed.

We'd rested well the night before our crossing at the quaint abode of Mrs Smithers, a dear old lady whose generous helpings of porridge, bacon and eggs, oat cakes and home-made damson jam had left us well-prepared for the long day ahead.

We arrived at the port early – around seven o'clock – with the intention of taking the late morning ferry to Stornoway on the Isle of Lewis. From there we would move on to the Isle of Harris and our first night's accommodation.

It was fortuitous that we had arrived in good time since that morning, just as the fishing fleet was making its way into harbour, the announcement had been made that the herring quota had been exceeded. By the time the fleet had docked, the local processing-factory had already switched its production and could now only accept cod.

Angry to be informed that their boats, which were heavily laden with herring, would have to return to sea and dump their costly cargo, the skippers had taken the decision to offload the catch regardless and make their point.

They chose to do it in a way which would stay with us for the entire holiday.

Activity in the port must have been feverish. Even at this early hour, the traffic queue – I guess some twenty cars – had backed up along the one, narrow road leading down towards the port and the waiting Caledonian MacBrayne ferry.

Empty wagon after empty wagon passed us, wending their way up the hill and out of the town along the road we had driven. By half past eight, the town was gridlocked.

The ferry was not due to leave until late morning, so we relaxed to Rachmaninov's 2nd Piano Concerto on the new car stereo. As the movements passed, intense discussion over the nuances of the interpretation had distracted us from the growing commotion outside.

Glancing up, we could see scores and scores of seagulls swooping and dancing just ahead of the queue.

As the last movement climaxed, percussive interference added to the screeching making it difficult to enjoy the deft finger-work of the accomplished Mr Bolet.

Raising the backrest of her seat to a sitting position, Marie gasped. The whole car, once immaculate black, had been peppered with yellow and white.

I peered out through the smears left by ineffective wipers. Ahead, the herring catch was being systematically dumped in the road and the seagulls were having a party.

Unable to contain their enthusiasm for the unexpected windfall, they had sought to download from a great height. As fast as they could gorge, they would discharge and return for a refill.

Outside, policemen were taking cover. Locals that once lined the street had retreated behind closed doors and were staring in disbelief through bespattered windows, shouting and waving as wagon after wagon passed empty, its tailgate flapping after spreading its load. I counted three, four, five... and more.

Against Marie's advice, I ventured to open the door for a moment to survey the damage. Immediately, the seat I had just vacated – my immaculate deep turquoise velour armchair – was hit, streaked from headrest to squab.

Ahead, other cars had suffered the same fate and in front of them, fully a hundred yards of herring stretched from edge to edge of the tarmac in a pile almost three feet high.

As the sun rose, so did the smell.

A digger had been tasked to move the heap but it was powerless to make an impression as wagon after wagon continued to arrive, each with its tailgate open.

By midday, almost an hour after our allotted departure time, the wagons departed and the digger was at last able to create a cutting through the squashed-herring mound.

A river of fish essence snaked its way down the hill, collecting in a small lake that spanned the entrance to the port.

Bedraggled police officers, now equipped with borrowed umbrellas, were endeavouring to marshal through the first cars.

With barely six hundred miles on the clock, our once proud symbol of French automotive chic had been reduced to a well-caked mobile dung heap. It had driven through its first shoal of fish and the underside was encrusted with scales.

Onboard, we abandoned the car in the bowels of the ferry boat and headed for the fresh air on the upper deck. It was a glorious crossing. The sea was like glass for the whole four hours it took to reach the Isle of Lewis.

The town of Stornoway, capital of the islands of Lewis and Harris, is built around the harbour. Brightly-painted buildings lined the perimeter and fishing boats idled at the quayside, motionless in the still water.

The Western Isles are a paradise for photographers. Open landscapes, pristine beaches, derelict thatched Black Houses, ragged cliffs with crashing waves below, unspoilt moorland, fascinating Iron Age Brochs – Lewis and Harris had them all and we were determined to explore every one.

But first we had to find our accommodation: Mrs O'Flaherty's B&B. We'd only been provided with general directions and the briefest address but it wasn't hard to find.

Excited, we opened the tiny gate and made our way up a narrow herb-lined path to the front door. It was quite a large, stone-built house, a little gaunt perhaps and in need of a lick of paint but we were content with our choice, close as it was to the shoreline.

We knocked.

Oi'll be out in a mo', came a voice from within, its dulcet Irish tones unmistakable.

Squeaking footsteps followed. The bolt drew back, the key turned and a second bolt slid noisily from its retainer. A chain rattled and the heavily-carved, circular handle that had caught my attention in the very centre of the door began to turn.

Hang you on dere and stand aside for da dog, wudya now? called the voice. *He's a-comin' out and he's not about ta spare da horses!*

We obliged, facing each other either side of the door as it creaked open on well-worn hinges.

A huge, shaggy, orangey-black beast leapt forth as if it had been attached by elastic to the telegraph pole at the end of the garden and proceeded to dance around excitedly, leaping first on Marie then turning its attention on me.

Git down ya mad beggar! yelled the voice. *Go and find a sheep ta play wid or sumtin!*

The beast tore off in the direction of the garden gate and pausing momentarily to leave its sentiments on our front tyre and sniff the essence-of-herring paintwork a time or two, bounded down the lane.

Top o' the evenin' too ya! My name's Mrs O'Flaherty, she announced loudly, *But you can call me Fanny.*

If the beast was a sight to behold, Mrs O'Flaherty – Fanny – had the edge on it. A great hulk of a woman with a figure more akin to a block of flats than anything recognisably feminine, she brushed aside a mass of rusting wire wool that cascaded over her face and reaching out a hand to shake, smiled a huge smile.

If the San Andreas Fault had had a face, one might imagine this could have been it. Somehow, things had slipped, the plates didn't mesh and there was a gaping crevice filled with crooked monoliths at its base topped off with a steel-grey moustache that spilled into stubble on one of several chins.

Heading south, it was impossible not to notice her voluptuousness. Busts like this didn't exist in real life. Two enormous mounds leered menacingly over the straining neckline of an alarmingly-pink garment but somehow, the bulk of the appendages seemed to be tucked beneath the strings of a grubby apron and both were endeavouring to escape through the pockets in either side. The garment hung at the sides like a marquee and descended to shapeless calves, its frilly edge coming to rest in natural shrubbery.

Has it took yer long to find us? she continued.

No, I confirmed, the instructions had been good.

Dat's good. The old dog writes a fine letter, now don't he?

The old dog? That dog? The one we just saw go tearing down the lane?

No, no, no! Not dat dog. The old dog over dere! She gestured towards a small plot of land on which a stooped figure was working. *Dat's him...Fido's his real name. Oi named da young dog after him so he's gotta be da old dog.*

Fido O'Flaherty. Fanny O'Flaherty. The names had quite a ring.

I was still trying to come to terms with everything when Fanny let out an almighty screech in the direction of the stooped figure in the vegetable patch: *Stop playing wid ya turnips!* she yelled. *Come over here and socialise ya good-fer-nuttin pillark. We got guests!*

Meekly, Fido Senior obliged.

Fido was a character and then some. Two piercing bright-blue eyes shone out like lasers from beneath untamed eyebrows. His complexion was pallid and his clothes hung off meatless bones. Beyond skinny, he didn't seem at all well-matched to the voluptuous Fanny. Whether his stoop was the result of years of subservience or whether it was the sight of Marie's well-proportioned hind-quarters in tight jeans wasn't clear but throughout our conversation his gaze remained fixed.

Is dat yer little lady? he asked, momentarily glancing up and extending a scrawny hand toward me for shaking.

As I reached over, his mouth fell open, then closed sharply with a click. A squelch followed.

Marie hesitated as the hand made its way in her direction.

Yes, he definitely had false teeth: the click was the top set falling on the bottom set as he gaped; and no, they were not well glued in. The squelch was confirmation they were back in place.

If ya get cold in da night, I've got a wee bottle in my room.

Fido! yelled Fanny.

Fido's eyes fell once more to the floor as if the elastic holding them had been severed.

Go and get da whisky. We'll have a wee dram t'gether den da luv birds can go off by demselves while oi prepare da room!

Whisky downed, we departed to explore. It was past ten o'clock and still light.

Rounding the corner with the house out of sight, I became suddenly conscious of the need to take a leak. Making my excuses, I negotiated a low dry-stone wall while Marie patiently admired the beach. I was just getting to grips with the task in hand when who should come bounding across the field in my direction but Fido O'Flaherty Junior.

If anything is designed to knock a guy completely off his stride, it's the sight of an eighteen-hands-high dog with orangey-black matted hair drooling at the thought of a live suppertime treat – but that wasn't what was on Junior's mind. Before I could withdraw and rezip, Junior had already decided there was something much more interesting on offer and proceeded to mount my left leg.

Marie, alarmed by the commotion, arrived to find me protecting my wedding tackle whilst endeavouring to extricate myself from the bear-like grip of one slobbering, horny Fido O'Flaherty Junior who, by this time, had satisfied himself mightily on my new black Wranglers.

The deed done, he bounded gleefully across the field from whence he'd come, leaving me to explain my infidelity and extricate my snagged assets from the evil teeth of a coarse trouser zip.

The sun had dropped below the horizon as we made our way back and it was much cooler, though the stench of fish hadn't subsided any as we passed the car. We'd been invited to join Fanny and Fido Senior on our return and headed straight for the drawing room where a peat fire was glowing in the grate.

With Fido Junior tucking into his evening meal in the kitchen, we sat down while Fido Senior poured whisky into two eggcups and handed them to us.

Fanny, who'd clearly had a few before we arrived, was well into a verbal assault on the neighbours, whom she'd nicknamed the Klaggies and for the next hour, she ran them down without pause while Fido Senior drifted off, occasionally grunting, clicking and squelching from the armchair by the window.

We had hinted on several occasions that we might like to see our room but each request had prompted a refill of the eggcups. In need of the bathroom, Marie finally made her excuses and escaped.

As the minutes ticked by and the eggcups drained, the conversation steadily ground to a halt. I could hear Marie calling so, thanking our hosts for their hospitality, I left, closing the door behind me.

We hadn't been shown where the bathroom was but from the exaggerated rattling and banging it wasn't hard to locate. She was locked in.

I reached down and pushed the handle. It wouldn't move. No amount of jiggling and pushing would release it. *Is there a window?* I asked, hoping there might be some other means of escape but there wasn't.

Back in the drawing room, Fanny had joined Fido Senior: rafter-rattling snores came from outstretched bodies in both corners. Realising I'd returned, Fanny awoke with a start, smacking a pile of spent eggcups and sending them hurtling across the hearth.

With some embarrassment, I explained the situation. *Ah, you English,* came the response. *You're all da same! Dere's no problem wid it. I'm a comin'!*

Pulling down the pink marquee, which had ridden up alarmingly to reveal an acre of thigh and yanking it over the exposed shrubbery, Fanny headed for the bathroom. *Hide dat pretty ass you've got, me dear,* she yelled, grasping the door handle.

A couple of wiggles and a solid yank – upwards – and the troublesome door opened obediently.

Lesson over, we started to make our way to the stairs.

Straight up, forst on da right, down da corridor too da end, Fanny yelled after us. *Dat's where you're at t'night – and don't forget now, to open da door ya gotta lift da handle!*

Grateful to have escaped from the endless eggcups, we followed the instructions, me as rear guard with the overnight bag. The absence of lights meant fumbling our way along the unlit corridor but at the end we found the door and groped for the handle. Sure enough, it turned easily – upwards. Just inside the doorway was the light switch. With an upward push, a solitary dangling bulb came to life.

The room was sparsely-furnished with a small wooden writing desk and chair in one corner and a large bed with wrought iron headboard in the other. There was no carpet but the bed-sheets had been ironed and smelled fresh. Ensuring the handle would allow us to exit, we closed the door gently and began to unpack.

I was about to deal with the zip that had earlier done so much damage to my potential when Marie tapped me on the shoulder. *Have you seen that?* she asked, pointing upwards to an open loft hole directly over the bed. She knew how I hated spiders and the very thought of hoards of palm-sized eight-wheelers bungee-jumping through the gaping loft access to the bed below as we slept filled me with dread.

Carefully, so as not disturb our hosts or the dreaded Fido Junior, we each took an end and manoeuvred the heavy bed away from the hatch. As it moved, my foot caught a large trunk that had been stashed underneath. We decided to leave well alone and proceeded to get ready.

The mattress was a saggy affair. It rested on noisy springs that groaned and twanged with every movement. As we crawled in to take up sleeping positions, there appeared to be something odd under the sheet below us – something hard. In fact, there were several. Suddenly, one of them made its presence know through the under-sheet as I laid down. It was painful. And there were more of them on the verge of biting.

This wasn't a bed either of us wanted to sleep in so, hastily, we dressed, repacked the overnight bag and headed down the stairs, intent on leaving and, if necessary, spending the rest of the night with the fishy odour in the car.

Downstairs, in the drawing room, the fire had expired and Fanny had slid feet first from chair to floor and come to rest in a heap. The pink marquee had ridden up again, taking with it the apron that held the mighty orbs in place. Revealed was a pair of blinding orange bloomers decorated with acid green spots.

Slowly, she awoke, rubbing her eyes. *Is dere a problem?* she croaked, still half asleep. We recounted our experience, adding that if another bed couldn't be found it was probably better if we left.

It was almost one o'clock in the morning. This was Harris. There were no street lights, no houses for miles, just moorland, shoreline – and quite possibly the evil Fido Junior who might be marauding, on the hunt for another unsuspecting Englishman to mount.

Don't be so hasty, now, spluttered Fanny, pulling herself up and rearranging the apron and the marquee. *Oi t'ink we can sort da problem for ya.*

Struggling to her feet, she began to fish around in the pockets of her apron. Whatever she was looking for was clearly not present, so off she paddled, intent on finding it. As she headed through the door and into the garden, we couldn't help but notice the pink marquee had become entangled at the back in the apron strings that kept the mighty orbs under control.

A formidable expanse of stern, clad in day-glow orange with acid green spots, had revealed itself and like two grizzlies fighting under a tarpaulin, they were attacking each other mercilessly as she made her way through the door.

Some little time passed when, from outside, there came a tapping on the window. It was Fanny. *Can ya open da door?* she called. *Oi've locked meeself out!* It was tempting to make a crack about the incompetence of the English when faced with door handles that don't work conventionally but I restrained. At least this handle turned. The door eased back with a creak and almost immediately a whiff of fish wafted in on the night air.

Fanny rushed past, momentarily knocking me off balance, and waddled up the stairs, the grizzlies still locked in mortal combat and on full view.

There wasn't room for all three of us in the room but from the other side of the door we could tell she'd lost something again and was rummaging furiously through the pockets of the apron for it. Whatever it was must have revealed itself and without pause, she undressed the mattress and set about attacking it with some determination while the springs twanged and groaned beneath.

The twanging ceased and Fanny emerged, triumphantly proclaiming the problem had been resolved. In one hand, she had several bits of coiled metal and in the other, a large pair of tin snips. *My son Seamus was sleepin' on diss bed for twenty years before he snuffed it,* she declared. *He sleeps under da bed now but he never complained about it when he was alive. Anyways, it's fine now. Get yer in dere and have a good night, da pair of yer!*

Suddenly, the thought of a night in a fishy Renault with a horny dog on the prowl seemed altogether more appealing than the prospect of sleeping with Seamus O'Flaherty (deceased) and the arachnids in a bed full of newly-trimmed ironmongery.

Paying in full to discourage any possibility of being pursued and with profuse thanks for generous hospitality bestowed, we hastily grabbed the overnight bag and left for the relative peace and tranquillity of the open countryside, the beach, a cliff face...

Reflecting on the adventure as we made our way back to Oban from South Uist, the rest of the holiday had been comparatively uneventful. It had been a pleasant two weeks, we'd used up dozens of films, enjoyed the peace and tranquillity of unspoilt places, photographed wonderful scenery and met lovely people and charming hosts with real beds and door handles that opened conventionally.

We'd even managed to find a pressure hose to dilute the smell of fish and wash off the residue from Ullapool's flying squad. But now we were heading back. In a few days, a new term would begin and our adventure in Scotland would be a distant memory.

I'm generally happier behind a camera than in front of it but the tranquillity, the colour, the scenery in the Scottish islands…just being north of the border always brought a smile to my face.

Hosing down the pride of French automotive chic after driving through a shoal of fish in Ullapool.

Chapter Six
Leaps of Faith

I can't say I was ever cut out to be a music teacher. It was a career I'd slipped into by default rather than out of choice, though there were classes I enjoyed teaching and students who rewarded the effort I put into their lessons with gratifying achievements. Nevertheless, there was always far more satisfaction to be had in teaching photography and towards the end of my time at Thirsk, I'd amassed quite a following through the evening classes I'd been running twice a week.

It was my escape, my chance to be creative and show others how to improve their skills. And it passed the time until the weekend when I could return home.

During my fourth year in Thirsk, encouraged by Marie who could see I was becoming very de-motivated by the unchanging regularity of the hamster wheel on which I could make no impression as an understudy, I started applying for Head of Music positions.

As a head of department, she reasoned, I would at least have more input, more control, more opportunity to achieve some of the things I'd pressed for over the last few years – and if nothing else, the pay would be better.

It takes ten years to become a head of department, the headmaster told me when I went to ask if he would be willing to provide a reference.

That was the red rag I needed. Determined to prove him wrong, I redoubled my efforts, typed up my CV and rigorously combed the recruitment pages as soon as the Times Educational Supplement landed on the staffroom table.

From time to time, positions would pop up in Leeds, Birmingham, Manchester, London. Proud recruiters would paint wonderful pictures of the facilities at their schools, the achievements and the expectations.

I ignored them all.

What I needed was a challenge that would wake me up from four years of coasting; somewhere I could make my mark, do things my way; a school that didn't have a music tradition – and, above all else, it had to be in the country. No fields, no trees, no fresh air, no application.

Is that the way to look for a promotion? Probably not but it was that cut and dried for me.

Eventually, a position did come up and it was in Norfolk – the third largest county in England and crucially, one of the most rural.

I remember the interview well. To my interviewers, it must have seemed like a bull had turned up in their china shop. I'd arrived with a list of demands that would give their school the most technically-advanced music department in the country bar none and with the county's music adviser on the interview panel – a dyed-in-the-wool traditionalist from Wales with a fixation on choirs – I sold my vision for a music department like no other: *this is what I will give you, this is what we will be able to achieve, this is what I need to do the job, this is how much it will cost.*

Thinking back, it was probably more of a brutal assault on the sensibilities of a trio of conventionalists than an interview per se but remarkably, they agreed to almost every demand and offered me the job.

I must have seemed very smug when, back in Thirsk, after three-and-a-half years as a junior teacher, I handed the headmaster my notice and confirmed I hadn't just moved up one point in the pay scale, I'd leapfrogged scale two and moved straight up to scale three.

Pretty much the whole of the summer holiday that followed I spent composing materials, writing worksheets and teaching materials, creating projects and sourcing the equipment we'd need for a keyboard laboratory, a composition lab, a listening lab and a four-track recording studio.

I was determined mine would be a department like no other and the course we'd offer would be a proper, joined-up music course that would give all pupils, regardless of their ability, the opportunity to play a keyboard properly, write their own music, perform it and record it.

It worked.

By the end of the first term, we'd recorded and produced our first record and hosted advisers from London who'd come to see 'Norfolk's answer to Benjamin Britten' – that's what the local paper called me – at work.

They were *my* pupils and it was *my* school that received the standing ovation from parents when the massed choirs from all the neighbouring schools performed the piece I'd written and we'd recorded that Christmas.

At long last, I'd drawn some tangible satisfaction from teaching music. It was long overdue.

But that summer hadn't been exclusively dedicated to paving the way for the first term. I needed somewhere to live. Mother, Father, Marie and I piled into the car and headed for East Anglia.

It was Father who first spotted the cottage. With everything else we'd seen either too expensive, too big, too small or too far away, we'd all but given up looking and were on the point of returning home when he persuaded me to call the agent. Hastily, a viewing was arranged for the same afternoon.

Semi-detached, two bedrooms and just south of the border between Norfolk and Suffolk, it had been bought as an investment and was newly-refurbished but essentially bland inside.

The original cottage was two up and two down but substantial extension to the downstairs and removal of the dividing walls between rooms had provided a long lounge that extended past a good-sized downstairs bathroom to a large kitchen. There was a loo, a basin and a bath in the bathroom and a base cupboard with a sink and tap in the kitchen.

That was it. No frills.

It was a blank canvas waiting for an artist to turn it into a home.

Standing with my back to the sink in the kitchen, Marie facing me, I remember my thoughts running wild. The cottage was fine – it was a big decision to make but it was not the cottage, not the work involved in turning it into a home, nor even the upheaval that preoccupied me.

In that moment, I had visited the future. I'd seen the possibilities and was gathering the courage to make it happen.

With Mother, Father and the estate agent involved in conversation in the lounge, I popped the question and Marie said *Yes*.

We were married the following April – April 1985, almost ten years after David had introduced us in the foyer at the School of Music – and now we had our cottage in the country.

Stark confirmation of our arrival in rural Suffolk came one bright and sunny Saturday morning shortly after Marie had moved down from Yorkshire.

It was May and we were laying in bed, awakening slowly and listening to the birdsong as it drifted in through the open window. The curtains were blowing gently in the warm spring breeze, occasionally parting to allow shafts of sunlight to dance on the floor.

Outside, one of our neighbours, Ivy, an elderly lady of tiny stature with one peg-like tooth that wobbled whenever she talked, was conversing with Arthur, another of the village elders.

Arthur, who was also in his early 80s, only had one leg. He always refused to use a crutch and whenever he wanted to get around the village he would sit astride his old bicycle. He couldn't ride it but he could shuffle it along.

On this particular morning, he'd stopped to rest against the garden gate and Ivy had brought him something to eat. Arthur had no teeth, so eating was difficult and made the non-stop dialogue between the two of them all the more unintelligible.

Fresh from the north, the Suffolk dialect was like a foreign language to us. All we could make out was a steady stream of vowels. Occasionally the *oo-arr-um-arr-oy-um-oo-ar* would be punctuated with guffaws of laughter, then they'd start again.

As the years passed, we steadily came to grips with the pronunciation. Almost 40 years on, I can *oo-ar* along with the best of them now.

If there was one thing the cottage needed more than anything else, it was character. It was painted throughout in bland magnolia, the ceilings were white Artex and fake beams had been added over the real ones. There was a modern brick fireplace in the lounge but every time it was lit, it filled the lounge with smoke.

With a school day that finished at 3.45 in the afternoon and a 15-minute hop over the border to home, that left evenings and weekends free to work – and work we did. Furiously.

We pulled down the hideous Artexed plasterboard to reveal the original beams in the ceiling and lovingly restored them one by one, staining and waxing each one until it shone.

Around steel trunnions that rose from the floor and supporting RSJs that spanned the ceiling, we added box-work and Spanish plaster.

It took three months to build a new stone fireplace, the stone arches either side of it and the wooden panel-work and swing-out bookcase but by the time we'd finished, it looked amazing.

We had a wood-burning stove installed and relined the chimney but to make the hood we used old copper water cylinders that we cut to shape, planished and polished so they matched the surfaces we'd built over the log stores either side of the chimney breast.

The cottage needed a completely new fitted kitchen, a new bathroom, a cabinet for glasses in the lounge and fitted wardrobes for each of the bedrooms. Anything that could be made from wood or panels, we made it. The panelled ceiling we designed and made to accommodate down-lighters in the kitchen wouldn't have been out of place in a stately home.

The first time the midwife arrived, the floor in the lounge was covered with wood shavings, dust sheets had been thrown hastily over the sofas and in place of a table was a workbench and a stack of sandstone left over from the fireplace we'd made.

Chipboard panels were piled against the walls and planks of timber lined the route to the kitchen, past the bathroom. A more unsuitable place to welcome a new baby it would be hard to imagine but by the middle of June '86, our first was due.

Marie chose the carpets from her hospital bed in the maternity unit. The carpet fitters finished just hours before she returned home.

I confess, until the birth of Christina, I had no idea the human neck could rotate through 360 degrees but in the 40-something hours it took her to arrive, mine must have been screwed round dozens of times.

I was the one making the noises, not Marie. If my nose hadn't been facing the other way at the critical moment, I'm sure she'd have bitten that off as well – but still she managed to give birth in near silence.

Christina's arrival provided an opportunity for trainee midwives to coo and cluck and it can't have been more than a few minutes after she made her entrance to the world that she was in front of an audience.

No one was prouder than me when the opportunity came to cradle her in my arms and show her off. It was an unforgettable moment.

My very first *Proud Dad* moment.

It was just as unforgettable when I returned to the hospital that evening to find Christina laying on her tummy, straining her neck and peering out through the plastic Tupperware container they'd put her in at the side of Marie's bed.

Babies don't generally do that for weeks, the nurse told me. *She's very advanced.*

At the time, I took her comment as little more than polite conversation.

Christina might have been ahead of her time but I was just in time: she took one look at me, grinned a huge toothless grin, strained and grunted. It was my first experience of dealing with a monster pickle.

Christina was a very happy baby, always laughing and giggling, always ready for a bounce in the bungee-jumper we'd screwed into a beam in front of the log-burner when I came home from school.

The only thing she didn't seem particularly interested in was food. It simply wasn't a priority for her, much to the consternation of my father who would call every few days to ask if she'd had anything proper to eat yet.

I remember very clearly him calling one evening and asking if she'd eaten. He was delighted to learn she had.

What did you give her? he asked, relief woven into his words.

During our usual after-school four o'clock cuddle on the sofa, she'd taken a slurp from my gin and tonic and gummed the end of a Twix bar.

Father was horrified.

Call me prejudiced if you like but I never wanted boys. I know, I know... every guy wants a son. I didn't. I wanted girls.

When Christina was on the way, I couldn't think of any boys' names. I knew it was pointless, anyway. She was going to be a girl and that was it. When she arrived, no one was more delighted than me.

When Marie became pregnant with our second some nine months later, I wasn't quite so confident we'd be having another girl. But I got my wish.

Christina had been very clingy and restless in the days just before the birth but my mother and father, who had come down from Yorkshire to look after her while Marie and I went to the hospital some five miles away, knew exactly the time of Catherine's arrival.

Christina settled immediately and went to sleep. She was accurate to the minute.

It wasn't until some years later that we started to realise Christina had some quite extraordinary abilities and this was just the beginning.

Christina and Catherine were always very close, as much friends as sisters.

Not wishing to miss a moment of them growing up, Mother and Father sold their house in Yorkshire at the first opportunity and moved into the village.

Every moment they could, they would spend it with the girls. When they were not feeding ducks together or out on picnics, they'd bake buns and cakes, paint pictures, leaf through the illustrated story books Father would paint for them and listen to the stories he'd make up about the adventures of Matthew Mouse, a character he invented to amuse them.

Christina loved Father's library. She would leaf her way through atlases, history books, books about ancient Egypt, science, nature... Her appetite for reading was insatiable.

By the time the kids at school had graduated from word pots to early readers, much to the surprise of Christina's teachers, who had run out of books for her to read, she was already into American literature.

Catherine had different interests. She loved cooking and baking but when she was not in the kitchen with Mother, she'd be playing with toy cars. At two or three years old, there were always traffic jams threading their way between the sofas in the lounge and along the fireplace and she liked nothing better than to steam up and down the garden in her pedal car, pausing occasionally to execute a perfect three-point turn.

Off-road biking, getting muddy, daredevil stunts that led to broken bones during gymnastic lessons... Catherine was in there. She couldn't wait to get a wheel in her hands and power under her right foot.

Family life was good. We had two beautiful girls but at work, strikes had disrupted teaching and the successes I'd enjoyed in the first years had become distant memories by the third. I'd become disillusioned by internal events, there

We were married in April 1985, almost ten years after David had introduced us in the foyer at the School of Music. Marie's sister Annette made the cake. It was a work of art.

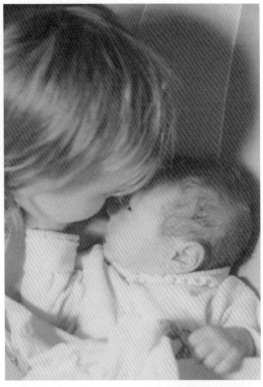

Christina and her younger sister Catherine were inseparable from the moment Catherine arrived.

The girls were always together, as much best friends as sisters.

*Much like me, Christina never really liked
having her photograph taken so the best
ploy was always to catch her by surprise.
She was always happier at the other end
of the lens and very quickly learned how to
spot and compose a good picture.*

were threats of the school closing, fears of teachers being demoted and departments – and their equipment – being disbanded and dispersed around the county.

At the same time, health problems that had seemed tolerable while I was at Thirsk were becoming more severe and eventually I ended up in hospital. Closure of the school was ratified shortly after and when I returned, the opportunity to leave presented itself, so I grabbed it with both hands.

I will never forget Marie's face the moment I told her.

She'd given up her job as a teacher, we had two small children, a mortgage, a car and no income. It was as if the world had come to an end for her.

To me, it was an opportunity to do something different, to grow what we'd already started, to build a business and swap the repetitiveness of a timetabled life for the excitement of a new and more colourful life in business.

It was the chance to finally ditch a career I'd contrived to be good at since leaving school and make something of a new opportunity that was opening up in front of us.

A year or so earlier, I'd written speculatively to a big oil company and been lucky enough to progress through the interview stages for a job.

Each interview included expenses-paid stays in fancy hotels in different locations and enjoyable discussions over pleasant dinners I could never have afforded as a teacher but not until the final interview did I discover the nature of the job.

In a very subtle way – a way that didn't seem at all like an interview – my recruiters had been looking not at the job I was doing, nor even the direction my CV suggested I should be pointing but at the skills I'd developed on the way and what I could bring to their organisation.

Qualifications – all the degrees, diplomas and bits of paper I'd amassed – proved I had a capacity to think creatively, work towards a goal and organise but that's all. The subject I'd studied was unimportant to them, other than to illustrate I was no stranger to detail, liked things right, would persevere until they were and had the confidence to perform to an audience.

Teaching proved I could explain and present, sell ideas, lead a group, convince – but it didn't limit me to life in a classroom.

It was the best part of four months before they revealed which niche I could fill but when they came up with an offer, it was for a job with a salary that delivered double what I was getting as a teacher.

It was an interesting job, too, a job in PR and marketing and one that would have seen my earnings rise exponentially – but there was a drawback: it offered a straight choice between no family life or a life for the girls in posh hotels for weeks at a time with nowhere to call their own.

That was unthinkable for me.

They needed their garden and familiar surroundings, their toys, freedom, somewhere to play, somewhere to have fun, stability.

By the time the confirmation letter arrived, I'd already decided I didn't want the job. If I could work for them – and they'd clearly spotted I had what it took – I could work for my family just as effectively, so I turned the offer down.

But the interview process had imparted a lasting impression on me. My interviewers had taught me to look beyond paper qualifications and achievements listed on a CV and concentrate on the applicant; to accept people for what they were and to help them realise what they could become.

That's something I adopted and took to heart in later life when it became my turn to recruit for my own company.

So, what was it we were going to do?

In the 14 months between getting married and the arrival of our first born, Marie and I had successfully transformed a bland cottage into a stylish home. We'd turned our hand to interior design, created atmosphere, built everything from ceilings and fireplaces to lamp shades and furniture.

She'd grown up around building – her father was a builder – and I knew cabinet-making from time spent in my grandfather's workshop. I'd always been good at technical drawing and illustration and the oil company had spotted I could organise, present and sell.

The furniture we'd made had prompted friends to ask if we could make things for them, so the direction seemed obvious.

Within a year, we had a small business designing bespoke fitted furniture – everything from fitted bedrooms and kitchens for friends (and their friends) to bars for millionaires – and we were using experienced cabinet-makers to make it and fit it for us.

It wasn't long before the cabinet-makers we were using cottoned on to the idea that if we could design and sell the products we were asking them to make, maybe there was a chance we could sell the products they'd already made.

Some were very expensive, finely-crafted pieces and we knew the home market would be a hard sell. It was, too, but the deeper we researched, the more it became apparent that there were accessible markets in wider Europe, the USA and Japan.

With the help of the Department of Trade & Industry's commercial attachés overseas, we amassed a directory of buyers in dozens of potential export markets and started to approach the most promising.

In a very modest way, we were successful but give your contacts to a buyer and you instantly make yourself obsolete. Without working on commission, which could

Catherine was much more at ease in front of a lens than Christina. I took this picture after she'd raided Marie's wardrobe and was trying on her high heels.

have presented a raft of problems to track, the business model was not sustainable. We figured there had to be a better way of presenting products and their makers to buyers in export markets that also allowed us to make a crust.

With the DTI keen to support any initiative that encouraged export sales, we turned to publishing – and the then very new concept of desktop publishing – for a solution.

It took two years of visiting workshops the length and breadth of Britain to find those whose products really were exportable, then take pictures and prepare appraisals before The Buyers' Guide to British Furniture Craftsmen was ready for print.

The first edition ran to 8,000 copies, the second to 10,000.

Against the advice of all the traditional book publishers we'd spoken to, we pushed the boat out and more than doubled our print run for the third and last edition.

The major booksellers couldn't see a market for it but on the strength of a PR campaign in consumer magazines, they cautiously took a handful at a time.

Re-orders were slow coming in but it really didn't matter. Consumers weren't our real target. Pressed by eager commercial attachés who wanted something to present to professional buyers, interior designers and specifiers in their markets, the DTI took hundreds of boxes for distribution through diplomatic post to British embassies in all the major markets.

By 1990, we'd successfully made the transition from music teachers to furniture designers to the authors, photographers and publishers of a book.

Three editions later, we were making in a month what I'd been earning in a year from teaching and the smile was back on Marie's face.

The girls would have been just six and seven when, with the third edition printed and at the mailing house, we decided to take them on their first long-haul holiday to Kenya. They were excited, we were excited and when we arrived, the first thing they wanted to do was play in the swimming pool.

We'd chosen a small, boutique hotel in the hope of a quiet escape away from crowds. Set in idyllic surroundings amid a forest of palm trees and richly planted gardens, 15 or 20 individual Makuti-roofed cottages, each sleeping up to four guests, had been carefully placed with enough space between to provide privacy.

They were simply furnished but comfortable enough and crucially, air-conditioned. At the centre of the complex was a kidney-shaped swimming pool with a swim-up bar. A large, open-air dining room overlooked it.

With no more than 40 or 50 guests in the hotel, it was the setting for a perfect escape; a little piece of paradise where we could enjoy time with the girls and relax.

The food was simple – edible but nothing special – and the girls were happy to have the pool almost to themselves. It didn't immediately strike us but after a few days, we began to notice that with each day that passed there appeared to be fewer and fewer hotel guests around the pool. On one afternoon, it was just the four of us and the bartender.

Fewer and fewer diners seemed to be dining in the restaurant, too. Asking around the handful who had arrived for dinner that evening, it transpired that one after another, guests were capitulating, retiring to their cottages with stomach cramps, nausea, fever and diarrhoea.

Dysentery had arrived.

Worried about the girls, we called the tour rep – a remarkably elusive character who seemed to know exactly when he was needed and always managed to be unavailable – to ask if a transfer might be possible.

There was no need to be concerned, he said, clearly unperturbed by events that had stricken most of the holidaymakers on his patch. *But I will come over tomorrow morning to talk to all the guests if it worries you.*

Of course, he never arrived.

It was on the fifth day that things suddenly took a turn for the worse: we'd arrived for dinner just in time to witness a huge commotion in front of the serving area.

Four waiters, a waitress, the chef and the kitchen helper were gathered in a semicircle by the buffet with their backs to us. They were shouting, agitated.

A machete was being waved around. There was blood on it.

The waitress was hysterical.

Suddenly, one of the waiters caught sight of us and immediately headed in our direction, waving his hands frantically as if to distract us from whatever was going on.

It was too late.

Through the gap he'd left, we could see the reason for the commotion.

On the floor in front of them was a snake, a ten-foot snake – a very dead ten-foot snake.

They'd beheaded it on the dining room floor.

The following day, we arrived for breakfast expecting to find tables laid and no trace of the previous night's incident but everything had been left exactly where it had been the night before. Used crockery was still on the tables. Even the buffet hadn't been taken away. By midday, still nothing had changed.

Dinner time arrived and in the 40-degree heat, the snake had started to make its presence known. Guests were complaining.

The buffet had been changed but no one wanted to eat. The situation was becoming ugly and the question everyone wanted answered was: *Why was it still there?*

It fell to the head waiter to explain: this was a Black Mamba. It was a very special snake. Only the medicine man could remove it but first he had to detach the bits he needed for his potions. The problem was, no one could locate him.

Realising things were not likely to get better any time soon, together with another couple from Yorkshire we led a revolt and the entire complement of guests decamped to the Indian-owned hotel further down the beach. It was bigger, it was busier, it was used by the same tour company we'd booked with but at least the management was understanding.

Back in England, after months of wrangling, the tour company finally capitulated and agreed to return part of the cost of the holiday. The following year, we vowed to opt for the safety of France.

A few months after our return, I was admitted to hospital for a minor operation. I've never been very good at idle time but we needed a route forward that would keep the financial momentum flowing, so, bandaged up and confined to bed for a few days, I started thinking about the massive database of furniture-makers and manufacturers we'd accumulated en route to publishing the book – almost 15,000 back then – and about the problems some of those we'd featured had subsequently encountered.

We'd provided the craftsmen with good, hot leads – in many cases, dozens of them. Export buyers wanted British-made furniture, they liked the work of the furniture-makers we'd presented to them but only a handful of the workshops had something to send out and an even smaller number had any clue how to respond.

One I'd visited a few weeks after we'd published the book had put 60 enquiry cards in a drawer and not knowing what to do with them, had left them there unanswered. It was a problem we'd never anticipated and we had to help.

Cue Furniture Journal, the first magazine we ever published.

Through the magazine, we could harness the expertise of the commercial attachés, who were now in possession of the book, and enlist their help once more with articles on their specific markets.

Alongside export articles that detailed how to sell to each market, the types of importers that might be interested, ways of doing business and the requirements of different buying-houses and retailers, we included articles on letters of credit and export documentation, business formats, legal issues, insurance and more – and we made it all free, financed by advertising revenue from those who sold machinery, materials, components and hardware.

And while the first edition of Furniture Journal was going through print and arriving on desks – the June 1993 edition – we took that long overdue holiday in France.

We'd been to France once before as a family and enjoyed two weeks in the pigeonnier end of an old farmhouse near Agen that had been converted to provide a taste of traditional France – and it was there, in the quiet of a private pool with the fragrance of a huge lavender bed behind, that the girls had learned how to swim. It was idyllic, characterful and enjoyable.

With the money we'd recovered from our Kenyan experience, we decided that this time we'd book a gite and try the Charente region, an area famed for its Cognac.

Our hosts, François and Jean-Paul, didn't tell us at the time that we were their first clients and it was only much later after we'd become friends that we learned how terrified they'd been to see a big, black BMW – a rare sight in rural France back then – making its way up the shingle driveway towards the courtyard and their tiny, two-room gite, a former cowshed.

They needn't have worried. We were not expecting five-star. But the welcome was five-star anyway.

From la cave in his barn, Jean-Paul brought decanters of home-made Pineau de Charente, a fabulous and very agreeable blend of Cognac and grape juice, sometimes white, sometimes red, made throughout the region. His English was basic, my French was basic but two glasses of Pineau later, it really didn't matter. We were already setting the tone for the friendship of a lifetime.

Within a couple of days, the girls had made friends with Coralie, the daughter of one of Jean-Paul's neighbours and as Jean-Paul and I advanced our respective language skills in French and English with the help of his Pineau, the girls took turns to leap into the swimming pool at the end of the garden while shouting words in each other's languages. It was a wonderful holiday, far beyond anything we could have expected.

The following year, with Furniture Journal now established as a bi-monthly magazine, we returned to François and Jean-Paul's gite, this time as friends.

Jean-Paul is a great guy. In his early fifties when we first met, he's a Frenchman through and through – but a very international Frenchman whose life has been enriched by friendships from all over the world.

Once upon a time he aspired to be a priest but then he discovered girls and never looked back. I kind of get that. My ecclesiastical aspirations only ever took me as far as organist and choirmaster but I'd have diverted too, given the chance.

He's very practical, in a country kind of way and is up for any DIY challenge. His house, an old farm dating back centuries, faces a courtyard bordered with barns and outbuildings, of which the gite is one.

Most rooms in the main house are furnished with antique Charentais furniture that has been lovingly restored (by Jean-Paul) with hinges that don't work, doors that fall off and the distinctive nibblings of woodworm retained for character. Light switches spark to the touch, the heating system growls like a hungry bear and the plumbing has a character all of its own – but in its own inimitable way, it's charming, different, enjoyable and the foibles add a certain *je ne sais qoi* to the experience.

On this particular occasion, the drive down had taken us longer than expected and we'd arrived late in the afternoon.

There was no time to unpack. In the courtyard, tables had already been laid and chairs had been placed in a long line beneath the sprawling branches of a huge tree. Our appearance immediately prompted the arrival of several decanters of Pineau from la cave and in the fullness of time, neighbours arrived, friends arrived, wine arrived and dinner arrived.

It must have been approaching two in the morning when, with the last glass of Cognac drained and the conversation slowing, Jean-Paul rose to his feet.

Tomorrow, mes amis, we has zee job to do, he announced, steadying himself on the table and raising a glass of his favourite William Pear liqueur.

Cheers followed and glasses clanked.

It was already tomorrow but everyone was well past caring.

We make zee new gite! he continued. *Zee cement...he arrive at aff past eight in zee morning.*

Most of the afternoon and throughout the evening, the Pineau, the Morgon and the Cognac had flowed. Spent glasses lay in evidence along the entire length of the table. The jovial banter had subsided but the murmur of conversation was still audible from the far end of the table. Everyone had heard the words but no one had really absorbed the meaning.

What did he say? Gite, as in house.

We're making one tomorrow, as in today.

Half past eight, as in six hours away, on a day when we'd already driven for 14 hours.

And, presumably, the builders were those of us still able to stand.

That wasn't many.

Alarmingly, Jean-Paul seemed serious.

Gradually the party dissipated. Half a dozen of the most intoxicated had already staggered arm-in-arm down the gravel driveway and arrived at the gate. Though fainter, their bi-tonal rendering of the French National Anthem could still be heard from the courtyard.

Laughter followed, then a commotion, then more laughter.

I didn't catch the words but with some indecipherable shouting and an unexpected surge of energy, the three guys from the far end of the table, who I'd taken to be past the point of no return, suddenly took off down the driveway.

Monsieur l'Expert, the main man who'd been tasked with leading tomorrow's grand enterprise, had failed to find the switch for the electric gate and while groping around in the dark, managed to point himself in the wrong direction, trip over a deck chair and fall in the swimming pool.

By the time the pool lights had been switched on, he had already been hauled out and was sitting on the grass, burping.

Half-past eight arrived all too quickly. Bleary-eyed, I hauled myself out of the door, coffee in hand, and headed for the gite-to-be. It was a huge stone barn, almost half of one side of the horseshoe-shaped courtyard. Inside the barn it was dark but, through small windows at the courtyard side, a roughly-levelled dirt floor was visible.

Beyond the door-less entrance, old beams and rough stone walls emerged from the gloom. I remember thinking how characterful they would look if they were cleaned and the stonework was re-pointed.

I could picture the entrance with a grand oak staircase and maybe a galleried landing leading to four, maybe five big bedrooms. It definitely had potential.

Eight-thirty had passed some time ago and nothing had moved. By nine I'd made it to my third cup of coffee. Nine-thirty followed swiftly. Then came ten and still no Monsieur l'Expert, no Jean-Paul and no band of merry men to help. And what of *zee cement?* He, as I recalled, was due to arrive at eight-thirty.

It must have been shortly after ten-thirty that Jean-Paul made an appearance.

Bonjour! he called, leaning out of an upstairs window and pushing aside the ivy that was growing around it. *Ca va?*

Fine, fine, fine… but where is the cement and where are the helpers?

He shrugged. *Ah, zee day he eez long. Soon zey will areeve. No problem!*

Approaching eleven in the morning, the first stragglers began to appear. Clad in rubber wellies and floppy hats and armed with spades and shovels, I couldn't help thinking how much they resembled The Waltons as they made their way up the driveway.

Taking up the rear was Monsieur l'Expert, a slightly-portly and rather vertically-challenged gentleman with a small moustache and a black beret. He'd obviously dried off overnight but seemed to be wearing the same clothes.

Within minutes *zee cement*, he arrived and Monsieur l'Expert was at once in his element, shouting orders from somewhere in the grass.

Having failed to find the button to open Jean-Paul's home-made electric gates, the driver of the cement wagon had been directed to the track at the opposite side of the building. He'd reversed carefully towards the barn, negotiating a route between the various relics of part-restored Triumphs from the '60s and '70s – one of Jean-Paul's other passions – and masterfully positioned the rear end of the wagon so it was ready to pour.

Zis, confirmed Jean-Paul, gleefully, *will be zee floor. We make him flat. No problem. We has zee expert. Ee eez your chef!*

Now that was a prospect that intrigued me – not Monsieur l'Expert being my boss, that didn't concern me at all; rather, a potential problem I couldn't quite wrap my head around: before me stood a cement wagon, its load churning in the rear. I could see the chute and I could see the driver judiciously positioning it in the general direction of the wall behind the wagon. He was poised to tip.

So far so good.

What I couldn't see was how he was going to get the cement from the wagon into the barn. The wall was solid. Very solid. There were no gaps, no holes, no doors, no windows and being an old barn, the walls were probably a foot-and-a-half thick.

Jean-Paul was quick to dispel my bewilderment: *No problem, mon ami! Eez your job to make zee window, eh? Zen ee put zee cement froo zee 'ole.*

I've never built a house, nor even carried out structural work much beyond the removal of stud walls and plasterboard ceiling panels but somewhere in the back of my mind I remembered the builders we'd employed to extend the cottage putting lintels in and bolstering load-bearing walls with props before attacking them with sledgehammers.

There were no lintels in sight. There were no supports. But soon there were four guys attacking the wall from the inside, two more accompanied me with lump hammers and stone chisels on the outside and from an appropriately levitated vantage point a safe distance away, Monsieur l'Expert shouted his orders.

It took a good half hour before we finally broke through and the supremely patient delivery driver was allowed to poke his chute into the newly-created window (known affectionately as *le 'ole* as a concession to the Englishman in their midst who hadn't yet learned the French word *fenêtre*) and begin pumping.

The last drop pumped, I followed the others back to the courtyard in the expectation we would start work levelling the vast heap of cement that stood in one corner of the barn. But instead of reaching for shovels and spades, they made their way towards a wheelbarrow that Jean-Paul had pushed from the kitchen to a central position in the courtyard. Here they gathered.

The sun rose high in the sky and the temperature hit the mid 30s. The heap inside the barn set about its business solidifying in the corner – but there were more important things to be done before attention could be given to it.

Glasses were being handed around. Pineau was being opened. Barely recovered from the night before, les français were setting about the important task of getting pickled once again.

Probably an hour or so later and now extremely merry, the happy band once more resumed its work under the direction of the staggering and even more vocal Monsieur l'Expert. But instead of levelling cement, we now had the task of shifting rapidly-setting shovelfuls from one side of the barn to the other.

Monsieur l'Expert, rather than directing the shovelling into boxed-off areas that one might expect should have been carefully levelled in preparation, was busying himself measuring up the wall six inches at a time from the sloping dirt floor of the barn.

Barely a couple of metres ahead of the dollop shifters, he was chalking level marks to which the dollops should be piled, occasionally retiring to a safe distance close to the wheelbarrow containing the Pineau on the pretence of checking for accuracy.

After copious quantities of pre-lunchtime libation, his idea of level was somewhat at odds with his spirit level but he was Monsieur l'Expert after all and I, just a humble dollop shifter.

With the cement eventually spread, the floor more closely resembled the surface of the moon than anything upon which tiles could be laid but Monsieur l'Expert was content. The heap had been big enough to spread from corner to corner.

Leaning against the back wall of the barn – his vantage point for checking the level of the floor and the Pineau – he shouted something indecipherable that seemed to indicate his satisfaction and raising a freshly-charged glass in acknowledgement of a job well done, took a satisfyingly long swig.

Outside in the courtyard, the long table we'd used the night before had been reset for lunch.

Tablecloths had been spread. Bottles of wine had been placed at even distances down its length. Food was arriving. Glasses too. And plates. Corks were popping and once more, while the still very uneven floor solidified, the French got to grips with the most important task of the day: eating, drinking and getting merry. Even more merry.

We must have been a good couple of hours into the meal when someone noticed there was a vacant chair at the head of the table. Monsieur l'Expert was not present. Nobody had seen him. He was not in the house. He was not in the garden. A quick check under the table revealed he wasn't there either.

I think it was Jean-Paul who discovered him. He was exactly where he'd been left but he'd slid down the wall and was now at something of an angle. Still resting against the back wall of the barn, his wellies embedded six inches deep in fairly solid cement, Monsieur l'Expert was snoring gently, oblivious to his predicament.

Leaving barely a mark in the now hardened surface, two of the band made their way across the cement and, realising his feet were rooted, hoisted him clear leaving his wellies as a permanent fixture in the floor.

Rumour has it they were lopped off and tiled over after we departed for England.

That December, the December of 1994, we returned to Jean-Paul's for the New Year celebrations. The weather was not as kind as it had been in the summer, in fact it snowed and the temperature plummeted but in the living room of the main house, with 20-something people gathered around the table and the fire stoked to capacity, nobody cared.

The *huîtres* [oysters] were good, the wine was good, the conversation flowed and in the best French tradition, as the clock struck midnight everyone linked arms and sang 'Auld Lang Syne'.

The concurrence of copy dates, production dates, on-press dates and publishing dates with school holidays was an infrequent event, so whenever the blue moon rose, we'd head off to far-flung places with guaranteed weather.

With both girls interested in swimming and snorkelling, for our next adventure we decided to take them somewhere that was famed for its beaches, friendly welcome and lack of behead-able Black Mambas.

It was with much enthusiasm that we arranged a trip to the Caribbean island of Barbados.

Barbados was beautiful. We found pristine beaches, we found limestone caves with streams and rock pools, we found a lovely old plantation house to explore and we had our pictures taken under a giant Baobab tree.

We enjoyed the local flying-fish and grilled lobster in the evening and the pink sands of Crane Beach and the colourful market in Bridgetown by day. We absorbed the local culture as eagerly as the warm sunshine. And of course, the girls enjoyed the pool and snorkelling in the shallow waters.

But there's only so much snorkelling an enthusiastic snorkeller with an adventurous spirit can do in the shallows before visits to the same rock with the same patch of weed start to lose their appeal. Snorkelling is fun but it's tricky taking pictures when you have to keep coming up for air.

The girls liked taking pictures.

Armed with £10 waterproof cameras, they snapped enthusiastically at anything that finned its way past, even if it was each other. Catherine wanted to feed the fish but there weren't too many that would hang around in the shallows to be hand fed.

Besides, she wanted to see bigger ones. Titanic, the movie, had just been released and both of them loved it. Everything underwater seemed exciting, different, and they wanted an adventure.

You can guess where this is going.

I'd been interested in diving since childhood. As a kid, I had a little plastic frogman who descended and ascended in the bath leaving a stream of bubbles behind him when I put a fizzy tablet in the removable tank on his back and I'd collected numerous books on wrecks, fish, dive sites and the underwater adventures of the inimitable Jacques Cousteau, co-inventor of the aqua-lung, and film-makers, Hans and Lotte Hass.

I'd even declared to my mother and father that one day I wanted to be an ichthyologist. I didn't know what it meant, at least not in any meaningful way, but it sounded good. It was the only thing I ever managed to impress my paternal Grandmother with – probably because she didn't know what ichthyology was either [the scientific study of fish, to save you looking it up] – so I wheeled it out often in her presence.

At the first opportunity, I learned to dive.

Seizing on the moment and my enthusiasm for the sport, the girls took their chance in Barbados and skilfully pestered until I gave in and took them to a dive shop.

At that time, they were far too young to go on a dive. Even a trial lesson should have been out of the question for at least another four years but we'd chanced upon a dive shop that had a lot of blank spaces on its week-planner and a young diving-instructor who'd spent a lot of time working on his suntan.

If I would agree to being in the pool with them and watching one of them while he worked with the other, he'd give them some basic pool training the following morning – but we had to be there early so no one saw and if anyone asked, they were both fourteen.

Immediately, their faces lit up.

The daredevils had talked themselves into an adventure.

The morning's brief was brief indeed. Two buoyancy control devices with tanks and regulators were already lined up at the side of the pool when we arrived and the girls sifted quickly through racks of equipment to find boots and fins that fitted.

I'd barely had chance to flash my diving licence and pay for the trial lesson before they were down at the pool, in the water, masks and snorkels on and finning around.

The trial lesson went well. Flooding and clearing masks came easily to them. They were soon swapping between regulators and snorkels on the surface, descending, ascending and getting to grips with buoyancy.

If I'd imagined one trial lesson would be the end of it, I couldn't have been more mistaken. I'd taken my wet suit, fins, BCD and regulator with me in case the opportunity presented itself to go on a dive. We'd found a dive school and the girls had impressed the instructor. With the bit between their teeth, they now wanted to go see some fish, feed some fish, visit a reef, see corals, take pictures.

By the end of the second session they were kneeling on the bottom of the pool, unhooking and reattaching weight belts, swapping regulators and having a go at buddy breathing – things I don't recall getting into when I did my dive training for quite a few sessions.

Everything the instructor gave them to do, they seemed to get it immediately, without hesitation and without hint of the panic I'd seen in so many dive students who, with half an inch of water in their masks, would head straight for the surface (in a swimming pool they could have stood up in) to gasp for air.

Towards the end of the session, with the exercises complete, the instructor gave them the freedom they'd been longing for and off they went, finning around the perimeter of the pool in circles a few inches from the bottom like a couple of curious sharks.

Back in dry clothes, the dive instructor turned salesman and steadily shifted the conversation to dive sites and availability. The Friar's Craig was laying in 30 metres of water near Lobster Reef, he told me. It was a good wreck dive. Or, if I wanted to see lots of marine life, he'd take me to dive the outer barrier reef at Mount Charlie.

It was tempting. Very tempting.

But what about a shallower dive – maybe a wreck with enough natural light for some good photography?

The Berwyn! Yes, of course, this was an easy dive. Lying almost upright in fewer than ten metres of water, he explained, the Berwyn had been deliberately sunk in 1919 by its crew. It was in Carlisle Bay, just off the shoreline near the dive centre. It was about 70 feet long and encrusted with corals. It was teeming with fish. The photography would be great. We could snorkel out from the shoreline in about ten minutes, or take the dive boat. When was I thinking of?

Persuaded by the opportunity to capture some good underwater photographs, we arranged a time and a date and agreed that we should hire the Zodiac so the girls could enjoy the boat trip while the instructor took me down to the wreck.

Enjoy the boat trip? Sit on the side? Count bubbles?

The daredevils were having none of it.

Marie always enjoyed a boat trip but wasn't interested in diving. She was quite happy to bob around in the boat while I was overboard taking pictures.

But the girls, they didn't want to sit out the opportunity to visit a wreck. They'd been OK in the pool. The instructor had been impressed.

It's an easy dive, Dad. The instructor had said so. It wasn't deep. They'd never seen a wreck before. There would be fish for Catherine to feed. We could all take pictures. They couldn't just sit in the boat and watch bubbles.

Quite how it came about or who persuaded whom, I can't recall but somehow, even the diving-instructor seemed to be going along with this idea.

It would mean there would be three dives and a boat to pay for instead of just one dive, he explained but if I agreed to two days instead of one, he could do a better price on all the dives and the boat would be free for the second day – or we could opt for a package and if the girls liked it, maybe we could all do a reef dive on the third day.

It was about that time I found myself wondering whether I should agree or just offer him a job.

The girls were nine and ten years old. They'd had a couple of pool sessions. They'd been fine, they were sensible but were they really ready for an open-water dive – a wreck dive?

He had totally captivated them. He reckoned they were ready. There was no going back. Before I knew it, my card was being swiped and the receipt was already printing from the machine.

I don't recall ever feeling nervous on a dive before. The thrill of expectation usually took over from the moment the whiff of neoprene escaped the unzipped dive-bag but on this occasion, I was uneasy.

The girls chattered excitedly as they looked for wet suits, boots and fins that fit. Christina was OK. Catherine couldn't find a wet-suit small enough. There were warm currents, the dive instructor assured and it wasn't deep. People often snorkelled this wreck in just a swim suit. She would be fine in a tee-shirt.

Over the dive site, the instructor tied the boat to a buoy while I triple-checked the girls' BCDs were properly fastened and their air supply was on and over the magic 200 bar.

It would be a shallow dive but if they were excited, they could still use air quickly. They knew the signal to give when their air supply dropped to 50 bar, the signal for OK and the signal for 'I need air'.

We'd talked about the backward roll off the boat, how to hold their masks as they rolled and the head-touch signal when they surfaced to confirm they were fine after the roll in.

We'd rehearsed buddy-breathing on shore just in case and the yellow alternate air-source regulators were visible at the front of their BCDs in case of emergency. They knew to descend together on the anchor chain. They knew to equalise ear-pressure regularly and stay together during the dive.

Throughout, the instructor had taken a back seat, become a spectator and let me assume responsibility for the dive.

I've never been motion-sick, air-sick, sea-sick – nor, indeed, been prone to queasiness of any kind – except when it came to the smell of two-stroke engines.

Combined with even the slightest swell, it was always guaranteed to make me feel nauseous. On this occasion, I was too apprehensive to take much notice as we tightened the straps on our fins and prepared for the backward roll.

First in, I waited for the girls anxiously.

I shouldn't have worried. One after the other, they rolled in like a couple of dive professionals.

The water was crystal clear as we descended the anchor-chain, pausing every now and then to equalise.

A short distance ahead, the wreck rose from the sandy bottom of Carlise Bay like a huge, sweeping wall, towering over us as we approached from a metre or so above the sea bed.

Following the instructor, we finned around the hull, ascending briefly to look through the port holes at colourful coral formations inside before descending again to explore the rudder where a shoal of tiny fish was playing chase.

With sunlight dancing on the deck, the open hatches were clearly visible and one by one, we peered through them. There was an anchor and a bell still on the deck. Approaching the bows, the capstans on the winch had become heavily encrusted with corals and the remnants of the prow swept up towards the sunlight.

Throughout the dive, we'd held hands but seeing the bows, Christina pulled away and seizing the opportunity for a photo shoot, positioned herself, arms outstretched – Kate Winslet on the bows of the Titanic – for Catherine to take a picture.

Taking turns to pose, they seemed entirely at ease and happy with their new underwater environment. I remembered how I'd struggled with buoyancy when I started diving. It was easy to them, effortless.

My moment of pride was short-lived.

The photo shoot over, holding hands again and with Catherine on my right and Christina on my left, we descended to the bottom of the hull for one more circuit before returning to the Zodiac.

Unexpectedly, without warning, Christina took off.

She'd seen her scrunchy hovering a few feet away just inches above the sandy bottom but in her enthusiasm to retrieve it, she caught my mask and regulator with her fin and in an instant, both were gone.

Almost ten metres down, I had no air and no mask.

By the time I'd retrieved my regulator and could see what was going on, she was already in front of me and making the OK sign with both hands. The scrunchy had been rescued and she was excited to have been its saviour.

Our instructor – our essential buddy whose duty it was to be close by in case of emergency – was nowhere to be seen.

We made a second dive on the Berwyn a few days later but livelier seas the night before had stirred up the crystal-clear waters in the bay and reduced visibility underwater, making all but close-up photography pointless.

We had taken some bread in a bag so Catherine could feed the fish but much larger fish with much larger teeth had swum in from the open ocean and taken the place of the shoals of little fish we'd seen playing around the rudder on our first dive. Without the protection of a wet suit, they bit.

The only way to stop them biting her was to tow the food bag a couple of metres away so she could watch from a safe distance as they gorged on its contents. It wasn't quite the refined tea party she had in mind.

On the third day, we went on the reef dive together. The girls enjoyed swimming around the coral formations and taking pictures of its inhabitants.

At eight or nine metres – the deepest point of the dive we'd planned – they were fine and I was comfortable with them enjoying the experience but the edge of the reef dropped away steeply.

With the superstructure of a large wreck appearing out of the gloom some 15 or 20 metres below us and my depth gauge already reading ten metres, when the intrepid three started descending towards it, I had to remind our enthusiastic and sometimes inattentive diving instructor it was time to start the ascent. Major decompression wasn't something I wanted the girls involved with on their third-ever pleasure dive, especially as we'd all used a good two-thirds of our air.

The following morning, Catherine had a hair appointment. She'd seen several girls with an unusual hairstyle that really appealed to her and with only a couple of days before we were due to fly back home, she'd managed to persuade Marie to allow her to have dreadlocks.

The owner of the hotel where we were staying recommended a salon and booked the appointment with Mama Lillybelle, a friend of his but concerned that Catherine was too young to be left on her own with someone we didn't know, I'd insisted on being there during the remodelling.

Mama Lillybelle was a big girl with the purest complexion and the most immaculate white teeth. We arrived early in the morning but already the sun was high and the heat was rising.

The salon was a tiny little building and inside it, the room where she worked

Catherine and me during a pool training session in Barbados. Diving came easily to both girls.

*Me diving the Berwyn in Carlisle bay, Barbados. Christina took these
pictures on on a ten-quid camera during the first two dives we did together.*

was no more than ten feet in any direction. There was a basin, a swivel chair for her client, a chair for her helper and a spare chair for visitors. There was no air conditioning and even with the door open it was baking hot.

Deftly, Mama Lillybelle got to work, twiddling away at Catherine's hair, her voluptuous hormonally-confused chest towering threateningly over the comparatively pocket-sized Catherine.

She was a barrel of laughs and giggled all the time she was working. Each sentence was punctuated with shrieks and giggles and the more she laughed, the more she jiggled up and down.

Finally, with a triumphant burst of laughter, she finished, spinning Catherine around in a flourish so I could admire from all angles.

Her creation was a work of art; an intricate succession of perfectly spaced quarter inch plaits, each impeccably finished with a colourful bead to hold it in place. Catherine had the full head of dreadlocks she'd wanted since arriving in Barbados and she was thrilled to bits.

She received all the attention from the cabin crew on the flight home.

It wouldn't be long after we returned from Barbados that Christina turned ten. Only too well, I recall the battle I'd had with the headmaster of her middle school in the months before our holiday when, with nothing further to offer – but desperate to keep his class numbers up – he refused to allow her to transfer to secondary school a year early and called in a child psychologist to help make his case.

If the psychologist had harboured any notion he might be in for an easy ride, he couldn't have been more mistaken.

Perched confidently on the black leather chair in my office, as coolly as any seasoned prosecution lawyer, Christina tied him in knots as I watched in admiration from the end of the desk. She had an answer for every question – as she always did – and delivered each succinctly.

At one point, rather than answering directly, she told him quite vehemently, *It would be futile for her to state what must be obvious, so what was the point in asking that?*

It was roguish, I admit, but I couldn't resist applauding.

She was just nine years of age, yet she'd successfully turned the interview on its head. The interviewer had become the interviewee.

The psychologist had been told Christina was shy, retiring, socially behind her peers because she didn't have many friends at school.

How do you feel about that? he asked.

Do you know where I live? came the response. *How far do you think it is? Doesn't it strike you as a bit impractical?*

He looked completely dazed as he left the room. She'd won her case – and my admiration.

Was that a Proud Dad look? she asked after he'd scuttled out. You bet it was. There were a lot more to come for both girls in the years that followed.

Chapter Seven
The Rise of the Journal

Since 1994 when we bought the offices and lit the blue touch paper under Furniture Journal, we'd seen growth every year. Advertising revenues were up, staff numbers were growing and our reputation in the industry was developing as fast as our portfolio.

It hadn't been an easy entrance to the market but we'd found a niche and our business model was working well.

Soon after the launch of Furniture Journal, we introduced a sister magazine, Bathroom Journal and in the years that followed there would be a Kitchen Journal, a Commercial Bathroom Journal, a Contract Kitchen & Bathroom Journal, a set of Kitchen Essentials supplements, a Design & Décors edition, a Tools & Machinery, even a Garden Journal (briefly).

We put forward proposals to publish Let's Fly magazines on behalf of several UK airports, then we set up offices and a sister company in Krakow and launched Furniture Journal Polska in Polish. We were on the verge of publishing a Cyrillic edition from offices in Lithuania – Furniture Journal Russia – when the winds of political change turned against us and it had to be withdrawn.

But they were exciting times. The company was growing. Furniture Journal was attracting advertisers from as far afield as the USA, Japan and Korea, adding to regular advertisers from the UK, Italy, Germany, Austria, Spain, Switzerland and Scandinavia, while Bathroom Journal and Kitchen Journal were winning advertising contracts from market-leading brands in Britain and beyond.

We recruited sales staff, editorial staff, designers, accountants, circulation controllers and admin staff, bought a company car, bought a company aeroplane and as the magazines grew in reputation, we started to travel wider in search of exclusive editorials to make the titles stand out, visiting exhibitions and factories around Europe and reviewing products.

The exhibitions were always the highlights of our features lists. They provided the best chance of finding new and unusual products and with almost all our major clients from one or other sectors in one place at one time, they always represented unparalleled opportunities for collecting materials and taking photographs. We worked them hard and our reviews became legendary.

Overseas exhibitions were always my favourites. They were hard on the feet and intensive days with no rest from morning 'til evening but they gave us access to much more technology and many more products. And they were always a pleasant few days escape from the office.

In an evening, after a hard day shuttling between hot stands and noisy halls, we would always make sure we had time to unwind, chill with a nice glass of something refreshing and enjoy the local cuisine. On one or two occasions, our evening chill time even proved to be quite entertaining.

Perhaps the most memorable exhibition we attended was one in Milan. It was a woodworking-machinery show, though it wasn't the show itself that proved unforgettable.

It wasn't Milan either.

Milan was never my favourite Italian city and that particular May it was especially hot and noisy. Parked cars strewn across pavements were a hazard that was difficult to negotiate and the paving stones they'd dislodged and up-ended through years of abuse made the half-mile walk from the hotel we used to the exhibition grounds treacherous.

Wheeled cases, heavy with cameras, lenses and flash equipment, were useless and had to be carried. We arrived at the entrance hot, sweaty and irritable – not the best start to a long day – and there was a lengthy queue.

Nothing seemed to be moving.

At least we had press passes and presenting the letter that came with them at the side gate where there was no queue would expedite our entry.

That's what it said, anyway. But this was Milan and controlling entrance through the gate was a young chap with a mobile phone at his ear.

Impossibly good-looking (as best a guy can judge another guy), slim, olive-skinned, black-suited and with immaculately-slicked hair and dark glasses, he was far too busy to let anyone past.

Press passes counted for nothing until his conversation had ended and that didn't seem as if it was going to be any time soon. As the minutes ticked by, more press arrived – three, four, five of them – but still the conversation continued.

Eventually, one of the newcomers must have caught wind of the conversation and yelled at him angrily in Italian. Someone else joined in. They wanted access, too. We all did. Finally, with a look of absolute disdain on his face, he ended the call and signalled irascibly for me to hand over the letter.

Though he'd barely given it a cursory glance, I'd naïvely expected the gate would be opened but instead, with supreme indifference written across his face and a dismissive shrug, he side-lined me and beckoned for presentation of the next letter.

Not until all the letters had been handed over did he signal for his colleague at the other side of the gate to open up while he stalked off with his nose in the air.

In his time, we'd finally managed to gain entrance to the exhibition we'd flown from the other side of Europe to see, proceeded to tackle the day's jobs and thought no more of it – that is until the evening when who should walk into the restaurant we'd chosen for its calming ambience but the same chap, now with lady companion.

Seated centre stage in the restaurant, and clearly aware he had an audience, with great verve and flamboyance he ordered the meal and the wine for himself and his immaculately-presented, long-haired, short-skirted tablemate and in due course it arrived.

She picked delicately at the neatly-arranged greenery while he flashed his immaculate white teeth from behind a well-tanned façade, posing and gesturing all the while, dancing the eyebrows and flashing the big brownies. She giggled dutifully. The more she giggled, the more he postured – and so it went on.

Then came the daddy of all disasters.

With most of the diners in the restaurant subtly spectating, he picked up his fork, twiddled the spaghetti the waiter had placed before him and gazing deeply and lustfully into his tablemate's eyes, put the fork to his mouth.

Fresh, Italian spaghetti isn't the ideal dish to order on a date. When liberally-dosed with tomato sauce and a slippery pesto it can have a mind of its own and has been known to exhibit wayward and sometimes anti-social tendencies. This delicacy was showing all the right signs.

Lustful glances turned to anguish as the offending worms refused entrance with the same conviction he had demonstrated towards us just a few hours before. Pout turned to suction, suction to panic and panic to embarrassment as first one strand hit his cheek, then another.

Finally, his lungs full, the last strand made its way to his mouth and with a defiant swirl of its tail, threw tomato sauce across his pristine designer shirt, wiping itself ever so thoroughly across chin and cheeks.

How we laughed!

How his young and beautiful tablemate laughed!

Soon, the whole restaurant was cheering and clapping, banging forks on the table, saluting him with their glasses.

Waiters rushed to the table, napkins in hand. Immaculate sun-tan gave way to intense shades of boiled lobster as the luckless lad mopped his brow and fought to recover some composure. But hardly was the episode at a close when he did it again.

With a deftness that had to be seen to be believed, he gently caught the rim of his glass with an ever-so wide double cuff and sent Valpolicella hurtling across the newly-replaced white table cloth to the waiting designer blouse of his delightful but now somewhat outraged dinner guest.

The scream she let out would have been enough to awaken the dead throughout Lombardy.

Staggering to her feet on enormous high heels and screaming at the top of her voice in words that seemed to complement her gestures admirably, the offended and somewhat soggy maiden wrenched the table cloth from under the remaining plates and dishes sending spaghetti, tomato sauce, pesto, parmesan, knives, forks, glasses – and the remaining contents of the Valpolicella – hurtling across the room.

All her date could do was gape in disbelief.

The restaurant buzzed as diners, male and female, took sides and cheered on their chosen champion. She, by now, was so involved in venting her wrath that she hadn't noticed her extremely short skirt had ridden up and was beginning to reveal a skimpy red thong (among other things).

It had not, however, escaped the note of her eagle-eyed date.

Desperate to reaffirm his gallantry, he struggled to his feet, determined to save her from further embarrassment. Tripping clumsily over the draped tablecloth, he lunged with both hands outstretched, grasped the tiny garment in his descent – and promptly yanked it clean off, baring a set of perfectly-formed and nicely browned buttocks.

With that, the fires of hell broke loose. The volcano erupted. Molten magma flowed. Arms and legs, like so much spaghetti before them, flew wildly. Screams and shrieks reached ear-splitting level.

The waiters fretted, mere helpless onlookers in a real-life battle.

Even protection of the remaining upstanding tables and chairs must have seemed futile to them as first one waiter, then another resigned himself to shuffling furniture in order to obtain the best possible vantage point.

It was only a matter of time before, over the noise of the intensifying battle, the sound of sirens could be heard. Lights flashed, blue-shirted Polizia arrived in force – two, three, four, five...more – but still the maiden would not relent.

'Hell hath no fury like a woman scorned', the English author William Congreve once wrote and this one had been scorned mightily.

But the end was nigh. The downing of the first officer in a melange of pesto and Valpolicella brought their patience to a close. It was left to the others to bring blankets...and two pairs of handcuffs.

There was no sign of the luckless lad on the gate at the exhibition the following morning.

We dined at the same restaurant that evening and the evening after, hoping that some drama would unfold to entertain us but it was not to be. There was nothing to compare with that first night.

It wasn't just exhibitions that provided the odd entertaining moment. Sometimes we got more than we expected during visits to see clients and their factories, too.

Editorial visits for Furniture Journal always had to be well-organised and to work like a well-oiled machine because, mostly, the people we needed to interview were either directors or production managers and their availability was limited.

Given an hour to talk to the right people and a tour of the factory to take pictures, we could usually achieve pretty much everything that was needed for a two, three or four-page article and invariably, our clients would help with the arrangements and ensure the right people were available when we arrived.

If we were visiting overseas companies, more often than not we'd need an overnight stay and if our hosts had the time, there was a good chance they'd book a nice restaurant and we'd enjoy some time together on the evening of our arrival and make the factory visit the following morning before flying home.

On one particular visit, the surprise that awaited was one I won't forget.

I'd flown to Germany to see one of the global market leaders in printed furniture décors with my publication manager. The plan was to meet the company's design director, who I'd known for many years, interview her about trends in the market, see the design department and the factory and take some pictures.

The entrance foyer was magnificent with its steelwork and glass but walking down the stairs, it wasn't the architecture that claimed my attention. Hiding under a dust sheet was a large piano.

I couldn't resist a peek.

Beneath the cover was a beautiful black concert-length grand piano – but this was not just any grand. This was a Steinway, the Rolls Royce of pianos and it was a very special Steinway. The sight took my breath away.

For a moment, I stood motionless, admiring, feasting on the visual spectacle.

But what was it doing in the entrance foyer of a décor printing company? It seemed bizarre, out of context.

It fell to our host, the marketing manager, to explain: the company sponsored local concerts from time to time. The CEO had bought this to attract performers. *Did I play?*

The next day, with the interview and factory tour complete, we made our way back through the foyer. The piano had been moved into a semi-circular antechamber. It was open and looked glorious. Chairs had been placed in a semicircle.

Was there a lunchtime concert? I enquired.

Yes, there was.

Who was playing?

We thought you might like to play something.

I couldn't remember the last time I'd played anything in public. It had been years. But this was a rare piano, a very special piano. Opportunities like this didn't come along often. The temptation was too much to resist.

Tentatively, I pulled out the piano stool, sat down at the keyboard and adjusted the height. That much I could still remember.

Stroking the keys, a pianissimo jazz chord rose from the strings, melting into honey as it resonated from the soundboard and dissolved in the vast acoustic of the foyer. The sound, the action, the balance… This was an instrument to savour.

Come on! Play me! it teased. *I want to sing!*

The subtlest touch brought a crescendo that grew out of nowhere. Creamy arpeggios rolled from beneath the lid, each note melting softly into the next with the slightest touch on the sustain pedal. I pressed the pace; the bite was crisp, teasing staccato and a flurry of counterpoint. A touch of left pedal and the softness engulfed the room in waves of sumptuous velvet.

Where shall we go next? Something big, something exciting, something to captivate the spirit and pull on the emotions, urged the temptress. *Give me Rachmaninov!*

Almost without thinking, the theme to the second piano concerto began to flow. Its lush, emotionally-charged harmonies and playful shifts developed like a tsunami from the keyboard, bewitching, beguiling, intoxicating…

I confess, for a while I was lost to her, this amazing creature. Utterly, totally, completely lost.

By the time I'd torn myself away and looked up, a small crowd had gathered and they were applauding. I have a notion it was not me they applauded. It was her, the curvaceous creature in the shiny black dress who'd dazzled and amazed, tantalised and enchanted.

The smile as I closed the lid and replaced the piano stool under the keyboard stayed with me the entire journey home. It had been a rare and very memorable trip.

Over the years, I've been privileged to have visited most of the countries in Europe and met, photographed and interviewed countless industry-leading entrepreneurs, engineers, designers, directors and CEOs. Many have taken me into their trust and presented designs, ideas, prototypes and projects that, had their competitors caught even the slightest scent of them, the competitive advantage – and quite probably many years of work – would have been lost.

To be taken into the confidence of blue-chip companies and market-leading global giants is an honour beyond words, matched only by the privilege of being allowed to write up and photograph ground-breaking technology and publish it first when it was ready for launch.

Furniture Journal has been in that position many times and that's something I'm especially proud of.

While many of the visits I made with my editorial hat on were to see the newest of the new, some were to see companies that were about to launch on the UK market and others were to conduct one-to-one interviews on different topics with specialists in their field.

Furniture Journal clients were always manufacturers of machinery, decorative products, components, hardware or materials so one thing I'd never had need to do was a dealer trip – a visit to a factory to see a new product line with a group of retailers.

With the arrival of Eddie, a new recruit to our advertising sales force on Kitchen Journal, that was about to change.

Eddie was a nice guy – mid-thirties, a bit nervous (probably the result of the endless stream of Coke bottles and cups of coffee he emptied daily) but generally easy to get on with and keen to make his mark on the world of advertising sales.

He'd been offered the chance to go on a dealer trip at ridiculously short notice by a client he was hoping to get on board but needed to take someone with him who could write up the product and take pictures.

His editor, a young lady I'd recruited a couple of years earlier to be my assistant editor on Furniture Journal and later promoted, was already out visiting multiple clients. Our editor-in-chief had arranged to visit a Bathroom Journal client on the day of the factory tour, so that ruled her out, too. Eddie was desperate.

Tentatively, aware he was the new kid on the block and not quite sure of his ground, he asked me what he should do, clearly hoping I would leap in to fill the void.

I'd been reliably informed by our editor-in-chief that dealer trips were likely to be a bit different to Furniture Journal's cultured factory tours and board-level interviews. They were, she said, as much an opportunity for retailers to let their hair down as they were for the host company to induce them to take a new line.

And they could be bawdy.

I can't say the opportunity particularly appealed – I was quite in my comfort zone with the furniture manufacturing industry – but the schedule wasn't the normal red-eye departure and the topic, a visit to a granite and marble-producing factory near the Italian town of Verona, was almost familiar ground, so I agreed to stand in.

No sooner were plane tickets organised than the schedule changed. The Thursday to Saturday that had been impossible for everyone except me turned into a Monday to Wednesday trip the following week. Feeling the lad still wanted my support and not wishing to mess his new customer about, I scratched out the previous dates in my diary, hastily rearranged my Monday and Tuesday meetings and blocked out the early part of the week for the revised trip.

From there on, everything went to schedule – well, more or less.

The flight arrived on time, the meeters-and-greeters were spread thickly through the arrivals hall of Brescia Airport and awaiting our arrival outside the terminal building were two enormous, chauffeur-driven Lincoln limousines, each equipped with a champagne bar, star-studded roof-lining and bubbly on ice.

I'd been forewarned to expect a degree of pretentiousness but it wasn't until we arrived in the narrow back streets at the heart of old town Verona that the folly of hiring flamboyant 30-foot monsters became apparent.

Shortly before arriving at the hotel, the lead limousine mounted a kerb while trying to inch its way around the 90-degree bend in a street that can't have been much wider than it was.

Completely wedged and unable to move, everyone disembarked in the pouring rain so it could be freed but with no possibility of it negotiating the bend and the limousine we were in stuck behind it, we had little option but to grab our cases and run for the hotel.

None of us had brought an umbrella, so it was a very bedraggled, if slightly intoxicated band that dripped its way towards the reception desk.

It was the evening of the second day, after the factory tour, that things took a turn for the unexpected.

We'd finished our meal, during which the Amarone had flowed generously and it was around midnight. One of the guys in the party suggested we should find a bar to conclude the evening. Another suggested a nightclub. I'd dressed casually for dinner but was perhaps a little formal for a nightclub compared with the other guys who were mostly wearing jeans and tee-shirts but it sounded like an interesting idea.

I'd never been to a nightclub before. Realising that was probably a bit sad at my age, I nodded my approval.

Our Italian hosts duly organised taxis from the hotel reception and issued instructions to the drivers, who spoke no English. Four of us piled into the first taxi, four more into the second and a couple into the third. I think it was around that time that Eddie said something about our Italian hosts not joining us.

There was room in the last taxi but sure enough, they were lined up on the edge of the pavement, smiling and waving as we sped off into the night.

The centre of Verona is delightful. Lining the square, the buildings are painted in warm colours of ochre, yellow and red, contrasting with the natural marble and granite slabs of the pavement. The windows have shutters to keep out the scorching summer sun. During the daytime, the Roman arena stands proud against a cloudless blue sky and music can be heard from within its walls.

The whole place buzzes with activity and there's a rich cafe culture. Even in the middle of February, the chairs and tables from countless cafes spilled out into the streets and whichever direction I looked, there were couples staring into each other's eyes.

Verona is a town famed for its romance and its Romeo and Juliet connections. The Romeo-and-Juliet balcony, framed within a small cobbled courtyard, is only a few metres from the centre. Romance is very much alive.

But to everyone's surprise, our small convoy was not making its way towards the centre; we were heading out of town, away from the cafes and the late-night serenades, two miles, three miles, four miles, more. Here the street lights were fewer.

Our attempts to communicate our consternation with the driver failed. He spoke no English, no French, no German and the best I could manage in Italian was *meno mosso* when he took a corner at high speed. It didn't work.

We must have been driving some 15 or 20 minutes, threading our way through back streets and winding roads when we caught sight of neon lights up ahead. The taxi slowed and turned into a narrow driveway. Either side, neon palm trees flickered in yellow and orange, bursting upwards along the length of their electro-fronds in showers of vivid colour like fireworks in the night sky.

With the driver paid, the elderly Lancia departed. The second taxi was nowhere in sight, so we waited by the entrance.

I'd always imagined night clubs to be noisy affairs where drinkers and smokers occasionally spilled out onto the pavement occasionally for a cigarette or a chat away from ear-splitting music inside.

Here, it was eerily quiet. There was no heavy beat music and no thronging masses spilled from the doorway. There was just a lone, formally-dressed doorman at the entrance who beckoned us to follow him.

Some minutes later the second taxi arrived, then the third. En masse, we followed the doorman toward the entrance. Somehow, I found myself at the front of the queue, leading the party with Eddie close behind.

Through the main entrance, we huddled in a small room to the left of which was a serving hatch – a ticket office, not unlike something one might expect to find in an old train station but without the luxury of breathing space.

The entrance fee was 15 Euros each. Two tickets arrived through the serving hatch in return for a handful of notes and coins and in heavily-accented broken English, we learned they included one free drink at the bar. And it was in that direction, through the double doors.

We were already pressed against the doors by the rest of our party and could hear music coming from beyond. Not loud, thumping dance music but soft jazz, played at a pleasant volume like one might expect in a salubrious restaurant. As the first door opened, Eddie stepped inside and I followed.

Inside, right in front of us, was a huge, imposing bar. Finished in white gloss and with a white marble top, it was bathed in subdued violet and pink neon light. From racks above the bar, hanging glasses sparkled in discreet down-lighters and there were palm trees placed strategically around the bar area. Intrigued, I took a step forward and immediately bumped into Eddie who'd come to a sudden halt.

There was no need to ask why.

Draped alluringly on every stool around the edge of the bar were half a dozen immaculately made-up young ladies with alluring smiles, perfect figures – and all were dressed to party. It took no second glance to work out they were all for hire.

I'm not quite sure where Eddie hailed from exactly. His accent suggested he was probably a Londoner. Me, I'm from Yorkshire and we Northerners don't hand over hard-earned cash without getting our money's worth. I'd just paid 15 Euros to gain entrance to my first ever night club and that included a free drink, so, whatever the intentions of the ladies at the bar, I was determined not to leave without a glass of something.

I made for the bar where already some of our compatriots had lined up and were ordering beers. With a Campari and lemonade in my hand, I retired a few feet to take stock.

A tall, dark-haired girl in a ridiculously long belt and heavy makeup drifted past, blowing a kiss in my direction.

I acknowledged politely and turned away, my disinterest registered.

Separating the bar area from a dimly-lit lounge was a wide passage lined with a dozen or so tub chairs. Two large fish tanks, each filled with spectacularly-colourful tropical fish, divided the bar from the passage, narrowing the entrance from both sides. A large, dark-coloured fish with a protruding bump on his head swam across the tank and for a while I followed him as he drifted easily between the smaller fish.

The Campari was generous and strong – the way I like it – and it hadn't been drowned in lemonade. I congratulated myself on having chosen well.

In the reflection on the glass at the front of the fish tank, I could see a young lady was approaching. A shoal of tiny fish descended from the far left of the tank, momentarily distracting my attention but from the corner of my eye I could see she had moved closer and was sliding easily between the other girls as if they were making way for her.

She arrived to my left and paused momentarily before leaning forward to peer into the tank. Consciously trying not to look but unable to resist, I could see she was slim and smartly-dressed in a well-cut blouse and knee-length skirt. She didn't appear to be like the other girls, though I felt a certain uneasiness as she edged closer.

A discreet few seconds passed while she assessed my reaction. Quite intentionally, I didn't react – or at least, not deliberately with any encouragement.

Maybe that in itself was encouragement enough.

As we watched together, I became suddenly aware of fingers running down the inside of my left arm, scarcely touching as they glided over my wrist and down to the palm of my hand.

Gently, she linked her right arm under my left and squeezed. *Bella, si?* she whispered in a hushed voice, barely audible over the music.

Behind us at the bar, the others from the party were all heavily engaged in conversation. More girls had arrived. It was busier. They were mingling, moving casually, stopping occasionally to engage when one or other of the party became free.

More drinks had been ordered.

Punctuated by false, ingenuous laughter, the discourse and the body language didn't seem apposite to any discussion about the products we'd seen earlier… or about the factory.

But my attention was being demanded elsewhere: a squeeze of the hand and my gaze was redirected towards deep blue eyes and fixed in an instant by dark pupils in the dimmed light. A shaft of pink neon broke over her right cheek, melting into subtle hues across her lip gloss. Cocking her head in a submissive gesture, she smiled, allowing me a moment to admire.

There was no denying it, she was pretty – beyond pretty: mid to late twenties maybe, petite, no more than five-foot four in heels and with very un-Italian softly-curled blonde hair that cascaded down both sides of her face and came to rest on her shoulders. It wouldn't have been hard to have imagined her appearing in the pages of a sophisticated ladies' magazine.

But somehow, this place, this situation, her approach didn't sit easily with my sensibilities.

The others were drinking, flirting, enjoying themselves. I suppose I was flattered by the attention but all I remember thinking was how awkward, how uncomfortable it felt. I was married, happily so, and I had kids. If I'd known nightclub meant this to our Italian hosts, I wouldn't have been so eager to take part.

I recalled them, smiling from the kerb as we departed, waving enthusiastically. They knew, of course. They'd ordered the taxis. They'd instructed the drivers.

I was contemplating a withdrawal to the bar and safety in numbers but there was no need. Bursting through the crowd and visibly flustered, Eddie arrived and much to the displeasure of the young lady I'd spent the last few minutes with, he landed right between us.

We've got to get out of here! he spluttered, repeating himself two or three times.

That was the conclusion I'd reached only a few seconds before his timely arrival but I hadn't figured out how to effect a retreat. The taxis weren't due to return for another half hour and subbing Eddie at the entrance had left me short of the where-with-all to pay for a return fare. I resorted to finding out what had rattled him so badly.

It's... it's her! he stuttered, pointing in the direction of the bar. *It's her!*

Perched on a stool at the corner of the bar, a very tall, leggy creature pouted dutifully in response to Eddie's frantic pointing, then in a flourish that could have come straight from one of Larry Grayson's drag acts, she looked away in a feigned show of coyness.

It was so comical that for a moment, I felt compelled to laugh.

With some difficulty, I managed to smother the desire and keeping a straight face, asked Eddie what the problem was. He was clearly embarrassed and shook his head. The more I pressed, the more he resisted but eventually, desperate to tell somebody about his ordeal, he capitulated and confessed: *She's just grabbed me by the nuts and asked me how about it?*

Ah... tricky. How to respond to that?

Not the way I did, most probably.

The thought of poor Eddie with his apples in a grapple was too much. Fighting back the urge to laugh any longer was futile. The Larry Grayson act at the bar, the hilarity of the situation, Eddie's reaction... It was too much. The impulse got the better of me and without the will to restrain, I burst out laughing.

Trying to regain some composure but still on the verge of another breakout, I glanced toward the young lady who had so shocked Eddie. She was another good-looking girl with immaculate hair and makeup, though the figure-hugging black PVC didn't really work for me. I couldn't help thinking it looked more like a stretched bin-liner than a garment and it left nothing to the imagination.

Recognising my unbridled amusement could only have been the result of her encounter with Eddie, she raised her cocktail glass in salute and blew a kiss in our direction. Instantly, I creased again.

What I really needed to do was rustle up some words of wisdom, some meaningful consolation for a new recruit towards whom I should at least have been sympathetic but I was teetering about on the edge of laughter and it just didn't want to be tamed. Every attempt I made at solemnity burst into flames before I could restrain it.

I'd given up any hope of returning to seriousness when the young lady at the end of the bar craned towards the barman so he could light her cigarette.

That's when it hit me.

There was something different about this girl, something out of the ordinary.

Was that...? No! Surely not!

I glanced in her direction again but couldn't focus properly at such distance.

Conscious I was staring, she pouted, blowing a plume of smoke into the air and scattering it around with a sweeping gesture.

But in that brief moment, I'd seen it. The silhouette had revealed her secret: she'd either swallowed a golf ball or...

At much the same time, the full reality of his encounter suddenly hit poor Eddie: on his first overseas dealer trip – indeed, his first-ever visit for the company – he'd had his tackle grappled by a ladyboy.

Eddie didn't last long with the company after that. Whether it was his Italian experience or whether some more appealing offer had been presented to him we never knew but a month or two later, he handed in his notice and left. And we were back to recruiting again.

It doesn't seem to matter how skilled you become at it, how much cash you throw at it or how scientifically you approach it, the recruitment process is always a roller coaster ride. Sometimes you get it right, sometimes you don't.

Occasionally, you'll recruit and you'll be lucky enough to find an employee who'll stay for years and grow with the company; other times, you'll give it your best shot and still find yourself recruiting for the same position three months later. It's a story that would draw empathy from most employers, I'm sure.

I remember our first job applicant very well.

We'd been approached by a post-service placement organisation that had begged us to provide work experience for one of their departing servicemen.

Then in his mid to late thirties, he arrived on the doorstep one Monday morning, white teeth glinting in the morning sun, polished boots, razor sharp creases in his trousers and standing to attention. *Good morning, sah!* he yelled at high volume from little more than a couple of feet away, saluting and stamping his feet as I opened the door. *Corporal Smith reporting for duty, sah!*

Fresh from the Logistics Corps of the RAF, Corporal Smith had been placed with us for 14 days and at the end of the trial period, if everything worked out well, we had the option to employ him with some limited on-going financial support towards his salary for a few weeks.

As the first week progressed, we realised things were not going at all well. Convinced there was little prospect of calming down the incessant shouting and stamping of feet, without hint of remorse, the following Friday we let him go.

Our second ex-service experience came shortly after in the form of an army guy by the name of Joe. I forget his last name but his rank seemed to change with every day of the week. When he arrived, it was very apparent he had the gift of the gab, so we gave him a thorough product-brief and some basic sales training and placed him at a desk with a phone.

One of his first sales calls was to a company supplying timber. In fact, as I recall, this was his only sales call, though he seemed to be making it a couple of dozen times a day.

Towards the end of the week, I took a call from the managing director of the timber company, asking if I was aware of what was going on. It transpired our rookie salesman had struck up a liaison with the managing director's secretary and after two or three late morning arrivals at work, he'd demanded an explanation for her uncharacteristic lack of punctuality.

Apparently, she'd broken down in tears and confessed: it was all our squaddie's fault. They'd been taking long, hot baths together with champagne and strawberries and spent two entire nights bouncing around like a couple of rabbits.

I think the secretary was invited to find alternative employment at more or less the same time as the advertising sales career of our errant private with the colourful private life came to an abrupt close.

From then on, we commissioned professional recruitment agents to search for us and although there were still no guarantees we'd find suitable candidates to interview, on a few occasions we did manage to recruit quite successfully.

It was always more successful when someone approached us, though, or we learned of someone who was looking for a job through word of mouth. We were lucky enough to have that happen a few times. We even had a couple of employees who left for greener grass at the other side of the fence, then returned. That was gratifying.

In those rare moments, it felt like we must have been getting something right.

I confess, as an interviewer, I don't think I've ever been exactly conventional, much to the consternation and bewilderment of my general manager and editor-in-chief, with whom I used to conduct most job interviews.

My approach was heavily influenced by my own experience as an interviewee with the oil company back in 1987 – that and the fact I've generally preferred to busk than follow convention when it didn't seem to be taking me where I wanted to go.

The oil company wanted to find out what I was like and what I was good at first, then see if I could be moulded into a position that would work for both of us rather trying to find a square peg to fit in a square hole. That always made sense to me.

While the GM and E-i-C stuck to the brief and diligently compared CVs with interviewees, measuring each candidate against the criteria in the job specification we'd set together, after the initial formalities of the interview, I'd take a back seat and observe. It's interesting how much more you can see when you're not in the driving seat for a while.

I was always more impressed when an interviewee treated an interview as a two-way street and asked questions as they came to mind. I took it as a good indicator that they were interested in the job and wanted to see how well they might fit in.

I still find it remarkable how few interviewees ever had questions they wanted answering – and just as remarkable how many had been briefed to ask something, anything and would pull a sheet of paper from a pocket and read out questions they'd dreamed up the night before that had already been answered during the interview.

Do people really expect to get jobs by ticking boxes on a must-do sheet?

Maybe that is the way to do it and it's me who's out of step.

Most times we were in absolute agreement about interviewees but just occasionally something would catch my attention and set me thinking about a new possibility, a new direction or the launch of a new product.

The panel always knew when I was away on a blue-sky moment. More than once, we interviewed for one position but ended up recruiting for another that didn't exist because the person in front of us represented an opportunity for the company to grow in a different direction.

There was even one occasion when, faced with two equally-good candidates, we offered positions to both rather than risk losing the chance of recruiting two good applicants.

It didn't always go that way.

I can quite clearly remember one very athletic young lady interviewee bouncing up the stairs two at a time and crashing through my office door while our receptionist was still calling her from downstairs. Dressed in a pale grey jogging suit and trainers and wearing a pink, fluffy headset, she sat herself down, switched off her music and announced *I'm ready.*

We did interview her but the interview was mercifully short. She was another one who didn't have any questions.

Then there was the applicant who wanted my job.

I remember the look of disbelief on my general manager's face when he announced it. I can't say I was especially fazed. I've always taken the view that if I can find someone who can do my job better than me, they can have it and I'll do something else. I was more than happy to explore whether that day had come when one very smartly-dressed young man presented himself.

He interviewed well, he was confident, he had experience, he'd started his own business at one point, he had an answer for every question and demonstrated he was adept at thinking out of the box. He fitted the profile of the job we'd advertised, he had the drive and the ambition and when I asked him where he saw himself in five years' time, he responded immediately: *Doing your job.*

Great, I thought. Maybe we really have found someone with the potential to take on the black leather chair.

We offered him the sales position he'd applied for with the expectation we'd be promoting him through the ranks quite quickly. Three months later, with not a single sale to his credit, he was gone. He didn't even work his notice. The recruitment roller-coaster was coasting again – and we'd blown another fat finder's fee.

Recruiting for our Polish sister company proved to be quite different.

In the UK, the problem had always been attracting applications from candidates who might have a sporting chance of possessing the skill set we needed and we would always count ourselves extremely lucky if we received more than a small handful of applications with potential. Occasionally, we received applications from university graduates, though paper qualifications were always less important to me than finding someone with the nous to do the job.

In Poland, the problem was the opposite: how to whittle down the scores of super-qualified applicants with real potential to a manageable number that we could interview over the two days we'd allocated.

Everyone who applied, it seemed, had two or more degrees and we could probably have taken any one of them from the sackful of applications we'd collected for the position of General Manager of our new Polish sister company. In the end, speaking fewer than four languages fluently seemed to be the only way to cut the numbers of relevant applications.

Late on the evening before the interviewees were due to arrive, I landed with a colleague at Katowice airport. We were due to meet a taxi driver who would take us to our accommodation.

By the time we'd cleared customs and collected our cases, only one person remained in the arrivals area. Tall, scruffily-dressed, with dirty jeans and unexpectedly orange hair, he wasn't carrying a card with our names on but as he was the only one left, I assumed he was our driver and diligently wheeled out the only phrase of Polish I'd managed to learn for the occasion. *Noclegi obok lotnitska proszę,* I announced confidently, assuming he probably didn't speak English and might need to know the hotel we'd been booked into was adjacent to the airport.

He smiled. *Yes, I know,* came the response. *Your colleague from England telephoned ahead to confirm.* His English was faultless.

I still wonder whether we should have recruited him and saved the cost of dinners and hotel rooms for applicants.

Establishing a business in Poland wasn't easy. I'd liken it to trying to swim up a waterfall in the dry season. The red tape was long, wide and very, very sticky and nothing about the process was straightforward or simple.

With our new Polish GM appointed, we set about deciding on a base. We didn't choose the city of Krakow for any reason other than because it was where he hailed from and the airport and rail links were good but the central square was extremely photogenic and our offices in the Puget Palace were quite swish. It was a nice place to be.

Steeped in history, Krakow was once the capital city of Poland. I've never been a city-lover but it made an instant impression on me. Krakow had character, it had architecture, it had culture and perhaps above all, it had art.

In the dimly-lit bars and cafés that lined its back streets, photographers rubbed shoulders with musicians, poets, writers, sculptors and painters. Impassioned discussions took place through an acrid fog of cigarette smoke, the participants leaning towards each other over rickety tables scattered with spent glasses of *Żywiec* and *Slivovitz*.

The vitality, the creative passion in Krakow, they were inescapable, like nowhere I'd ever been. In every bar, every café, art lived and breathed. Just being there was inspirational. It was easy to imagine how 19th century Paris must have been in the days of Monet, Matisse and Toulouse-Lautrec.

In the summer months and early autumn, chairs and tables spilled into the central square and throngs gathered every 15 minutes to await the arrival of the trumpeter – the local fireman – who'd blast his fanfare from the top of the tallest church tower. And on market day, the place buzzed with activity.

Krakow is very much a city of learning and the Poles prize their education, a fact that hadn't escaped us when we were recruiting. In this city alone there were no fewer than 12 universities including one of the oldest in Europe.

At the same time, makeup, hair, clothes, deportment – they were as important as education to the ladies of Krakow and with few exceptions, they went to great lengths to look their best.

The contrast between them and the male population was stark. Most of the men seemed content to wear torn clothes, dirty jeans and immense beetle-crushers. Suits and ties were largely shunned, except in the offices of banks.

Metro-sexuals, the arty set would call them; city slickers.

In the early years of the new millennium, the Poland I saw was a land of extremes and disparities. It was also a land of rubber stamps and bureaucrats.

Things may be different now but back then it was impossible to establish a limited company without having a bank account. It was just as impossible to open a bank account without having established a limited company.

Everybody understood, to break the impasse the bank manager had to confirm to the notary that an account had been opened and the obligatory 50,000pln had been placed in it. The notary would then accept the fictional bank account details and proceed to draft documentation to ratify the existence of a fictional company.

The documentation then had to be delivered to the bank manager, who required a company stamp to be made before the account could be opened. To commission the stamp, one had to know the office address – but it wasn't possible to sign an agreement to rent the offices until the company had been formed.

For the best part of a week, we shuttled constantly between offices and banks to piece together the puzzle and unknot the red tape before, finally, the business of setting up the official company began.

With the articles of trading drafted by legal-beagles, it fell to a notary to read them out, word by word, then they had to be signed. Everything had to be carried out with the help of an appointed, certificated, authorised, rubber-stamped translator – my punishment for being a foreign Prezes Zarządu.

My recollection of the event is still vivid: the vast room painted in cream with pond-green dado rails; the enormous desk parked at an angle on its own in one corner; and behind it the notary's pristine Magnus Magnusson chair in black leather with burr-walnut arms, burr-walnut figuring on the star base and castors in gold plate.

It felt like we were awaiting the arrival of the Queen of Sheba.

Sadly, there was no Gina Lollobrigida in a flowing white gown, a golden crown and big dangly ear-rings for us. We got Rumpole of the Bailey in a skirt.

Having a translator seemed to be something of a pointless exercise since I couldn't hear most of the translation and the bits I did catch suggested the translator was having as much trouble with the speed of the delivery as I was. Every now and then, the notary would pause and look up over her horn-rimmed spectacles. *Spooky!* she'd say, staring directly at me with an intentionally solemn face. *Spooky!*

How do you not laugh when that's the only word in a 15-minute monologue you actually recognise?

I later learned it was *spółka*, the Polish word for company but the pronunciation, the frequency of its occurrence and the unintentional comedy in its delivery made it more than a tad difficult to maintain a straight face.

With the establishment of a Polish sister company and the first couple of editions of Furniture Journal Polska published, we set about adding to our portfolio of titles in the UK.

Buying and selling companies is a notoriously tricky business. I've sold a couple but can't say I particularly enjoyed the experience. Every title we'd ever published had been researched, invented and launched by the team we'd grown. We had no experience of acquisitions.

We already had a clutch of successful titles and our business model made good profits but when two guys approached us with a view to selling a title they'd owned and worked on for a couple of years, we decided to take a closer look and invited them to our offices for a discussion.

Stuart, my general manager, had been through the accounts and I'd had a chance to call a few of the advertisers discreetly to canvass their opinions on the effectiveness of the title. Clubbing and Pubbing were a bit outside our comfort zone but we decided to meet the owners for an exploratory chat. A couple of days later, they both arrived.

Marty was the advertising sales guy. Slim and trim, he walked through the door in a leather jacket, insanely tight jeans and a tee-shirt. His eyelashes were far too long to be home grown and he had a beard that plummeted vertically from his ears, banking around his jaw line to a just-on-the-lip moustache that never once deviated from its eighth-inch thickness. His hair was a mass of heavily-moussed black locks and he had the wiggle of a catwalk model.

Hello, darling! he called, extending a cold, clammy hand in my direction and placing it delicately in mine. I'd never been called darling in a business meeting before.

Rod was the editor. He was much more laid back. He used to be a DJ and was into heavy rock. It was the angry stuff that lit his candle, he said. I could quite imagine it. Dagger-like badges were sewn up the sleeves of his flying jacket and beneath unkempt hair, he had sullen, craggy features. I'd seen better teeth on a donkey.

Marty and Rod were not business folk. They admitted that. But they had a magazine, it was losing money and they were desperate to sell it. Sell it but keep it – just in case there was a chance they could dump the risk but still get rich when someone else showed them how.

We have no business sense, we don't know where we're going wrong but we're very passionate about it. That was Marty's attempt at justification for the £60,000 debt the title had saddled the two of them with.

If that was his opening gambit, I reasoned things had to get better from there but it turned out to be the full extent of his sales pitch.

We just know the magazine's a winner, interrupted Rod, realising Marty's admission was perhaps not the best introduction. *Everyone tells us how wonderful it is.*

As the meeting progressed, we could feel the passion and they certainly had ideas – pretty good ideas – of how they could develop the title. But we needed to know more about how they saw the numbers working and started to delve. The analysis went straight over their heads.

Ooh, it's like being back in school! exclaimed Marty, recoiling in his chair, eyes wide with disbelief. *You are putting us on the spot, aren't you?*

Rod leaned forward as if he was about to make a point, then flopped back in the chair, his arms slumping to his sides.

It was all very dramatic, not at all the grown-up discussion we had expected but neither of them knew where they were financially, where they were heading or what they hoped to achieve from the meeting. Sales forecasts, production costs, expenses, salaries, margins – they were a foreign language.

Marty was getting flustered. *Ooh! It's not looking good, is it?* he squealed, raising a hand to his lips in an act of feigned shock. He was sitting on the very edge of his chair at an angle, his right leg wrapped around his left like ivy up a tree trunk, when quite unexpectedly it scooted backwards, dumping him on the floor just in front of my desk. Like the wartime cartoon character Mr Chad looking over the wall, two hands clasped the desk edge and he hauled himself to his feet. *It's a good job I'm tough,* he exclaimed, dusting himself down, lips pursed and a hurt look on his face.

Rod lolled back in his chair, staring at the ceiling, arms folded.

With patience running thin, Stuart launched into a succinct summary: *The upshot of it is this, gentlemen: the magazine isn't making money. It's losing it hand over fist. You have a £60,000 debt and it's on the increase because you're taking more out of the business than you're selling in advertising. You can't be surprised your bank won't continue to support you because you haven't yet told us how you hope to turn it around. You don't have a company to sell because it's not been set up properly, so there are no shares to buy. You have sleeping partners who own part of the debt but you don't know how much. And from what little you've told us, you'd like us to buy the debt, show you how to make it profitable and leave you both as part owners of the publication. Is that correct?*

Ooh! That's a bit harsh! Marty was back on his chair edge, looking indignantly down his nose, both hands on crossed knees, lips pursed again. *We've spent two years making this work. Everyone tells us how wonderful it is. If you had kids aged 16-23, they'd tell you it's just simply brilliant. Rod's done a brilliant job. Just brilliant.*

I never like to close doors on opportunities, regardless of how slim they might appear but this one had started to look slimmer than Marty's skinny jeans.

The two of them had an unswerving belief in the product and seemed committed to it but the little research we'd done had already led us to question its reader-appeal and effectiveness for advertisers.

We had ideas and with a firm hand on the finances and some proper planning, there was a prospect it could be made to work but with these two…they had the background knowledge but getting anything more than pouts and poses out of them had proved to be a struggle. Neither of us could imagine working with them.

Thanking them for their time, Stuart extended a handshake to draw the meeting to a close. Rod sniffed, turned away and headed for the door. Marty reached out, then seeing Rod's reaction, withdrew his hand and followed. It was all the confirmation we needed that meaningful collaboration would have been impossible.

At much the same time, we started investigating a publishing project in Lithuania.

We'd found a European export marketing grant, research had confirmed Lithuanian furniture manufacturers were eager to access it and the Lithuanian Embassy and Chamber of Commerce in Vilnius were supportive of the idea we'd come up with. Unfortunately, access to the grant had become entangled in bureaucracy that made it almost impossible for manufacturers to avail themselves of it, so with little prospect of untying the red tape and some regret, we had to admit defeat and pulled out.

With all the magazines performing well, we took a punt and embarked on a very different project. The idea was to broaden the company's portfolio laterally in a way that might allow us to break into consumer publishing.

I'd amassed a collection of several hundred aerial photographs taken around Norfolk and Suffolk that provided a different perspective on the local landscape. Unsure whether they might be more appealing as straight photographs or photo-art – watercolour and printed canvas – we set about organising a series of exhibitions that we hoped would provide a steer for the book.

The exhibitions were modestly successful, especially for the charities to which we'd decided to donate the profits. In a couple of days, we outsold the local gallery by a good margin and raised several thousand pounds for the Eastern Air Ambulance and the local branch of the Royal National Lifeboat Institution but the abstracts sold just as well as the aerial photographs.

Another publisher pipped us to the post with a book of aerial photographs before we could publish, so with no clear indication of what ours should contain and another book on the same subject already in the market, we abandoned the idea.

The profits from six days of exhibitions filled the fuel bowser for the Eastern Air Ambulance and provided a few thousand pounds towards upkeep of the Lowestoft lifeboat, so we managed to achieve something worthwhile.

In later years, we teamed up with a young entrepreneur from Lithuania and set about establishing a new company through which to publish Furniture Journal

Russia. The idea was so well received by our European clients that almost all the advertising in the first edition was sold in a couple of days during an exhibition.

We'd just arrived at the point of putting the first edition together when Russia invaded Crimea. Within a couple of weeks, tit-for-tat border controls and threats of sanctions had killed that project, too.

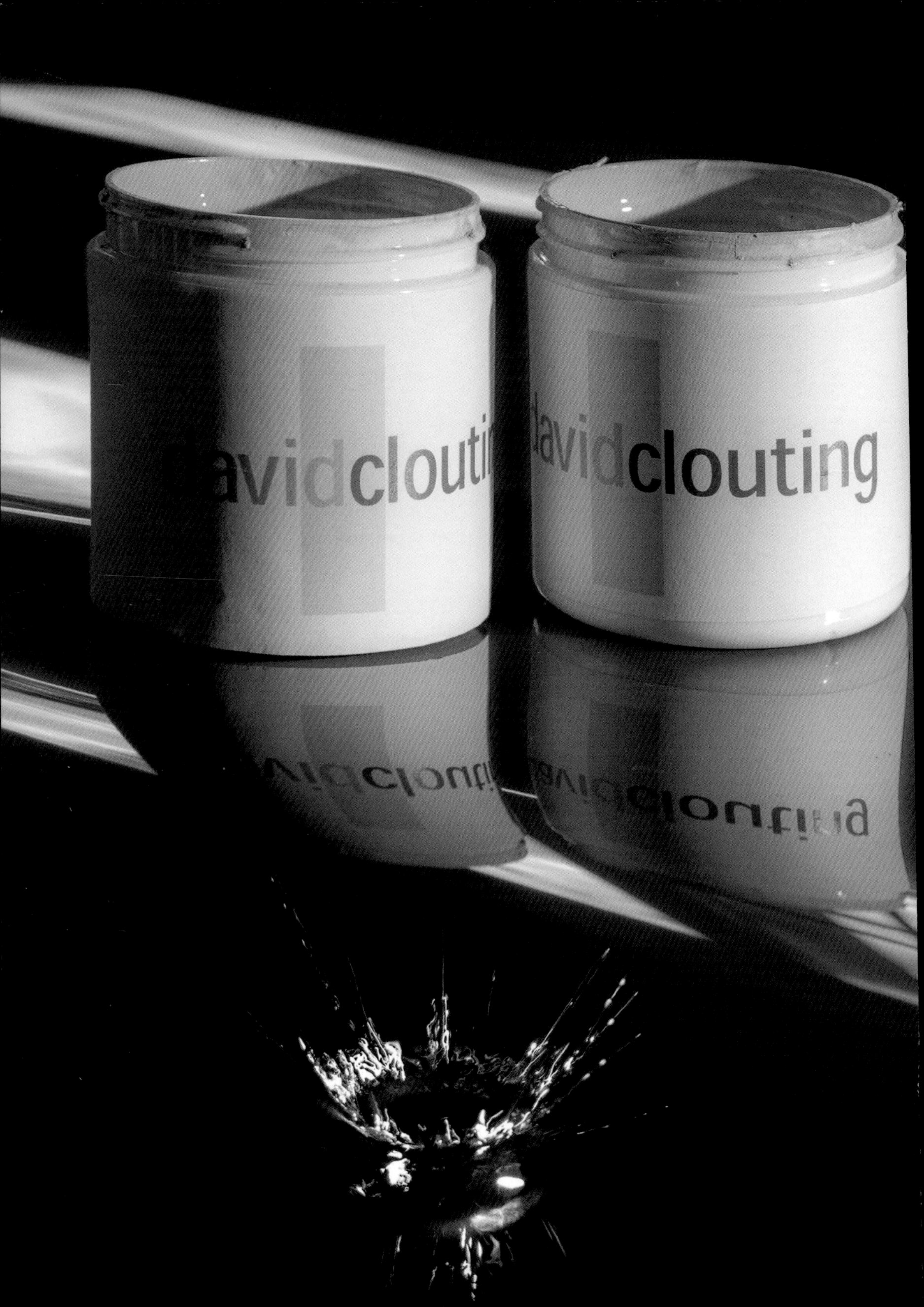

I enjoy the challenge of commercial and advertising photography, especially when clients give me the freedom to be creative and I've taken all manner of subjects.

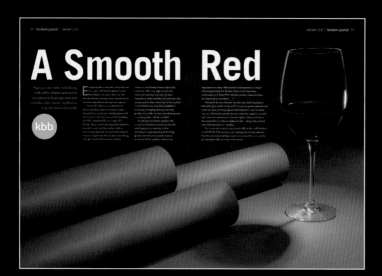

I always enjoy coming up with concepts and finding ways to bring them to life with a camera. I've put on photo-art exhibitions before and would do more if time allowed.

Chapter Eight
Friends and Flying

I can't say I was ever a gregarious creature, at least not in the truest sense of the word. Sociable, yes; gregarious, no. At school, much like Christina, I was always very selective about my friends. Up to the age of 11, the kids I met were an unreliable bunch who seemed incapable of playing anything for more than a couple of minutes without switching to something else or falling out. I quickly tired of them.

True friends I could always count in single figures and I remember all of them: Ken, my employer and mentor in all things photographic when I was a teenager; Parvez, whose father owned a restaurant; Helen and Tony, who I met through Marie – the soups Helen created were amazing and Tony could mend anything with four wheels; David, my organ-playing pal from the School of Music, with whom I played a good many of the cathedral organs in England; and Sally and Doug, who lived in the same village – Sally's desserts were always divine, though she'd never admit to it, and Doug is just the nicest and most helpful chap you could ever wish to meet.

In later life, I more frequently made good friends through business: Jean-Paul, whose gite we hired and whose friends adopted us as their own; Steve and Jayne from Guernsey, without whom we'd never have bought an aeroplane; Janos, the Hungarian-born pilot from California who delivered our first aeroplane from Switzerland to Norwich and later told me he'd never have signed the paperwork if he'd known how good it was; Alejandro, whose Spanish company printed Furniture Journal and several of our other periodicals for many years, and his Cuban-born wife, Ly-Sandra; Jock, the inimitable Scotsman who offered his services as a freelance on Furniture Journal long before I had any appreciation of just how much experience he really had; Linda, my American pen-pal, to whom I first sent many of the anecdotes I'm recounting to you now; Dmitry, who came to us from Russia on President Gorbachev's Russian President's Training and Marketing Initiative – his appreciation of Abbott Ale is matchless; Hinrich, a fellow photographer and videographer extraordinaire whose industrial clients featured for many years in Furniture Journal; and Paul, Steve's colleague from Aradian Aviation, who found and sold other aircraft for us.

I've often smiled at just how much fun this disparate, eclectic but exceptionally enjoyable international band of like-minded folk really is.

Get a few of them together at the same time in the same room (as we have from time to time) and it very quickly became obvious that it's only the politicians and the bankers in this world who create boundaries, build walls between people and exaggerate unimportant differences for their own ends.

People are just people, wherever they are from, whatever their tongue.

Friendship doesn't recognise borders, it celebrates cultural differences and embraces and enjoys the diversity in them. I feel privileged to have met them all.

I have aviation to thank for bringing me together with some of my closest friends.

It might seem like a slightly whacky idea to buy an aeroplane you can't fly but in the era before low-cost airlines came into their own, the idea of flying to an exhibition or to visit a client on the Continent and being back home the same evening without the inconvenience of booking hotels held a lot of appeal.

We could escape hours of wasted time in airports waiting for aeroplanes to arrive and without restrictive airline schedules, the flexibility having our own aeroplane offered was on a scale that just wasn't possible by car.

All I had to do was learn to fly.

From a very early age, Christina would accompany me on my Saturday morning flying lessons out of Shipdham airfield. Sometimes she'd take a book to read or look out of the window when we practised manoeuvres but most of all, she liked circuit-training.

She'd strap into the back seat and at the end of each lesson, my instructor would give his debrief, then Christina would hand me her paper: marks out of five for each landing and a drawing at the side of each mark to illustrate the point.

A thud got me a one or a two – and a picture of a broken aeroplane. I'd lose marks if I was too fast on the approach, if I hadn't nailed the climb speed or if I'd overshot circuit height on the downwind leg.

She'd draw the Air Speed Indicator or the Altimeter, usually with an exclamation mark at the side of it and a reminder of what my airspeed or my height above ground should have been. Sometimes I'd get a four or a five and a picture of an aeroplane with a big smile beneath its propeller. She was a demanding examiner.

The critique could be merciless if a crosswind had tipped the wings more than once or twice on final approach. One time, I dropped all the flap on the takeoff roll instead of leaving one stage down during a circuit training session. She tore up the paper in front of the instructor.

My real examiner was kinder. He passed me.

David, my good friend from organ-playing days.

Helen and Tony.

Sally and Doug.

Jean-Paul is a great guy – a Frenchman through and through but a very international Frenchman whose life has been enriched by friendships from all over the world. It was inevitable we'd become friends.

Alejandro and Ly-Sandra from Spain. Alejandro's company printed Furniture Journal and several of our other periodicals for many years – and the first impression of this book.

Jock Gallagher, the inimitable author, journalist and broadcaster who inspired the writing of this book.

Hinrich, a fellow photographer and videographer extraordinaire from Germany whose PR clients featured for many years in Furniture Journal.

Linda, my American pen-pal, to whom I first sent many of the anecdotes I'm recounting in these pages.

Dmitry (in the foreground), who came to the UK on President Gorbachev's Russian President's Training and Marketing Initiative, pictured with me.

Paul, Steve's colleague from Aradian Aviation, who found and sold aircraft for us, pictured with his daughter Alyssa.

I'll never forget my mother's face when she saw the first aeroplane we bought. As a small child, I suffered badly with constipation and to get things moving when the cork wouldn't pop, she'd sometimes incentivise me with a toy car, a toy aeroplane or a toy boat. The bigger the job, the bigger the toy – so of course, I'd hang on 'til the last minute.

At 33 feet in length and towering 13 feet to the beacon on its tail, the twin-engine eight-seater we'd bought filled half the hangar at Norwich Airport. *My Goodness!* she exclaimed as the hangar doors slid back, *You must have done a big one to get that!*

The Piper Navajo that had so impressed Mother was an entirely different beast to the single-engine Warriors and Cherokees I'd learned to fly in – and the instrumentation was far more complex than anything I'd used for instrument-training.

With two crew seats separated from passengers by a cabin-divider, four seats facing each other in the main cabin with extendable tables between and two further seats behind, there was space to move around, space to put things. There was even a toilet, washing facilities, hot and cold water and a small drinks cabinet on board.

Compared with the aircraft I'd been flying, it was luxurious and offered immeasurably more space than flying Cattle Class in a commercial airliner.

Buying the aircraft had been a serious challenge, though and at times the experience had been as exasperating as it had been disappointing. Most of the aircraft sales agencies I'd approached didn't care whether the aircraft they sold fitted with what we needed so long as they made money out of the deal.

Looking for something or matching our needs to a particular aircraft was unimportant to them. The only thing they wanted to sell was what they had on their books. As far as I could tell, they were an unscrupulous bunch of Arthur Daleys.

We'd been to see a few aircraft and on each occasion, we'd come away from the experience frustrated and disappointed. Some looked good on paper but weren't where they were supposed to be when we arrived or they were totally different aircraft from the ones advertised.

On a couple of occasions, the interiors and exteriors had been swapped over on the sales literature and when we arrived for a test flight, the exterior looked good but the equipment in the panel was nothing like the sparkly new avionics in the picture.

Others were shabby relics that offered little hope of ever leaving terra firma in safety but they'd been photographed in a romantic sunset from their best sides and looked good on paper.

The owner of one aircraft flew it over to us for an inspection and the main landing-gear on one side collapsed as he was taxiing in.

It seemed the whole industry was riddled with charlatans, sharks and shams.

When price tags for aeroplanes start in the tens of thousands and slide up to seven figures and beyond with remarkable ease, it wasn't at all what we'd expected.

I was on the point of giving up hope of ever finding an aircraft when, more by good luck than good management, I came across a chap called Steve. He had a relatively new aircraft brokerage called Aradian Aviation on the island of Guernsey. Talking to Steve was like a breath of fresh air.

He asked questions none of the others had thought to ask: *How many people do you want to carry? How far do you want to fly? What kind of runway will you be operating from? What kind of experience do you have as a pilot?*

It seemed that at long last I'd found someone who was knowledgeable and helpful and might actually be able to find an aeroplane that worked for us.

I knew nothing about buying aeroplanes. I needed a lot of help, not just to find the right aircraft but also to find one that wasn't a flying junk box. Steve knew exactly what we needed and it wasn't long before he had found a bird that was available.

It seemed to be in good order and matched our mission profile but part way through the negotiations, the Swiss owner decided he no longer needed a broker now a buyer had been found and cut Aradian out of the deal.

Still in need of help, I asked Steve if he'd switch sides, shepherd the purchase through and train me to fly the aircraft if I paid the commission he'd otherwise lose on the deal. He agreed.

Not only did I get first class instruction, I also found a good friend.

I remember sitting in the pilot's seat for our first flight as the aircraft stood outside the hangar in the sunshine. It was February 1998. Steve sat at the side of me, the girls, Marie and Steve's wife, Jayne, were in the back.

Steve and Jayne had flown over from Guernsey and the plan was that we'd all fly back together and Steve and I would work from Guernsey Airport for a week while the girls explored the island. At the end of the week, I'd have a flight test and with a bit of luck, I'd be the proud holder of a multi-engine pilot's licence.

But staring at the vast array of instruments, gauges, switches, knobs and levers at both sides of the panel and the sets of multiple radios and navigation equipment in the centre, the task ahead suddenly seemed much more daunting than I'd imagined.

This wasn't just an aeroplane, it was a small airliner – a far cry from anything I'd flown before. I didn't even know how to start the engines.

Training with Steve that week was intensive.

The weather was superb: wall-to-wall sunshine, light winds, perfect. By day we'd fly out to The Needles to practise manoeuvres, single-engine flight and simulated emergency procedures. In the evening, we'd retire to the hotel for something to eat.

Dinner over, Steve would pound me with questions from the Pilot's Operating

Steve and Jayne from Guernsey, without whom we'd never have bought an aeroplane.

N63560, the first aircraft we ever bought. It was luxurious and offered immeasurably more space than flying Cattle Class in a commercial airliner.

Handbook: *What's the best rate of climb? What's the blue-line speed? What's the procedure if the undercarriage won't go down? Talk me through de-icing…*

A hard taskmaster with thousands of commercial flying hours to his credit and a CV that included a stint as the sales and demo pilot for Beechcraft's UK operation, he left no stone unturned. Every night, I died on the pillow, exhausted.

At the end of the week, we all piled into the aircraft and took off for Exeter Airport where I was to take the flight test with an ex-RAF examiner.

By the time the examiner arrived, the weather was already beginning to turn. The windsock was waving about horizontally as the wind whistled across the runway, then the clouds rolled in and the rain started. Pre-flighting the aircraft by torchlight in the wet was no fun at all.

I knew I'd be in for a rough ride when, with the cloud-base barely above circuit height, we climbed straight into instrument conditions. Visibility outside was zero. It went black. Rain hammered on the windscreen. The turbulence did its best to throw us off course.

This is fun, isn't it, old chap? the examiner chuckled over the intercom in a voice that could have come straight from 'Reach for the Sky'. With my eyes glued to the instruments, I didn't get the chance to see if he'd morphed into Kenneth More.

By the time we'd emerged from the gloom and into smooth air above the clouds, the sun was already beginning to set and we were at 9,000 feet, ten miles out over the English Channel. It was an incredible sight but there was no time to admire it.

I'd no sooner levelled for the cruise than, without any warning, he cut an engine – not a careful pull-back of the throttle to the idle position to prevent shock cooling but a sharp tug on the mixture-control that cut the fuel to the critical left engine.

Instinctively, I corrected the yaw as Steve had taught me, trimmed up and with the stationary propeller feathered, we carried out the manoeuvres I'd rehearsed with Steve on one engine.

Jolly good! he announced, clearly happy I'd survived the challenges he'd thrown at me. *Seems ya got the hang o' that. Let's crank up the donkey and head back for a few circuits.*

Unfortunately, by this time the donkey had ideas of its own.

Back in Norwich, the engineer who'd given the aircraft a full annual inspection and service when it arrived in the UK had replaced a noisy electric fuel-pump on the left engine with a new one but he hadn't told me the replacement wasn't new and at the critical moment, with nothing but water in every direction, it failed.

Without the electric pump to prime it and after half an hour at sub-zero temperatures, the left engine would not start and no amount of carrot was going to get this donkey to fire up without a squirt of fuel in the pipes.

Suddenly, I had a real emergency to deal with.

Well, Captain, that's a bit of a bother, isn't it? came a voice across the intercom. *Wotchya gonna do now?*

Handing over control to the examiner with the request he maintained straight and level flight, I leafed through the Pilot's Operating Handbook Steve had pounded me on until I found the section on cross-feed priming.

It detailed the procedure involved in pumping fuel from one of the tanks in the right wing to the dead engine on the left. Get it wrong and there was a strong possibility the right engine could quit and we'd turn into a glider.

With the English Channel around us in all directions and Exeter Airport 30-something miles to the northwest, it wasn't a prospect that appealed much.

Following the checklist meticulously, I rehearsed out loud and satisfied I'd got everything in the right order, worked my way through each step.

With some relief, the fuel-pressure rose and the left engine started at the first crank. It was a tense moment, at least for me, but my examiner was completely unfazed. *Jolly good*, came the response as he folded his arms and handed control back to me. *Fly us home, old chap. I'm gasping for a cuppa!*

Janos was another gem I met through aviation.

Yes, there was an element of the Hungarian gypsy in him and he loved to wheel and deal (I lost out to him a couple of times) but essentially, he was a family guy with a passion for aeroplanes that was easy to identify with.

When he and his co-pilot delivered the Navajo to Norwich Airport on December 23, 1997, the bank couldn't organise the transfer of funds until the end of the day on 24th. The weather closed in before the transfer was confirmed, preventing them from catching their flight home to California and it was almost inevitable they'd end up spending some of Christmas with us.

But in those few days, we cemented a friendship that contained the seeds of a business venture and over the coming years, we bought and sold several aircraft together and with the girls, visited some of them in California.

It was on the first trip we made to the USA with the girls that I decided to use one of the aircraft we'd bought – a twin-engine Cessna 310 that Janos had picked up at a good price from someone who needed cash more than wings – to convert my British licences and ratings to the American system.

Janos knew a multi-engine instrument instructor who'd won his spurs flying Dakotas during the Second World War and would be happy to put me through the FAA instrument rating.

Old Ned, he told me, could fly anything and what Old Ned didn't know about aeroplanes and instrument flying wasn't worth knowing. I'd be in good hands.

A few days into our three-week holiday, with the girls enjoying the swimming-pool in the morning and Janos's wife on standby to take them to the shopping mall in the afternoon, Janos and I flew out to Twentynine Palms airfield to meet Old Ned.

I can't say I particularly liked the aircraft. When filled with fuel, the tuna tanks on each wing made it dance around at the slightest touch on the rudder pedals and the avionics were the originals from the early '70s. The radios were Cro-Magnon compared with the suite of King avionics I'd become used to in the Navajo but I figured it would do the job and it didn't have to be hired. Just add fuel, Janos had said. So we did.

The heat in the desert was intense as we taxied to the parking area at Twentynine Palms Airfield with the door ajar. The moment the propellers stopped, the hilly terrain on the rising slopes of Joshua Tree National Park to the south melted in the rising heat from the starboard engine cowling, turning into a blur of swirling eddies.

It was half-past two in the afternoon and more than 40 degrees Celsius when we landed and we were at almost 1900-feet above sea-level. The engines were not turbocharged and the westerly runway was 500 feet shorter than Norwich. And one of the favourite tricks Old Ned used on his rookie students, I'd been warned, was to kill an engine on the climb out.

It was baking inside the shed that passed for a terminal building. There was no air-conditioning, no fan but I'd found an old chair, dusted the sand off it, sat myself down with the aircraft handbook and taken a few minutes to comb through the performance data and takeoff roll charts while Janos went to find Old Ned.

All that heat, the thinner desert air 1900 feet above sea level, no turbos, 70% fuel load, two on board, 5,500 feet of tarmac… With two engines running we'd be fine but I didn't give much for our chances of getting any climb if Old Ned did his party trick.

I was still rehearsing the what-ifs when Janos appeared in the doorway with Old Ned. The question of just how old Old Ned might be had never come up in any conversation with Janos and I'd never thought to do the maths when he mentioned Old Ned used to fly Dakotas during the war.

Skinny, wrinkly, browned by decades under the desert sun, he definitely had experience on his side.

Janos must have noticed the moment when the other what-if suddenly struck me.

Hey! You wanna be go do some flyin' or you gonna be sit there pullin' faeces? he croaked. Janos always croaked and his eclectic fusion of Hungarian-American and English often led to some amusing pronunciations, *faeces* being one of them.

I'm quite good at accents but I could never imitate his. It was as if he had a mouth full of marbles.

You so damn' picky, picky, picky! he muttered, heading out to the plane and leaving Old Ned to make his own introduction.

Old Ned was a man of few words. When he spoke, everything came out like black treacle from a pot, glued together, indecipherable. The crackly intercom just made it worse. Three times I asked him to repeat his instruction as we taxied out to the holding point for runway 26, pushing my headphones back for the third attempt so I could hear what he said over the noise of the engines.

First, he wanted to see a short-field take-off followed by a soft-field landing, then we would climb to 8,000 feet on a northerly heading to start manoeuvres.

With Old Ned's party trick uppermost in my mind as we started our takeoff roll, I steadily pushed the throttle controls fully forward to the stop and knowing it wasn't a particularly good practice, blocked them, the prop controls and the mixtures with my hand before releasing the brakes so he couldn't kill an engine.

Slowly – ridiculously slowly in the heat – we cantered along the centre line, me holding the nose off until we had enough airspeed for the wings to generate lift. Diligently, I called out *airspeed rising, V1, rotate, positive rate of climb, wheels up, trim...* the checks I'd learned by heart from Steve in Guernsey a year or so before.

If yo' talkin' to me, boy, ah cain't hear a dang thing, Old Ned yelled over the screaming engines.

It was about then I realised his headphones were plugged into the top pocket of his short-sleeved shirt.

Established on the downwind leg, I prepared for the soft-field landing while Old Ned fished around for the headphone socket. *Yo' done yer GUMP yet, boy?* he crackled across the intercom.

He was with me at last.

GUMP? Ah, yes, the acronym for Gas, Undercarriage, Mixtures and Props that American pilots use as a basic pre-landing checklist. Janos had explained what it stood for when I queried it on the approach to Corona airfield the day before.

I'd just started reciting the British version for Old Ned when, alarmingly, on reaching the U for undercarriage, the red undercarriage unsafe light stayed on. Recycling the gear handle did nothing. Still no green lights appeared. None of the circuit breakers had tripped. On the third try it was still red. It could only mean one thing: one or more of the wheels wasn't locking down.

There was no one on the Tower frequency but for the benefit of any approaching aircraft, I made an open call to say we'd be departing the circuit and climbed away to the north, as planned.

With more altitude, we'd be out of the way of any circuit traffic and could go through the emergency checklist step by step in safety – and if all else failed, I told myself, we'd just crank the undercarriage down manually with the handle and fly back slowly. But it was not to be.

With the emergency checklist exhausted and the manual crank at its limit, the red light stayed stubbornly illuminated.

There were no suggestions coming from Old Ned's direction and with steep dives, pull-ups, even a couple of aggressive departure stalls failing to lock the wheels down, there was no alternative but to make a Pan call and ask the military to foam the runway in preparation for an ungainly arrival.

Time was on our side. We had two hours of fuel to burn off – and burn it off we must. The prospect of arriving at dusk with runway lights that could ignite fuel tanks if they ruptured as we slid across the margins with no wheels wasn't something I wanted to contemplate.

Old Ned was still admiring the view out of the starboard window as I made the emergency Pan call. In an instant, he came to life: *Wotchya tell 'em that fer?* he spluttered, clearly disturbed.

I thought it was obvious. I'd forgotten this was California. The prospect of a real live crash was a spectator sport and Old Ned didn't fancy being spectated upon. The military would be there. The media would be there.

Dang photographers be everywheres by the time ya get back, boy! he growled, folding his arms and glaring at me briefly before turning his attention once more to the view from the side window.

Crew Resource Management was definitely not his strong point.

Approaching the airfield, the high ground of Joshua Tree National Park looked spectacular in the setting sun and the desert had turned from golden yellow to a rich, red ochre. Despite the awkward situation, I felt oddly relaxed. It was calm at 8,000 feet, detached, comfortable in a weird kind of way.

Diligently, I briefed Old Ned: we'd use minimum approach speed; I'd cut the mixtures and feather the props as we crossed the end of the runway; he'd switch the mags and the fuel off before we touched down. Three times we went over it. I wasn't entirely happy we were on the same plan but we both tightened our safety belts and just as the sun dipped below the horizon, we started our approach.

Over the line, I cut the mixtures, feathered the props and concentrated on keeping to the centreline. The touchdown was sweet – one of the best I've ever done – and the main gear held. Gently, as the speed bled away, with no functioning nose-wheel, the nose lowered to the tarmac, kicking aside the foam as it ploughed along the centreline and we ground to a halt.

It had been an adventure but we'd made it and we were both in one piece.

I don't remember him getting out but by the time I'd secured the aircraft, switched the fuel and the mags off that he'd long since forgotten about and found my jumper, Old Ned had legged it and disappeared into the night air.

Outside, it was dark and the temperature had plummeted. In stark contrast to the day, it was seriously cold. Stood on the wing, I could see the props at both sides were bent back at the tips. We'd wrecked the engines for sure and remodelled the underside of the nose but the rest of the plane was untouched.

I was still struggling with my jumper when, quite suddenly, a small crowd started gathering around me. There were flashes, cameras were clicking, a microphone with a big foam ball was thrust in my direction: *Gee, what does it feel like to land in foam?* some idiot asked from out in the blackness.

I'd just spent the last three hours trying to rescue an aeroplane that had no intention of co-operating and the best he could come up with was *What was it like to land in foam?*

In that moment, the only thing I could think of was *Go take a *------ Jacuzzi!*

I don't even remember how it slipped out but by the time I was back at the car, Janos was already recounting the story with some delight. He'd heard it – the full account, radio calls and everything from the moment we started our approach – on the local radio station while driving in and the invective I'd hurled at the young reporter had amused him.

But you gotta be call Marie now, he cautioned. *She gonna be see a news. You splattered all over it!*

Indeed, I was: *Cool Brit crash lands in foam at Twentynine Palms.* My claim to fame in the Americas.

Without the pressure of an instrument-rating to pass, the rest of the holiday was more relaxing. We drove up to Big Bear, the girls enjoyed the ski-lifts and tobogganing down the slopes, we visited the lake, bought souvenirs.

Away from the traffic jams on the freeways, up in the mountains the air was clear, free from the smell of traffic fumes and the orange dirt kicked up by the Santa Ana wind that had just started to make its presence felt. It was a place to breathe, to savour, to enjoy.

A year or so later, Janos had located some better aircraft for us to buy and we took the girls out to California again. He'd found a smartly-painted Golden Eagle with youthful engines and a clutch of ex-flight school two-seaters he was confident of selling quickly.

Two had sold before we arrived but there was one nobody seemed to want: a Cessna 152 with basic instrumentation. The paint was faded, the interior was scruffy but it flew so well and climbed the 8,000 feet to Big Bear airport so eagerly with the two of us on board that I couldn't leave it idle in the baking Californian sun.

I had it repainted and a new interior fitted. The girls chose the colours and the upholstery fabric. Janos found an engineer who could dismantle it and put it in a shipping container and we brought it back to the UK. That was my payment for the insurance he'd banked from the Twentynine Palms write-off.

With much more room inside, the Golden Eagle enabled us to take the girls exploring. First on the list of places to visit was Catalina, a small rocky island a little larger than Guernsey, about 30 miles southwest of Long Beach in the Gulf of Santa Catalina. It was famed for its buffalo and the girls wanted to see them.

It was also renowned for its diving. There were wrecks and giant kelp forests and the girls liked that idea too but they still weren't old enough and America wasn't Barbados. The rules were applied more rigorously. Besides, I told them, flying and scuba diving wasn't possible on the same day.

The approach to Catalina airport was a wild ride. The girls loved it.

Whenever there were clouds in the sky back home, Catherine would beg me to fly through them. It was like she lived for turbulence and they both liked big dippers and scary rides that flung them around and dropped them from great heights.

They couldn't get enough of the theme parks in California and we did them all (I remember the hour-long queues for each ride – ugh!) but as we descended towards runway 22, the headwind off the Pacific suddenly turned to wind shear and without warning we found ourselves looking at cliffs in the windscreen rather than tarmac.

Fortunately, the Golden Eagle was nothing like the ageing Cessna 310 that had come to a sticky end at Twentynine Palms on our previous trip. With a light payload, easing the throttles to the firewall unleashed 850 surging horses and fired us skywards over the airfield.

The second approach was successful but at the westerly end of the runway we'd seen evidence of those who hadn't been so lucky. The wrecked carcases of several aeroplanes were still strewn over the slopes, a warning to any pilot who didn't take Catalina seriously.

The ride down to Avalon, the capital of the island, can't have been more than eight or nine miles in a straight line but there was nothing straight about the roads on Catalina and the short trip took the best part of an hour.

It was rough terrain and the taxi driver was adamant, if we wanted to see buffalo we'd have to take the scenic route. It twisted and turned through a series of hairpins, winding its way first in a southerly direction through scrub and forest, then southwest, south around botanical gardens named after William Wrigley Junior – the chewing gum magnate who once owned the island – north for a while and finally east where it descended into the town and turned into a crescent at the seafront.

We hadn't seen much in the way of buffalo but at the far end of the crescent stood an imposing circular building. That was the casino, Janos told us. It was famous. Did we want to go?

I've never won anything in my life, apart from a large and very sharp panel-saw at Belle Vue Zoo during a brass band competition in the early '70s and getting that and my euphonium back on the bus was more trouble than it was worth.

Cards, dice, fruit-machines, betting…they've never been my thing. They've never been Marie's either, so we declined.

You so damn' picky, picky picky! came the response. It was a stock phrase Janos would wheel out whenever his ideas met with resistance and he clearly fancied the idea of a flutter.

So, what we gonna be do?

The girls had seen a poster offering submarine rides to see the fish and like a couple of sniffer dogs on a trail, they followed it. *If we couldn't go diving, Dad, could we at least go in a submarine?* It sounded like fun, an adventure and they both liked adventures. It was on the pier. *Could we go?*

Stopping briefly to grab a bite to eat and admire a couple of large motor yachts that were moored in the harbour, we made our way along the tree-lined waterfront and onto the pier. The girls were already there when we arrived. Their disappointed faces said it all. We'd missed the last tour of the day by five minutes.

The following day, Janos had arranged to meet the owner of another aircraft that was for sale. It needed new paint, he cautioned and the interior would need to be refitted but the engine and airframe times were good and the avionics fit was recent. It was a King Air, an early model C90a.

It was well under a million dollars and it could be our first turbine.

It was over at Grand Canyon. We'd love the scenery en route, he assured, there would be plenty of turbulence for Catherine and we could have lunch there. On the way back, we could drop into Las Vegas, walk down the Boulevard, see the lights on The Strip when it went dark and maybe catch the fountain show.

Viewing aeroplanes didn't appeal to the girls – generally, most things to do with aeroplanes and flying failed to spark much interest as they got older – but the way Janos had painted Las Vegas had caught their attention.

The route from Corona to Grand Canyon took us more or less east, over the Mojave Desert and into Arizona. A more arid and inhospitable place it's difficult to imagine – even from 18,000 feet up in air-conditioned armchair comfort – but in its own way, the landscape has a beauty like no other.

Leaving California, complex patterns in yellow and ochre gave way to a canvas of subtle oranges, pale reds, hues of purple and brown with incised meanders that snaked between the steeply-sloping sides of rugged peaks. Deep fissures spread outwards from each summit, as if a craftsman carver had been at work on them. Nearer the airfield, forests added touches of green to the patchwork of lines and shapes.

Father always found patterns and lines fascinating and drew much inspiration from them. It was easy to imagine him snapping away enthusiastically through the window with his camera.

Leaving our cruise altitude, buffet from the rising heat off the desert hit us hard. Shrieks from the back seats denoted some enjoyment from flying had returned and the lower we descended, the more turbulent the air currents became. At one point, every time I reached for the throttle controls, a kick from beneath rammed them up beyond my grasp, then the tail would get a whack and we'd slew sideways or a wing would lift and we'd be rocking and rolling.

Landing more than 6,000 feet up at Grand Canyon National Park Airport proved to be as entertaining and colourful as the desert had been on the way but the touchdown was a greaser to be proud of. Janos had certainly found us a nice Golden Eagle and it flew beautifully.

Unfortunately, the King Air we'd gone to see wasn't one of his better finds. It had EFIS on both sides – a full glass cockpit – but with brush-applied stripes in barely matching colours that covered flaking paintwork beneath and an interior that left me itching and scratching after the briefest of excursions to the flight deck, he certainly hadn't overstated the cosmetics.

As for the low airframe and engine times, they were easily explained by several years of missing service records. It pleased the girls, though. The meeting was short.

In the late evening sun, the Grand Canyon was spectacular. Jagged pinnacles rose dramatically from dark ruby chasms, becoming vivid orange-red as they broke into the skyline. The power that created this incredible landscape is beyond the imagination and its unparalleled vastness took us all by surprise.

Gradually, the sun slipped below the horizon and gave way to stars in an infinite black sky as we set a westerly course towards the bright lights of Sin City.

A blaze of light confirmed Las Vegas was ahead. No sooner had we been instructed to intercept the Instrument Landing System on runway 19 right than we were shifted to 19 left to make way for a small jet. Then we were bounced back to 19 right as another arrived out of nowhere.

The girls didn't care. They were glued to the windows, watching out for Caesar's Palace and the sights on The Strip.

That evening, we must have photographed everything between the Luxor hotel and the Interstate 515 at least twice. They were mesmerised by the spectacle.

As with Janos, Steve and Jayne, my friendship with Alejandro grew out of a business relationship.

Alejandro worked for a printing company in Bilbao where he headed up the export sales team. Small, slim, olive-skinned, always smiling and eternally patient, I remember the many conversations leading up to our first meeting very well. By the time we eventually met it was more like a reunion of old friends than a business discussion.

Although he knew long before he set foot in Norwich that changing printers was a bit like changing wives for us, he remained quietly persuasive and had good reason to be optimistic.

He'd presented his company and its capabilities well and even our seasoned general manager, who'd spent his entire life as an inky, was impressed with the quality from the Spanish print works. All Alejandro needed was the opportunity and he knew he'd be in.

We'd been working with a Polish printer for some time when his opportunity arrived unexpectedly. A series of major quality issues and a couple of unexplained late deliveries had been followed by repudiation of all responsibility.

That didn't go down well.

I've always worked on the principle that there are no problems, only unfound solutions, so to watch our trusted print partner washing his hands of any accountability for another avoidable disaster when we could have worked towards a resolution with a little more willingness from his side, that turned an already flashing orange light red.

We'd persevered, tried and tried again but with frayed nerves and patience at an end, it was time to cut the cord and Alejandro's reward for patience had arrived.

A few days later, Marie and I hopped in the plane and flew down to Bilbao to see the print works and the bindery.

Satisfied the facilities and the production and pre-press staff could provide the quality, service and delivery schedules we needed, we ratified the contract and headed off with Alejandro towards La Rioja for lunch and a wine-tasting.

It would be the first of many visits – and many wine-tastings that eventually earned me the distinguished title of 'The Man Who Smells A Lot' from Alejandro.

A little over an hour's drive through undulating scenery to the south of Bilbao lies the town of Laguardia. A few miles to the north-west, amid an almost-uninterrupted landscape of row upon row of neatly-trimmed vines that seemed to extend almost seamlessly from the Basque region to La Rioja, we arrived at our destination: the

The Cessna 310 parked up at Twentynine Palms, its nose damaged and its propellers bent back at the tips after the crash landing.

Janos, the Hungarian-born pilot who lived in California and delivered the Navajo, N63560 from Switzerland to Norwich.

Marie with one of the two-seaters Janos found for us to sell. This was the one we had repainted and shipped to the UK in a container. It was a dream to fly.

Catherine, Marie and me at Mâcon-Charnay, our stop-over for Chamonix en route to Corsica.

Through the window at Heredad Ugarte winery (now Eguren Ugarte) in La Rioja: a glorious view towards the mountains where eagles soar effortlessly on the rising thermals – a spectacle to be enjoyed over good wine and traditional Basque cuisine.

Heredad Ugarte winery and restaurant, nowadays better known as Eguren Ugarte.

It's hard to appreciate just how hot La Rioja is from the comfort of an air-conditioned car. A wall of heat hit us the moment we opened the doors. Crossing the car park, the sun bit mercilessly as we made our way towards the shade of the entrance.

Ahead, a small party of visitors was eager to start their wine-tasting tour. In their impatience, they'd completely missed an elderly gentleman stood to one side of the entrance door. Clad in well-worn blue overalls, he was leaning on a broom stick and watching them file past from beneath a wide-brimmed hat.

I remember thinking what a characterful face he had and wishing I'd brought a camera. Intense sunlight was bouncing off the sun-drenched car-park, illuminating the underside of the brim of his hat, mellowing the shadow on his face and warming his already-tanned complexion. In that moment, his would have been a magical portrait.

Noting my interest, he smiled. I smiled back and reached out to shake his hand. A powerful hand clenched mine, engulfing it with a formidable grip. He was not especially tall nor even heavily-set but this was a serious hand, a big hand with a colossal span. It had done some serious work in its time, though the years had not tempered its authority. For a few seconds, we clasped, unable to speak each other's language but reading the moment.

Had we come for the wine tour and the restaurant or did we want to see his garden? he asked tentatively, releasing his grasp.

Alejandro translated.

Would we like to refresh first?

Approaching the garden, he beckoned towards two signs affixed to the side of a high rocky mound: Caballeros and Señoritas. The doorways to both were obstructed by enormous stone blocks. There appeared no obvious way past.

Seeing our bewilderment, he smiled. Pushing his shoulder against one of the blocks, it pivoted slowly, allowing just enough space to enter. The intensity of the sun made it difficult to see what lay beyond but gradually, as scorched eyes accommodated to the darkness, the interior past the Caballeros sign appeared in all its glory. Roughly hewn and cut deep into the rock, it was a small but fully equipped man cave; a rustic restroom like no other. It could have come straight from a Flintstones movie.

Refreshed, we started our tour of the garden.

Winding our way along the pathways, our guide pointed out the features: a beautiful little chapel with a vaulted ceiling, an altar, exedras with statues cut in the walls and simple bench-seating for wedding guests; a banqueting hall, perfect for weddings; a small lake with a jetty; a boat and an island that had been individually crafted so the groom could row his bride to a secluded spot away from wedding guests; and here, he said, pointing towards the edge of the garden, would be a hotel.

In some detail, he described it: the pillars at the entrance; the bedrooms, some with balconies overlooking the vineyard; the restaurant with views over mile upon mile of vineyard; and the tower – its crowning glory – from which the panoramic vista towards La Rioja would be magnificent.

When he'd asked if we wanted to see his garden, I'd naïvely imagined pretty flowers, rockeries, a few palm trees, a pond and maybe some nice seating areas.

This wasn't just a garden. It was a triumph of civil engineering. The buildings were massive undertakings – substantial edifices with vaulted ceilings that provided sanctuary from the fierce temperatures outside, all set against beautifully landscaped backdrops planted with colourful bushes, native trees and shrubs.

Through Alejandro's translation, he explained how they'd been made. It was immediately apparent why the huge hand that had clasped mine so warmly had such power.

First, he'd created small hills using colossal earth-moving equipment. With cranes and bulldozers, he'd covered them with massive boulders. Then he'd injected tonnes of cement between the boulders to set them in place before scooping the earth out from beneath with enormous track-driven earth-movers.

This wasn't gardening as I knew it. It wasn't gardening as most people might know it. He'd undertaken a major mining and engineering operation and its impressiveness was both imposing and awe-inspiring.

But who was the creator? Who had masterminded its construction? And who was the gentleman who had been so kind as to show it to us?

As we made our way back past the lake and along the pathway, curiosity got the better of me.

With Alejandro translating, we learned the unassuming gardener whose portrait I wished I'd been able to take and whose illuminating tour we'd enjoyed so much – the gentleman in the old blue overalls who was leaning on a broom stick and watching visitors file past from beneath a wide brimmed hat when we arrived – was none other than Victorino Eguren Ugarte, the owner of the winery.

Humble, unpretentious and masked as the sweeper of the yard, we'd been treated to a unique guided tour from the architect and vender of everything we'd surveyed. And what an incredible fellow he was.

I confess, I do enjoy the wines of La Rioja – not the pithy things stocked by most supermarkets, the proper ones from specialist producers.

The intensity, the uniqueness, the combination of fruit and oak in a really good Rioja fuse into a powerful and instantly-recognisable taste experience that, for me, embodies the very essence of northern Spain.

It cries out for the right food and in the Heredad Ugarte restaurant, the simply-prepared Basque cuisine complemented the various wines that came with it perfectly: toasts with paté, raspberries and fig; asparagus with olive oil; roasted peppers with olive oil and garlic; butter beans and potatoes in a soup with roasted peppers, paprika, chorizo and green chillies on the side; salted lamb chops grilled over vine timber and served with a simple salad; and Crema Catalana to finish.

The pause between courses provided opportunity to enjoy the glorious view towards the mountains, to watch eagles soar effortlessly on the rising thermals and to chat through the finer points of the print contract we were there to arrange.

The only English speakers in the restaurant, we very soon came to the attention of the adjacent table where a suited gentleman was entertaining two others. Leaning over, he introduced himself: he was Heredad Ugarte's export manager.

Were we enjoying the meal? He asked in very broken English.

Indeed, we were.

How did we like the wines?

He was clearly struggling so Alejandro translated.

Yes, we were enjoying those, too. *Was it possible to buy them in England?*

Sadly not. But he'd like to export to England. *Did we know any wine importers?*

Wine importers were a bit off my radar but I had bought from a recently-established wine merchant and I'd been in contact with the wine buyer only a few weeks before when we'd met at a wine-tasting evening in Norwich. Perhaps he'd heard of them?

No, he'd never heard of Virgin Wines.

Trying to jog a connection, I started to explain…

Virgin Wines, like Virgin Atlantic, the airline – the same brand.

No, he hadn't heard of Virgin Atlantic.

What about Richard Branson, the entrepreneur who owned them?

No, he'd never heard of Mr Branson.

It would be about then that the next course arrived. Hastily, we exchanged business cards and I promised to send an email contact and phone number via Alejandro when we returned home.

With their meal finished, the three departed and we followed shortly afterwards for a tour of the winery.

Much of the winery was underground and there were recognisable parallels between its construction and that of the garden. Hundreds of yards of subterranean passageways connected little bays that were simply furnished with rustic seats and tables.

Here, aficionados could bring friends and family and in perfect temperatures and absolute privacy, taste and enjoy their own collections.

There were enormous vaulted cellars where barrelled wines could gather distinctive flavours and small, gated recesses along the route where old vintages dating back a century or more could rest undisturbed. It was a fascinating experience, a world away from the intense heat and unrelenting sun outside.

As we were about to make our exit, the receptionist, who'd seemed quite haughty and aloof on the way in, rushed towards us, a big smile on her face. In her hands was a five-litre bottle of Crianza. This, she explained with some reverence as she presented it to us, was a gift from the export manager and he'd signed and dated it for us as a thank-you for our visit.

Grateful and flattered but not quite sure why it should be coming in our direction, we accepted her generosity and with profuse thanks, headed for the car.

I think it was a couple of weeks after we'd returned home that Alejandro conveyed the email address and contact details I'd promised to send to the export manager and called me to confirm they'd spoken.

I remember that phone call well.

He could hardly hold back his amusement.

Somehow, everything had become knotted in the export manager's understanding of our disjointed, part-English, part-Spanish, across-the-table exchange.

Richard Branson, the entrepreneur, had morphed into Charles Bronson, the actor; Virgin Wines had become Charles Bronson's home in the Virgin Islands. And our offer of help (and hardly deserved celebrity status among the rich and famous) was the reason for the unexpected presentation.

We opened the wine to share with a couple of dozen friends who arrived from far flung parts of the globe some years later and recounted the tale as the cork popped. As always, Jean-Paul performed the honour in his capacity of Maitre de Vin. A very good wine it was, too.

One of the band of friends who'd flown in for our international party was Linda. Linda hails from America and although we've only met a handful of times, over the years we've got to know each other – and each other's families – modestly well.

It was 1998 when Marie was first diagnosed with MS. Although she'd not been well for some time, the news hit us both like a bolt from the blue. Suddenly, the future had become uncertain. One week she was fine, the next I was teaching her how to walk.

Desperate to find something – anything – that might make things better for her, I embarked on a quest that eventually took me to Linda's door.

Linda was working for one of the leading research hospitals in the US and through her connections, I learned much more about the disease and the research paths that were being explored. She was a real gem and on many occasions, she went out of her way to track down the right people, ask questions and relay answers.

In the course of our email conversations, we inevitably touched on family issues and it wasn't too long before we became pen pals.

Neither of us could write short letters. Often, we'd punctuate medical updates and emails on more serious topics with anecdotes from life.

On one occasion, with little time to read two or three of the longer letters I'd sent but a lengthy business flight ahead that would afford her the opportunity, Linda vowed to take them to read on the plane. She recounted afterwards how her laughter had reached the ears of other passengers and how the letters had made their way from the rear of the cabin to the front, then back down the other side, always with the same effect.

Their entertainment value hadn't escaped the cabin staff, who, intrigued to know what had so amused their passengers, asked if they might also read them.

Linda agreed – but only on condition no one passed them to the captain until after the plane had landed.

Some years later, we mooted the idea of collating the letters we'd written to each other in a book. We made a start but a computer crash wiped out many of Linda's anecdotes, then events in our personal lives halted progress. Eventually, with more pressing issues taking precedence, we put the idea on ice.

One thing that did seem to help Marie's condition was altitude. Whenever we flew together, she'd notice the difference within minutes of leaving terra firma. The continual pain she suffered would diminish and the stiffness in her hands would relent, especially if she held them over the instrument binnacle in the sunlight.

It wasn't a phenomenon that held much interest for the researchers where Linda worked but it did intrigue the Civil Aviation Authority Medical Examiner who conducted my pilot medicals. Together we hatched a plan to carry out a series of tests on several volunteers that would better indicate whether altitude was a tangible benefit or whether it was simply feel-good factor at work.

With Marie's help, we organised a flying day for a willing bunch of volunteers, all of whom had MS. Taking six at a time and the CAA Medical Examiner, I flew them around Norfolk and Suffolk for an hour while he repeated a series of simple, non-intrusive tests that had first been administered, measured and recorded while everyone was still on the ground.

Even at 3,000 feet, several of those who had dexterity problems found they could manipulate their fingers better, while others who had no sensation in lower limbs could feel the touch of a feather after ten or fifteen minutes in the air.

Some had problems putting numbered cards in chronological order on the ground but in the air, they managed the same test faultlessly. Only for one or two was there no measureable difference.

Did it lead us to a conclusion? Sadly, not one that advanced the science of neurology or won much attention from the cutting-edge researchers Linda worked with but it was good to see smiles on the faces of the volunteers when we landed. They'd had a good time and that was ample compensation for the lack of a conclusion.

That summer, Marie and I decided to take the girls on holiday to Corsica, stopping off en route at Chamonix in the French Alps for a little more altitude therapy. At around 3,000 feet, the difference was immediately obvious to her. We made a video as she ran up a hill.

A few days later, she'd adapted to the thinner air and slipped back, so we took her higher to see if more altitude would promote an improvement.

I remember waving goodbye to the three of them as they disappeared in cloud, suspended on a steel rope inside a cable car and thinking what an intrepid bunch they were. A few thousand feet more made all the difference but the effect was short-lived.

I didn't get to see it.

I'm happy enough flying inverted, looping and barrel rolling in an aeroplane. I don't have a problem poking around inside a shipwreck, providing its not strewn with old fishing nets. But to be enclosed in a metal box that's being dragged between two mountains on a string rates second only to leaping from a bridge with an elastic band attached to my ankles.

It's not for me.

I prefer to have a modicum of control over my own destiny.

The next leg of our trip took us to Propriano on the south-western corner of the French-speaking island of Corsica. We'd never been before and as the holiday had been hastily arranged in peak season when all the hotels were already fully booked, we decided to take a couple of tents.

Camping was a privilege the airfield bestowed upon visiting pilots and the price of the pitch was included in the landing and parking fee. The beach and the warm Mediterranean Sea were only yards from the end of the runway, so we figured the girls might enjoy an outdoor experience as part of the holiday.

They'd enjoyed camping before when we'd visited Guernsey – there were hot showers, hair-driers and electricity in Steve and Jayne's house across the grass – so we reasoned the idea of camping under the wing with the sun setting over the airfield would be a romantic experience for us and compensation enough for the boredom of the two-and-a-half-hour flight from Mâcon-Charnay to Propriano for them.

There was a small restaurant and a shower-block on the airfield. It didn't promise five-star luxury but for a couple of nights, we reckoned they'd cope.

We couldn't have been more wrong.

Have you been in there, Dad?

There's no lock on the toilet door!

The water pressure in the showers is rubbish!

Where are we supposed to plug our hair-driers in?

The mirror is broken!

The lights don't work!

Engulfed in a sea of complaints, we entirely missed the moment when the sun dipped below the horizon.

The instant darkness engulfed the airfield, frenzied activity commenced. The French mating season opened.

From every direction, the sound of couples engaging enthusiastically beneath flimsy canvas carried across the still night air and from their tent a few yards away, we could hear a running commentary from the girls:

Which tent is that?

They're behind us.

Could she make any more noise?

He's as bad.

This one's at it now.

Are they the ones from the red plane?

Ooh, that didn't sound good!

Hope it wasn't the cooker that went over.

What was that noise?

A zip.

They're outside!

Are they on the wing?

Aren't there things sticking out of a wing?

We'll know soon enough.

Yeah, told you! [Laughter follows]

Shh! Dad'll hear you!

Dad has heard you! Go to sleep!

[More laughter.]

It must have been well into the early hours before the mating frenzy subsided and calm descended on the airfield. We didn't stay to find out whether it was a nightly ritual. The following morning, we filed our flight plan for Mâcon-Charnay and with the restaurant closed and the girls refusing to go anywhere near the shower block, we left.

In the autumn of that same year I took a second stab at passing my American Instrument Rating. With some diligent tutoring from Tom, an American instructor who'd set up base in Norwich, I'd worked hard to familiarise myself with the differences between the British and American systems, passed my written exam and perfected my approaches on his simulator.

With the required number of under-the-hood flight hours clocked and simulator work repeated in the air, all that remained was to prove to an examiner that I was up to the FAA standard and the problems of blasting off through clouds that had so often seen us waiting on the ground for the weather to clear would be behind me.

That meant another trip to the USA.

It was a few weeks after 9/11 – the back end of October 2001 – that I flew over.

After my experience with Old Ned at Twentynine Palms and the aeroplanes Janos and I had bought either unavailable or unsuitable, there was no point in heading for California again.

For my second attempt, I decided to take the FAA instrument rating in Delaware. Everything had been arranged through another friend who'd just moved to the US after a distinguished flying career with various European airlines. All I had to do was get there.

It wasn't easy arranging flights. Services were massively disrupted with some airlines no longer in business, routes cancelled and other carriers still trying to reposition aircraft.

I'd expected huge security upheaval but aside from a short delay in Norwich that almost saw me miss my connection in Amsterdam, the flight to Chicago, then on to Philadelphia ran like clockwork.

To be honest, I was surprised – shocked – at how low-key the security was on the American side of the Atlantic only a few short weeks after such an apocalyptic event.

The officials in Amsterdam were rigorous but at every point I landed in the US, I was waved past with nothing more than a cursory passport check.

A hire car was waiting for me on arrival in Philadelphia and in not much more than an hour and a half, I arrived at my hotel.

My first flight was an orientation flight and it was booked for the following morning. It would be the only time in a whole week of flying I'd get to see out of the windows, so I was determined to enjoy it – and enjoy it I did.

Delaware was a riot of colour in the autumn and flying beneath the 700-foot military zone near Dover Air Force Base provided a spectacle beyond compare. The coastline bordering Delaware Bay was a string of nature reserves from just south of Delaware City in the northwest to Rehoboth Bay and the Coastal Highway at the eastern edge of the State and it was breathtaking from the air.

Dusty, my instructor for the week, had been tasked with getting me up to examiner Jim's exacting standards for the oral exam and the flight test. Jim, he told me, was a hard task master who let nothing slip. If I passed, I could consider myself airline-ready. Jim didn't take prisoners, he cautioned. Make a mistake, hesitate, deviate from designated altitude by more than a few feet and he'd stop the test.

That afternoon, I saw the proof.

I'd been working with Dusty on approach charts, when a young chap – probably in his early 30s – returned to the clubhouse with tears rolling down his cheeks. He'd failed. Jim was not amused as the pair of them went into his office for the customary debrief.

We couldn't hear what was being said but the following morning I learned nerves had got the better of Jim's student. After his ground exam, he'd been sent out to pre-flight the aircraft. Pre-flight checks completed, he'd returned to the clubhouse to collect his examiner. The two of them had boarded and closed the door. Jim had sat there while his student fumbled about with checklists and organised charts.

When asked if he'd preflighted the aircraft, the student confirmed he had. Jim opened the door and left.

There were two almost identical aircraft on the apron and his student had boarded the wrong one. Realising his nerve-racked examinee had already made the ultimate error, Jim had sat there for a while, waiting to see what would happen next. It wasn't until the student tried to start the aircraft that he realised the electrics had been disconnected and there was no engine on the left wing.

It was an intensive but extremely enjoyable week spent pounding approaches, flying holds and correcting awkward flight attitudes with Dusty. He was a good instructor, a patient instructor and as the week progressed, the tasks he set me became more and more automatic.

Quite intentionally, he'd distract me with stories and jokes and as the week passed, the banter in the cabin grew in parallel with my ability to cope with increased workload. Through the experience, we gradually became friends.

At the end of the week, my moment came and I boarded the aircraft for the last time with examiner Jim.

If ever you hear anyone commenting on how much easier it is to pass the American instrument rating than the British one, take it from me, they've never done it.

After a solid hour of questioning for the oral exam, the flight test took two-and-a-half hours. In that time, every conceivable approach was thrown at me, three times I was dumped in a holding pattern, we'd recovered from some extreme flight attitudes – even a departure stall at 700 feet under the hood.

Mentally exhausted, we landed at Dover and as the sweat poured off me in the baking cabin, I turned to Jim and asked if I'd passed yet. *You passed half an hour ago,* came the reply. *You seemed to be having a good time so I thought I'd sit back and enjoy the view.*

That same afternoon, with no more than a few minutes to shower and change my shirt, I started my journey home.

Hastily dumping the hire car at Philadelphia and with the usual grind of tickets and passports behind me, I perched myself on the most advantageous seat I could find at the departure gate.

Dressed in smart black trousers, white shirt and black tie with a pilot case that had my CAA wings on the front, I couldn't help noticing a uniformed lady staring at me from the other side of the desk.

She was huge – seriously huge. Gigantic, mountainous bazoinks threatened from beneath a blouse that had probably been the sail from an ocean-going yacht in a past life, wrenching at the buttons. Enormous thighs challenged the fabric of trousers that her voluptuous acres were never intended to occupy and as she headed towards me, I swear I heard the creaking of seams from 40 feet away.

I tried to bury myself in a book but the only thing I could find in my flight case was FAR AIM 2001 – the Federal Aviation Administration rule book. It was a futile act. She'd locked onto me like an air-to-air missile and was closing in fast.

Yo dare, honey! she called across the almost empty waiting area in a deep Southern drawl you could have cut with a chain saw.

I pretended not to hear.

Yo dare! Ah's a-towkin' ta yo!

I looked up. *Me?* I mouthed.

It couldn't have been anyone else. There was no one else.

Dere am nobody else roand hare! she yelled back, half-amused but with more menace than elation in her voice. *Ah gotta wand yo!*

Repacking my FAR AIM into my case as slowly as I could, I made my way across the narrow corridor that separated the waiting area from the gate, boarding card in one hand, flight-bag in the other.

Yo hurry up now. Dere am a plane waitin' for ya! she urged, impatiently. *Don't ya want ta get on it?*

You know how it is in Hollywood movies when two cowboys are squaring up for a shoot-out in the main street of a ghost town. Somehow, the only thing that was missing from the moment was tumbleweed.

Yo can stop dere! she announced, a commanding hand raised.

Obediently, I stopped. About six feet separated us.

Yo speak English, honey? she demanded, waddling closer.

Yes, I do. And French. And German.

Oh, dat am a byootiful English accent ya got, honey!

English accent? I don't have an English accent! I protested. *I <u>am</u> English.*

I realised it was dumb to comment before it left my mouth but it was too late.

Spread dem legs! she ordered. I'd obviously riled her.

Before I could oblige she was already in the descent, wand in hand. Hoping she had air brakes to slow the rate of decent before her nose-cone head-butted my wedding tackle, I gritted my teeth and stood my ground.

Most security checks I've ever been through start at the top with collar, arms, back and chest and work down. Not hers. Inside legs first. Nothing beeped. With a snort, she moved to wand the outside. Still nothing beeped. I remember shifting my gaze to the ceiling lights as her search moved north.

Ya good ta go! she snorted, stepping back. Clearly, she'd found nothing more foreign than an Englishman with a byootiful English accent inside the neatly-pressed black trousers and white shirt.

It probably wasn't the smartest thing I've ever done, especially as I'd been cleared to board, but I felt compelled to ask: *This wand of yours… how does it work exactly?*

Ah show'd ya! came the response. *Ah jos move it op and doon. It tell me if ya carryin' danger-arse metal t'ings.*

It must be different to the ones we have in the UK.

Why dat, honey?

Well, you see that little light there…

Dere am no light!

Yes, that's my point. I think you're supposed to switch it on!

Only a few short weeks after 9/11, with security alerts in every airport around the world, I'd managed to find the one security officer who hadn't been told airport security isn't only about putting on the uniform and looking menacing.

Chapter Nine
Family Life

Mother and Father were a tremendous anchor at the centre of the family and for both girls they played a crucial role in developing their sense of values and family life. They were always there, ready to help, support and advise. It was good having them around.

Whenever the weather allowed, they enjoyed nothing more than a barbecue in the garden. Neither of them drank much, so when Father got a glass of wine inside him the corny jokes would come out.

He's been licking bottle tops, Mother would quip, rolling her eyes in a momentary show of feigned tedium.

What's that about organ stops? Father would retort, intentionally mishearing – he misheard often but sometimes he'd capitalise on the amusement value. It was always in good humour.

I remember one barbecue in particular. It was late summer and one of those idyllic days that make you glad to be alive. The sky was a cloudless deep blue. Martins darted playfully in and out of the nest that had been their home beneath the eaves since the late spring.

It was relaxing sitting by the pond, watching the fish, admiring the stripes I'd just rolled in the lawn and listening to the waterfall. The marigolds were at their best and tumbling from half barrels and big earthenware pots against the south-facing white walls of the house were petunias, lobelia and allysum.

It was the perfect afternoon to be in the garden and we'd invited Mother and Father for six o'clock.

Father was always early. It's a family tradition. At five-thirty they arrived, Mother in a long flowery frock she'd made herself and Father wearing his cream Del Monte Man panama (tied under the chin with a piece of brown cord) and a pair of sawn-off cream trousers.

It's not that he couldn't afford a pair of shorts. Not wanting to throw anything away is a Northern-dad thing.

When the long pants passed their sell-by date, Mother shortened them. Mother's eyesight wasn't all it used to be when she was dress-making and one leg of the shorts was slightly shorter than the other. At least, we assumed it was the shorts that were at fault.

What's matter? Don't you like them? Father asked, pulling a face to show his amusement.

They're very trendy, Grandad, responded Christina.

Bendy? Who's bendy?

No, trendy, Grandad. Trendy, not bendy!

That's what I said. Well I like them. I can get out of them easily.

[Laughter followed.]

Is that one of your party tricks, Grandad?

Don't be cheeky. I heard that! Pardon?

Father didn't wear one deaf aid, he wore two. He also kept a small collection of dead and dying relics in his pocket along with assorted batteries, most discharged. They all frustrated him mercilessly but the standby models generally came in useful when one or other of the new digi-versions had been ripped out of his ears in exasperation and lobbed somewhere.

With the sea bass browning over the coals and skewered crevettes ready to go on next, Father discovered he hadn't brought his tablets. Christina had taken him home earlier to get them – just a short walk down the lane – but somehow, he'd managed to return without them. Mother wasn't amused.

How can you go home for your tablets then forget to get them? she scolded.

I can't hear you. I'm deaf.

I know you're deaf... but what about the tablets?

Yes, I know about the tablets. They're on the dressing table.

But you went to fetch them!

What?

The tablets...you went to fetch them!

Another glass of wine arrived and the subject changed.

Fish, Dad?

What? No, that's what I went home for.

You went home for a fish?

That's not what you said the first time.

Barely able to restrain herself from bursting into a cheeky giggle, Catherine spooned out the couscous. Sea bass laced with lemon and black pepper arrived on Father's plate and a thick wedge of crusty bread was added with a salad garnish. Marie and Mother opted for salmon while Christina headed for the couscous and the char-grilled peppers. She was a veggie, though not for any political reason. She just didn't like meat, even as a toddler.

How's that, Grandad? asked Catherine.

Grandad didn't respond. He'd taken a first mouthful and was fishing about in the pocket of his lop-sided shorts, the plate perched precariously on his knees.

Have you lost something, Grandad?

What?

Have you lost something?

I hate this thing!

What thing?

My hearing-aid. I can't find it.

It's in your ear, Grandad.

It's what?

It's in your ear.

Oh, yes. I hate it! he snapped, unaware of the volume of his response as he wrenched it out of his ear and, like an Olympic discus thrower, hurled it over his shoulder in the general direction of the rockery.

This entertaining custom was normally reserved for Christmas dinner. In years gone by, numerous deaf aids had met their end at the bottom of the gravy boat or in the rum sauce. One was even found in the loo – but that was apparently an unintentional loss rather than the result of one of his Olympian launches. Mother had bleached that one and sprinkled it with aftershave so Father never knew where it had been. Remarkably, it survived.

This particular model, one of the latest generation digital deaf-aids, had felt the G-force on its way to the rockery but had only made it as far as the fish pond. A gentle plop announced its arrival.

It was almost guaranteed that the unfortunate object would land in the deepest part of the most inaccessible place. Four feet out and two feet down, it had spiralled into the mud at the bottom of the weedy end. Momentarily, the barbecue was abandoned as all hands diverted to its retrieval.

After a few minutes of intensive search-and-rescue and some fishing around with a net, the deaf-aid was salvaged and handed back. Father, who'd almost finished his sea bass and couscous by that time, shook it vigorously to get rid of the pond life, switched it on and stuffed it back in his ear.

Talk to me someone, he yelled, still unaware of his capacity for volume.

Come in Beagle Two, Christina responded. *Is there life on Mars?*

Who do you think I am? Pillinger?

Another cork popped. More giant crevettes were heaped on his plate. The rosé was getting to work. The Del Monte Man hat had been squashed and was sitting side-saddle on his head like the field service cap he used to wear in the RAF and between the crunching of crustacea, Father grinned. It was good to see him enjoying himself.

With the main course finished and cleared away, Catherine returned with her dessert. She was good at desserts. She was good at anything to do with cooking and baking but she especially excelled in desserts and this time she'd invented an intoxicating pudding that included alcohol-soaked plums, thick double-cream and jelly. I forget what she named it but it immediately caught Father's attention.

The first serving slipped down easily and with it the banter around the table intensified and the volume grew. Mother giggled. She never giggled. Father grinned from ear to ear.

More dessert anyone? Catherine asked.

Please. Father's hearing-aid was at peak performance. *See if Grandma wants some first.*

Mother nodded. Catherine served.

We'd almost finished the second helping when Father burst into Malay, a relic from his wartime service days in the Far East. Normally, he reserved it for visits to the local Indian restaurant where it never failed to dumbfound the waiters – most of whom were born in Bradford. To the uninitiated, he was quite fluent and often added to the authenticity of the moment by wobbling his head from side to side.

Seeing the effect, curiosity got the better of me. What had Catherine put in the dessert?

Oh, it's just plums, cream and jelly, Dad.

It was at about that point that Father hauled himself to his feet and started towards the fishpond. His feet didn't respond well. Abruptly, the adventure ended and he fell back in the chair with a grin on his face.

It was rather good. Is there any more?

Catherine reached for the spoon but before she could serve, Marie leaned over to take Father's dish. It didn't get her far. He wasn't letting go and clasped it to his chest.

Before you give him any more, I think we should know what's in it – I mean exactly.

Christina giggled. *Grandad's on tablets, Catherine. You'd better say.*

Well... Catherine started.

Could oi have another portion o' dat dessert, Patrick? Catherine had become Patrick and Father had switched accent from Malay to Irish.

You were about to say...Catherine...

Well, I used Pineau to soak the plums.

Is that it? Pineau isn't usually so strong.

It's the jelly. Ask her what's in the jelly, Mum, Christina prompted.

Well, Catherine?

It's er...vodka jelly. Good or what?

It was indeed good. Powerful, in fact. Mother was hanging off the side of her chair, I was feeling decidedly woozy, everybody was giggling. Father was wasted.

How much did you put in? Marie asked, trying to make a stern face. It didn't work.

Father leered at her with crossed eyes, mouth open and head wobbling from side to side. Instantly, she dissolved into an un-suppressible titter. Marie never did titters. This was serious.

Can I no get a wee dollop o' your jelly? Father chimed in, this time in broad Glaswegian, but no one took any notice. Everyone wanted to hear Catherine's confession:

I used that small bottle on the bar.

Suddenly, I'm wondering which *small* bottle. There was a large, part-used bottle of vodka and two smaller bottles that were presents from a Russian visitor we'd entertained the year before. I never drank vodka – didn't like it – so they had just sat there where the last visitor had left them.

The one with the red top.

My present from Andrei?

Guess so.

How much did you use?

I used it all.

Anything else in it?

Nope, just jelly.

Oi don't wonder it was smashin', responded Father. (We were back to an impersonation of the Reverend Paisley.) *Now can oi finish dat off cos it's dinimishing in proofability all da time we's a-talkin' 'bout it?*

Dinimishing? Now it was Mother who was tittering. *Do you mean dimininishing, dear?* she giggled, realising her own error was even more comical than Father's.

Sumtin loik dat!

With no one else taking notice, Father decided to serve himself but his lunge for the jelly missed. Unintentionally, he caught the long-handled serving spoon that was hanging over the edge of the bowl and it catapulted across the table. Wobbly, orange alcohol shot straight down Christina's top. She squealed.

Oh, goodness gracious me! Father was back to the Indian impersonation again. The spoon had continued its journey over Christina's shoulder and landed in the barbecue but standing up to retrieve it proved more difficult than he had anticipated.

To applause, he fell back in the chair, a pleasured grin the only thing that could be seen beneath the brim of the Del Monte Man hat. *Ah, 'tis a grand party, so 'tis! I must invite you all to another some day!*

Deafness is a dreadful affliction. It's impossible to imagine how difficult it makes life for those who suffer hearing loss but Father was always one to make light of it. The girls, Marie and I had all become accustomed to translating the reinterpretations he'd come out with and making sense of things that usually dumbfounded others.

There was one phrase, however, that took us all by surprise when its true meaning was revealed – one we'd all taken at face-value for years – and it took a trip to the local hospital to discover our mistake.

Father wasn't often ill. In fact, apart from low blood-pressure and occasional arrhythmia when he overdid the Drambuie, he seemed to enjoy the rudest of health. The one time he was taken poorly, it turned out to be the result of some pills his doctor had prescribed to slow his heart rate.

I confess, I'm not in the least medical and popping pills has never been on my priority list, aside from the odd allergy pill when I've come in contact with cats. I don't have the slightest idea how medicines work – chemistry was lost to me after the rocket-and-glass-cabinet incident that got me banned from chemistry lessons at school – but to me it didn't seem a particularly logical move to be prescribing pills that would slow his heart rate when his symptoms included low blood-pressure and an irregular heartbeat. But, like I said, I'm not medical and for a while after he started taking them, he did seem more perky.

Things took a bad turn when Father decided to double the dose *to get better quicker*.

It was the early hours of the morning when Mother phoned me to see if I could go over and take a look at him. I arrived to find him a bit grey and sweaty. In the absence of a night-time phone number for the local surgery, we bundled him in the back of the car and headed off at high speed to the local hospital.

It was only ten minutes away (12 to the maternity ward – I'd got that down to perfection) but by the time we'd arrived he'd gone all limp and gooey. Anxiously, we took our seats outside the treatment room while a group of white-coated doctors got to work on him.

It was about an hour later that one of the doctors popped his head around the door and told us we could go in and see him.

Miraculously, they'd sorted him out.

Father was sitting bolt upright in his hospital bed, apparently none-the-worse for his experience, and was entertaining four junior doctors who'd gathered around his bedside to learn about the origins of a medical problem that had been bothering him for years: his jungle toes.

Father attributed the problem to his time in Java, Sumatra, Ceylon (he never could bring himself to call it Sri Lanka) and India during the war years. The junior doctors seemed fascinated by this apparently unheard-of ailment that turns one's toenails a murky, striped yellow and induces them to curl downwards.

Having had his pump regularised, he was only too pleased to help further their medical education when one of them asked if he could examine the aforementioned yellow curly objects.

The intrepid pack-leader, a young man whose family probably originated from the very region in which Father had spent some of his five service years, lifted the lower bedclothes and proceeded his digit by digit examination.

Please to be telling more of jungle toes, he asked in a strong accent that immediately caught Father's attention.

Mother's eyes turned heavenwards, as if on springs and remain glued to the flickering strip-light on the ceiling as Father launched into an explanation worthy of any medical dictionary.

It transpired that, in rare moments of respite from the defence of Her Majesty's provinces, he and some RAF pals had built a canoe. It wasn't a very good canoe and after about half an hour of paddling around, it would start to fill with water. Undeterred, Father would keep paddling until it was on the point of sinking, then run it up the beach where he would roll out and the canoe could be decanted.

The murky waters of the river, he revealed, caused the acute discoloration and years of squelching around in jungle boots forced a downturn of the nails. Hence, the condition was known as Jungle Toes.

The conversation that followed between the junior doctors was not in English but Father didn't care. He'd clearly been wherever it was that they were from. He knew how to order a meal in an Indian restaurant and now his pump was working at full throttle, there was absolutely no holding him back from taking an active part in the discussion.

In quick succession, he bid them good morning, good afternoon, invited them to sit down at his table, enquired after the health of their various relatives and asked if there was any chance he could have *secangkir teh* with *susu* in apparently fluent Indonesian, all the while wobbling his head from side to side and grinning from ear to ear. It clearly impressed his audience. They'd understood every word.

Mother's eyes were still on the ceiling when through the door arrived the consultant. The stern face, the white-coat and the dickie-bow brought a hush to the private bedchamber. The shuffling of Father's jungle toes making their way back under the bedclothes broke the silence.

Please can you explain, sir, started one of the junior doctors tentatively. *We are learning about jungle toes. Very bad. Very, very bad.*

The consultant looked disdainfully down his nose. *Jungle toes?* he queried in a creamy basso profundo voice, lifting the end of the bedsheet to reveal the curled set that had made its way back down the bed.

Gentlemen, if you are referring to these fine specimens, they are not jungle toes, they are <u>fungal</u> toes. That's fungal with an F and I hardly think they are worthy of the attention of four highly-paid NHS interns, do you?

After decades believing Father's exotic condition to be the result of wartime experiences in the Far East, an unfortunate set of circumstances had led us to discover the legendary jungle toes that we'd all taken to be a genuine medical condition were little more than a vernacular distortion resulting from his deafness that had gone un-corrected.

Father, of course, was completely unconvinced by the diagnosis and continued to recite the tale of the jungle toes almost as regularly as his mother – my paternal grandmother with the glass eye that fell in the salad bowl – had presented her favourite ailment, Hardening of the Eyeballs.

As they grew older, the clothes, the hair and the makeup took pole position for the girls and it was always a pleasure – if an expensive one – to take them shopping.

Maybe I'm eccentric but I enjoyed seeing them look great, seeing the pleasure on their faces as they tried on different outfits and the excitement when we returned home for the fashion show.

It was never quite so straightforward when they accompanied me to buy something.

Unless it was cameras, cars or aeroplanes, I never found shopping held much interest. Whenever I found a pair of trousers I liked, I'd buy half a dozen pairs to save going again. Shirts? I like my Tyrwhitts. They fit, so I don't look elsewhere.

Big-name brand labels, well…I can't say they were ever important to me. I possess a couple of pairs of Wranglers and a few years back I bought a Rado in a reckless moment. I liked the design and wanted something a bit smarter to go with my dinner suit than the five-quid market watch that had served me well for ten years. My favourite aftershave is one from Armani's Privé collection. None of these really make me a brand-addict.

I did once end up with a brand label on my nose, though but that was entirely down to the girls.

I was probably in my mid-to-late 40s when it first became apparent I needed more than just the contact lenses that had given me bottom-line-of-the-chart vision for a couple of decades.

Somehow, although it was not a point that had ever come up in discussions with my outfitters, my arms must have shrunk because the arm's length reading I'd never had any problem with had suddenly become difficult.

I'd done well to manage so long, my optometrist told me but now was the time for some reading glasses over the top of my contacts – *and while you're here, it would also be a good idea to have a new pair of glasses in case you need to rest your eyes from contact lenses for a while.*

Father in 2009: he was an accomplished artist with a wicked sense of humour.

Father, pictured in Ceylon (he never could bring himself to call it Sri Lanka) in 1942. He often wore his panama side-saddle like his RAF field service cap.

Catherine (left) and Christina: lively, amusing, effervescent and fun to be with.

Perusing row upon row of gleaming new frames with designer names proved how long it had been since I last bought a pair *in case I needed to rest my eyes from contacts for a while*. Gone were the almost indestructible frames I used to wear as a kid. Only flimsy wirework was available.

Give it an Italian name and suddenly the ricketiest of frames attracted a price tag of two or three hundred quid – and don't shop assistants look strangely at you when you ask what you can get for a fiver?

She gasped, she gaped, she yawed, she staggered a little, then she glanced outside at the gleaming new S-class Mercedes Benz I'd parked half way up the kerb outside the shop and stuttered, *But sir... these would suit your lifestyle so much better*.

My lifestyle? How will they suit my lifestyle better?

When I'm half asleep in a morning, I lurch downstairs looking through my spectacles as little as possible, trying hard not to open more than one eye at a time as I grope for the coffee. Back upstairs, mug in hand, I rummage around the en suite for my contact lenses and slap them in while I'm still on autopilot.

The aforementioned spectacles rest just above the bidet for most of the day, undisturbed. They hardly qualify as essential to my lifestyle.

Last thing at night, I take my lenses out, stick my spectacles on my nose and shut the lights out before negotiating my way to bed in the dark. I know my way from the creaks in the boards. I don't need £300-worth of wirework with see-through dinky blue tints on my beak to find my perch for the night.

And yet, ridiculously, with the girls at my side, I parted with £300.

Just as I was about to leave the shop, having signed up for my bargain basement plastics, who should come through the door but Christina and Catherine.

The review of my spectacular purchase began.

Retractions were elicited. Forms were shredded. I found myself being towed past row upon row of gleaming Gucci goggles, then toward even higher-priced works of art. As I read the labels without assistance I began to question what had driven me to visit the optometrist in the first place. *You could buy a car for that,* I protested. But to no avail.

Not one I'd drive... and you wouldn't catch Mum in it either!

I thought I'd finished and the job was done but suddenly, I found myself powerless to resist as my beak became the resting place for numerous bits of wirework.

They're no good, I protested. *Too small. Not value for money. Anyway, I can see over the top!*

They look great, Dad.

But am I not supposed to be able to see out of them?

No. Not necessary. You said yourself you only wear them in the dark.

Try these.

They're awful.

They look great. Don't be such an old fart.

But...

We'll take these, please!

But...

Come on, Dad. Now we can show you what we've bought!

What?

You'll love it. Well... them!

Behind the counter, the assistants tried hard to control themselves. Amid the titterings of barely-suppressed amusement, my bargain-basement purchase had disappeared, new forms had been drawn up in readiness, they'd got my credit card and it was going through the machine.

Sign here, please.

But...

Oh, I'm sorry sir. This line... Would you like to borrow some reading glasses?

How kind.

By the time the girls had reached university years, the banter and the humour had grown like their confidence. They were lively, amusing, effervescent and fun to be with. The house was always full of laughter.

First to fledge the nest and go to university was Christina.

I remember the interviews well. We covered hundreds of miles trekking from one university open day to the next, shuttling between Bournemouth on the south coast and Preston in the northwest. She liked London but the course wasn't what she wanted. Sheffield had a good reputation but it was biased towards print journalism and she wanted broadcast experience as well. The others on her list were soon whittled down.

Preston's UCLAN won the day.

I don't think I could ever have imagined quite how emotional I would be at seeing my eldest start the engine of her car and leave the family home for a new life at university.

I knew she'd be fine, I knew we'd see her at Christmas, Easter and for the summer holidays but as she headed off down the lane and disappeared out of sight and I turned for the door, there seemed to be an emptiness to the house I hadn't felt before.

Standing in her room, the clothes gone from her wardrobe, I found myself reminiscing: the time I taught her how to ride a bike across the village green;

collecting her from the roadside after she'd taken control of events when one of her boyfriends had gone into meltdown after crashing his mother's car on the way back from a date – he didn't last long after that; her first driving lesson and the first corner she took when she forgot to turn the wheel and we ended up on the verge; the time she went to a party dressed as Little Red Riding Hood. There was no time for a proper photo session but we managed to get a couple of pictures in the garden before she left.

Crazy things. Random things. Special moments a Dad remembers but is supposed to be too man for them to affect him.

I looked forward to her weekly phone calls. We'd talk for hours sometimes.

Then there were the times she'd take me completely by surprise and put me on the spot with a phone call in the middle of the day:

Dad, I'm presenting a programme on campus radio with my best friend, Lorraine and the Indian chef I was supposed to be interviewing about curries has let me down at the last minute. He promised he would tell us how to cook a chicken bhuna. Would you be able to do a radio interview?

How long have I got to prepare?

Say yes and we're on air!

They were fun times. I remember being asked to take part in several interviews when one or other of her contacts had let her down at the last moment.

The role of wine specialist was one of the most challenging. I'd just prepared myself for the part with my best French accent on standby when she announced she was interviewing Helmut somebody-or-other. Out went Chablis and Gigondas. In came Spätburgunder and Eiswein.

You did that well, Dad, she told me afterwards. *Lorraine was well impressed!*

I didn't let on I'd spent most of the interview reading labels from the wine fridge in the kitchen.

The following year, it was Catherine's turn to choose a university. Manchester was the first of several trips we had to cram in before I was due to fly out to our Polish office for a few weeks. Catherine and I were booked to stay in a little place called Longridge. Preston wasn't far so on the evening of our arrival we collected Christina on the way.

Longridge is nice – my kind of country – with rolling hills, sheep, cows and just enough distance between farms to be isolated from neighbours. The farm we'd chosen was probably 250 years old, or thereabouts and it had immense character.

So had the landlady.

Hello, luv! she greeted us warmly. *You must be Mr Earle and young Miss Earle.* The rolling 'r' denoted we'd definitely arrived in Lancashire.

Why don't you sit by the fire for a few minutes while we finish off your rooms? Can I get you some tea and buttered scones or will you be heading out for something to eat?

After a long journey, tea and scones sounded good, especially by a roaring applewood fire in the snug but Catherine wanted to explore the restaurants in the vicinity. She'd spent the last couple of years working part-time alongside the chef in a restaurant near home while studying for her school exams and had become quite proficient as a sous-chef. The subject she was applying to study at university was Hospitality Management and she reasoned, there was no time like the present to check out the local eateries.

There's a very good restaurant not far away, our landlady told us. *Would you like me to book you a table?*

What she didn't know about the local area didn't seem to be worth knowing. If you wanted a walk, she had a route. If you wanted a sight to see, she had a book full. If you wanted a restaurant, she knew the best... and she had a friend who worked there!

No sooner had we booked than she rang the restaurant to ensure we were given the best table – and primed the head waiter to greet us in person.

Ah, you must be Mr Earle. Your table is ready, sir. Come this way... I understand Miss Catherine is seeking to enter the hospitality trade – and you, Miss Christina, you must be the journalist.

He'd been well-briefed.

It's Preston you're studying, isn't it? And you're staying down by the river. Very nice, if I may say so.

It was a nice restaurant – a tasteful blend of contemporary styling with the essential character of the old building retained – and we'd been given to understand the chef had quite a reputation locally. The words Michelin Star had even wafted past. Expectations were high as we took our seats.

Hm. Very Nouvelle Cuisine, announced Catherine as she scanned the menu.

Very meat! Christina mumbled, somewhat less impressed. *I can't eat this. It's snorted, mooed, clucked and quacked. Where's the veggie section?*

Would Miss Christina like me to see if the chef can prepare something special?

Miss Christina would, yes please!

The meal was a spectacle; a masterpiece of presentation with ingredients formed into exquisite shapes. They tasted as good as they looked. Christina's vegetarian dish arrived. Catherine chose the duck.

How is Miss Catherine enjoying the Mallard? asked the waiter.

It's a sports duck and it really needs to be pinker, she replied, almost without a second thought. *The jus is a little on the thick side but it tastes good. Eight out of ten.*

The waiter poured more wine and retreated to a discreet distance while Christina spooned long beans from her plate to Catherine's. It was good the chef hadn't prepared leeks. She detested leeks – something to do with a very wet week spent on an outward-bound course in the Welsh mountains, as I recall.

The fruit sorbet had just the right amount of bite to clear the way for a smooth and silky Creme Brulée – and it was another work of art: atop the white ramekin was a perfectly torched brulée decorated with a Cape Goosberry. On the assiette, a trickle of fruit coulis had made its way artistically around the sorbet and two perfect leaves of mint ascended from a stencilled sugar pattern, the crowning glory to a visual spectacle.

It met with instant approval. A glow of pride returned to the waiter's face.

By the time the coffee had arrived, he was chatting away happily with the girls about their prospective careers. The questions seem unusually probing and directed, a fact that had not gone unnoticed. As he refreshed the coffees, I glanced up just in time to see Catherine wink at Christina.

There was something other than coffee brewing. He still had the cafetière in his hand when Catherine played her card.

You know you were saying a few minutes ago that your chef was over-stretched? I could give him a hand in the holidays if you like.

There was no reaction.

Christina has just passed her bar exam. She's pretty good front of house and could probably work weekends. So, what do you think?

He didn't appear at all fazed but the pause for thought seemed particularly long.

Could Miss Christina start Friday? he asked. That wasn't the response I'd expected.

Depends on the rate.

Five pounds an hour?

Six.

Five twenty-five.

Five seventy-five.

Five fifty, plus petrol from Preston.

OK. What time do you want me here?

I was still reeling from the unexpected post-dinner negotiation when Catherine started her bid.

I could work half-term. What rate do you offer your chefs?

It really depends on what you can do, Miss.

Say six-fifty to start, rising to eight when you've seen the proof.

What can you do?

Everything you've served today. 100 covers a night.

I think we could accommodate that.

Result! When do I start?

Back at the farm, our landlady greeted us at the door. *Did you enjoy your meals? You were both offered jobs, I hear. Well done!*

Neither of them took their job offers up but the way they'd played the moment, that was an occasion to bring out the *Proud Dad* look. And I did.

If I'd expected it would be easier by the time Catherine's turn had come to fledge the nest and head for university, I couldn't have been more mistaken. It wasn't.

We'd brought them both up to be independent, stand on their own two feet, take on the world with confidence but no one had prepared *me* for the moment they'd actually go and do just that.

I knew she'd be fine, just like her sister and I was immensely proud that she'd been accepted on the course she really wanted at her first-choice university but as the second little turquoise Peugeot left the driveway and set course for Gloucester, emotions got the better of me.

Suddenly, we were empty-nesters, rattling around in a three-and-a-half-thousand square foot house that, for the first time since we'd bought it, didn't feel quite so much like a home.

As the weeks and months rolled by, the small successes mounted and from time to time we'd hear of the odd accolade being won. They'd both found friends, good friends and were enjoying their time at university.

Christina was about five-and-a-half-hours drive from home, Catherine was a good four hours away, so quick trips home for either of them were out of the question, especially on a Friday with rush hour traffic.

But Catherine lived ten minutes from Gloucester Airport. She still had friends back home. With lectures finishing mid-afternoon on a Friday, she could go see them on the Saturday and be back on Sunday afternoon if I could collect her – *and it's only an hour's flight, Dad. You said so yourself.*

She never really liked the two-seat Cessna. She might have helped design the paint scheme and chosen the colours and the upholstery fabric but there were no tables, there was no inch-deep carpet, no fat leather seats with armrests and no space to spread out.

The Puddle-Jumper, she called it. Compact it might have been but it was reliable transport and with a cruise speed of about 120mph and no need for convoluted routes that took advantage of motorways and main roads, it was a lot quicker than driving.

The flight was a straight-line hop from Norwich and in good weather, there was no need for the rigmarole of filing flight-plans. All it took was a quick call to Gloucester to book us in.

Christina was never interested in aeroplanes – or cars, come to think of it – but from a very early age, Catherine had been crazy about cars and couldn't wait to start driving. I thought at one point the convenience and speed of flying compared with the drudge of traffic jams and stop-start motorways might persuade her to take lessons and the two-seater was the perfect plane for her to learn in but it didn't.

On the flight back from Gloucester, I asked if she wanted to take control but she wasn't interested. She seemed perfectly content to chat and watch traffic jams like the ones she used to create in the lounge when she was little grind to a halt as we flew over them.

On another occasion – I think it was her third year, her work experience year – she'd been working late at a club on the south coast and someone had helped themselves to the keys of her flat when her back was turned. The spare set was in her bedroom at home. The Puddle-Jumper came in useful then, too.

It was 2005, Catherine's first year at university, when we sold the twin-engine Navajo. It had been a fabulous aeroplane and had served us well.

At considerable expense, we'd had both engines overhauled and zero-timed, given it a pair of new, black, three-blade propellers and a luxurious executive-jet interior with cream leather seats, deep-pile carpets, polyester-finished burr-walnut cabinetry and gold-plated seat buckles, lights and air vents. The interior alone had cost us almost £40,000.

It looked amazing and it flew every bit as well as it looked but more and more we were finding we needed to get higher, into airways where there was a much better chance of escaping the weather. The Navajo could get us there but no one wanted to wear oxygen masks for a couple of hours at a time so we could use it to its full potential. The time had come for us to look for a pressurised aircraft.

With some regret, we put it on the market.

It was Paul, Steve's colleague at Aradian Aviation, who sold it for us and its new owner, Carlos, hailed from the Mediterranean island of Menorca.

It was a glorious day Carlos had chosen for the delivery flight, so we decided to stay low and fly on Visual Flight Rules rather than filing an instrument flight plan. Filing IFR invariably meant fighting with Brussels and they almost always changed something within half an hour of departure that would have us heading in a direction that suited them better than us.

We'd planned an easy route from Norwich, coasting out over Dover, heading almost due south over the English Channel and on to L'Aigle via lower airways in France, across to Nantes and descending into La Rochelle to uplift fuel.

Knowing there could sometimes be problems filing flight plans in France, we'd filed the plan for the second leg – La Rochelle, Toulousse, coasting out somewhere near Girona, then a straight line to Menorca – and completed the immigration clearances from Norwich at the same time as the first, so the second flight plan only needed to be activated 15 minutes before we departed La Rochelle. All that took was a call to La Rochelle Tower.

The weather was forecast to be good, except for a patch south of Toulousse where thunderstorms were predicted in the afternoon. If we managed to stick to our timing, I figured we'd be able to avoid them.

Everything went well en route to La Rochelle. We'd enjoyed wall-to-wall sunshine all the way. Conditions had been calm. On the approach to the easterly runway, we were treated to a fantastic view of the Île de Ré bridge and the landing was a real greaser. The refuellers were already on standby when we arrived to give us a quick turnaround.

I always liked plenty of fuel on board whenever we were flying over water, especially when the stretch over water was the last stage of the flight. One of my first flying instructors had drilled it into me that there were two things you never wanted in aviation: fuel in the bowser and runway behind you.

Fill to your load limit, he always told me *and use all the runway, because running out of fuel before you reach your destination is as unhealthy as demolishing the runway end lights.*

With the inboard and outboard tanks in each wing both filled to capacity, we called La Rochelle Tower, activated the flight plan to Mahon and taxied out to the holding point. Over the radio, the Tower confirmed the flight plan was active and cleared us for takeoff, handing us over to Bordeaux a few minutes into the climb.

Nearing the edge of Bordeaux's radar-coverage, the controller handed us off to Toulouse. Then all-hell broke loose.

Toulouse couldn't find the flight-plan.

We hadn't filed a flight plan.

We had to file a flight plan.

Where were we going?

No, we couldn't go to Spain without a flight plan.

We had to land and file a flight-plan.

I think we were more or less at the extremity of Toulouse's radar coverage and ready to abandon them for a less neurotic controller when, after almost half an hour of stress and continual distraction and with the on-board weather radar indicating lightning clusters and heavy precipitation either side of our course, Toulouse found the flight plan – and immediately dumped us without a hand-off so we had to start afresh with the next radar controller.

The rest of the flight was easy. We'd told Carlos, the new owner, we'd be in Menorca at 2.30pm and at exactly 2.30 the wheels kissed the tarmac and we taxied in.

Carlos was there to meet us, a big smile on his face. His new baby had arrived and in the afternoon sunshine, it looked a picture. After almost eight years together and hundreds of flying hours, it was a sad moment as we parted on the tarmac.

Unfortunately, Carlos had taken the decision to swap the aircraft over from its American registration to Spanish. It had been a relatively easy task swapping it from the Swiss register to the American register after Janos had delivered it to Norwich nine years earlier. Carlos wasn't so lucky.

A couple of months after we'd delivered it to Menorca, he called me. The registration couldn't be completed because the Spanish authorities wouldn't accept the new three-bladed propellers we'd had fitted when the zero-timed engines arrived back from the USA. He needed the originals. Did we still have them? How much would we charge him for them?

Fortunately, they were still boxed up in shipping containers and sitting in the hangar – and they'd been overhauled. I had no idea how to value them, so I told him he could have them if he'd pay the shipping costs to Menorca and let us borrow one of his villas for a holiday the following Easter.

He was happy with that and a few weeks later, I booked flights for Catherine, her university friend Caz, Marie and me, and we headed off to Menorca for a few days away from the coalface.

Menorca was every bit as characterful as I remembered from the time Marie and I first went there in the late seventies. We were lucky enough to have picked a week when the weather had started to warm. The villa was in a nice village and in the low season, it offered tranquillity.

The island had, of course, become much more touristy with large areas devoted entirely to holiday villas. It's a common story but at least the village we were in was calm and characterful.

Tourist hot-spots have never really appealed to me – neither of us, in fact – but most of the developments were around the coastline. The central part of the island was still largely unspoilt. Small, white farm-houses nestled between rolling green hills and cows, sheep and horses grazed the tiny, stone-edged fields that distinguished Menorca from its nearest neighbour, Mallorca. Menorca was a lush island, rich in greenery that contrasted with the orangey-red earth of its newly ploughed fields.

The fishing industry was very much alive and we often saw elderly pescadors enjoying tapas and pungent Spanish cigars in corner cafés shaded with white-arched terraces and lemon trees. The country folk sold beautiful cheeses from the roadside. They seemed more than friendly but in a genuine way that's become all too rare these days.

Along the coast, just a few short miles from the tourist towns, dark vermilion fields met the naked stone of cliffs that plunged dramatically into an azure Mediterranean. Over thousands of years, the pounding white foam had etched caves, bays and outcrops to delight the eye at sunset.

On the other side of the island, the landscape turned into a moonscape of fascinating rock formations surrounding tranquil inlets where colourful boats idled along the shoreline. It was a photographer's paradise and while the girls enjoyed the sunshine, I snapped away happily.

Carlos was something of a local celebrity, not least for his acquisition of the Navajo and the hangar he'd already built at the airfield in anticipation of its arrival. Then probably in his mid-fifties, he had a singing voice to rival the best of Italian baritones.

After dinner one evening, he and his wife took us to a bodega. It was very quaint – originally an old cave that had been painted white inside and given a door. There was a bar to one side with a curious canopy in green-painted timber and various candles scattered around in crevices that had atmospherically blackened the whitewash on the walls above them.

The strong aroma of Spanish cigars created an intoxicating melange with burning candle-wax and Sangria. It all added to the ambience.

Two elderly gentlemen – I guess well into their eighties – were entertaining their late evening clients with a voice and guitar duet from the farthest corner of the cave when we arrived, singing songs of old Menorca.

Carlos couldn't resist. He found a pair of maracas and deftly began to add a rhythm. By the chorus he was in full voice. It was a fine sound that filled the space; a most enjoyable and unexpected impromptu concert.

A few days after our arrival we came across a nautical-centre offering boats for sale and mostly out of curiosity rather than any urgent desire to buy, we decided to take a look around.

Although we have never really been boaty people, Marie and I had occasionally toyed with the idea of buying a small speedboat but just as quickly as the subject had been raised, we would consign it to the same resting place as the villa abroad.

I thought a villa would be a great idea, especially if we could find somewhere in the depths of rural France that offered tranquillity and was close to an airfield with a runway we could get in and out of easily enough. Marie had always been set against it. We'd spend the first week gardening and cleaning, she'd say and that's not a holiday. Besides, did we really want to go to the same place whenever we found the time to go away?

She had a point.

But here, in the boatyard, the French salesman was very persuasive. He'd seen a prospect and was quick to inject a spark into what I'd intentionally kept as a very low-key conversation.

It's a villa you can move around, he told us, latching onto Marie's argument against villas and gardening immediately. She was definitely nibbling the hook.

We have a sea trial tomorrow, a new twin 275 horsepower Menorquin 160 motor yacht, he pressed, twitching the bait in front of her. *Would you like to accompany us?*

I knew it was not an offer she'd want to turn down. Catherine and Caz weren't going to say no to a boat trip either. He'd got his passengers.

Morning arrived and with it came the phone call: meet at 9.45 on the quay and look for the dark blue Menorquin. We'd recognise it easily because it would be the only traditionally-built motor yacht on the quay that morning. He'd be there and we could look around while he prepared everything.

It's a good thing he was there. I didn't know enough about boats to distinguish a traditionally-built motor yacht from any of the other boats on the quay – and they were all blue.

I have to admit, it was nicely appointed. The woodwork gleamed in the morning sun. There were luxury cabins with en-suite shower rooms and shiny brass-fittings, there was a master cabin decked out in solid teak and polished brass, a galley with a gas hob, an oven and a fridge-freezer, a helm with some vaguely familiar instruments in front of it, an upper-deck from which to steer while enjoying full-on sunshine – even an aft-deck large enough to accept a dining suite for a bunch of guests.

She is fully air-conditioned and sea-going, came a heavily accented voice from up on deck. *We are ready to cast off. Would you like to accompany me on the bridge? Maybe the ladies would like to sit on the fly?*

*Cast off…bridge…fly…*The sudden plethora of boaty terms hit me like a bolt of lightning. It was alarmingly unfamiliar territory; a stark reminder that underlined just how little I actually knew about boats and sailing.

Aviators never cast off. My grandmother used to cast off when she'd finished knitting a jumper. We did chocks away and brakes off.

Bridge – I could kind of get that one. It was the flight deck.

Fly? That had a familiar ring to it, if for no other reason than it seemed to be more or less skywards.

Eagerly, the girls bounded upstairs and onto the fly.

Deftly, our French captain eased the yacht out of its mooring while I admired the view from a deeply-upholstered white settee.

As we poddled through the harbour at a stately two or three knots, a couple of centuries of British history drifted past: the house where Nelson had stayed; the British quarantine hospital; the old fort.

Compared with the continuous workload getting airborne involved, it all seemed very relaxed, almost soporific. There were no checklists to work through, no communications, no airfield and departure plates to check and no instructions from Air Traffic Control to note, repeat back and expedite.

In next to no time, we were in the open ocean. *Would you like to take the helm?* asked our French salesman, keen to ensure I got the whole experience.

Advancing the throttle levers in a big motor yacht is a lot like advancing the throttle levers in a plane but without the immediate breath-taking surge that nails you to your seat and sends the corners of your mouth into an involuntary smile on takeoff.

There was no rapidly-diminishing tarmac ahead, no centreline to follow, no feeling of elation when land turns to sky and no full-on thrill as a couple of massive hair driers drag you off the runway but there was definitely power under us. It growled.

As the speed rose, the bow began to pitch up, limiting forward view. Over each wave, it dipped sharply, scooping cold, salty water and throwing it high into the air as it rose again to mount the crest of the next wave. At 16 knots, the squeals intensified from upstairs. I'd steered into a wave the wrong way and soaked them all from head-to-toe but they seemed to be enjoying it.

Entering the harbour on our return to port, we joined the girls on the Fly. Catherine took the helm. *Wow, this is great! Can we have one, Dad?*

Marie smiled. She'd enjoyed it, too. And the thought of a villa that could be moved around, especially a luxury villa with as much space on board as a small house, clearly held some appeal.

I could feel the surge in my wallet. The dollar levers were being eased forward.

Back at Carlos's villa, armed with hard-bound books full of glossy pictures taken in exotic locations and aviation-style price-lists that read like telephone numbers, we began to explore the world of the luxury motor-yacht. It was as heady as the world of private aircraft.

There's no denying, they are fabulous. There was nothing that couldn't be included for a price. At 50-something feet in length and 16 or 17 feet wide, the one we'd spent the morning on offered space to move around in and there were home comforts aplenty.

The idea of a yacht certainly ticked a lot of boxes.

But it wasn't long before common sense started to dawn.

Was a motor yacht really a practical option for a family that holidays for a few days here, a few days there and seldom has the luxury of a couple of weeks in a straight line? Did it make sense to be spending seven figures on a motor yacht that would pass most of the year tied up and unoccupied?

You could easily sail to Turkey in a Menorquin 160, the salesman had told us. It sounded impressive. And the thought of all those tiny Greek islands on the way and azure blue coves in which to over-night spiced the dish. That was the romantic image but somehow, it didn't feel like a sensible proposition for a novice with zero experience of sailing across anything much more challenging than the municipal duck pond.

My thoughts turned to practical considerations: the flight we'd made the day before in Carlos's single-engine Cessna had taken just forty-five minutes over water from Menorca to Mallorca. It would have taken almost seven hours in a calm sea running at three-quarters power in a motor yacht.

Seven airborne hours in a twin-engine aircraft like the Navajo we'd sold to Carlos would get us from Norwich to Naples and the Navajo wasn't the fastest of twins by a long way. A short hop from Italy and we'd be in Corfu, Kefalonia, the Greek mainland or any one of those Greek islands the salesman had mentioned.

And I had enough flying experience to get everyone there safely.

Then there was the weather to think about. Weather can change a lot in a few hours. If you're only making ten or 12 knots, the options are a bit limited when you're a long way from port and a storm arrives. There's no going around it, flying between it, climbing over it or turning back to escape it like you can in an aeroplane.

You're in it and that's that. It's a sobering thought to anyone who hasn't spent his life around boats. I hadn't.

Almost as quickly as enthusiasm for the idea had bubbled up, it fizzled out.

A line was drawn under the mobile villa and the glossy brochures were abandoned.

18 months later, with help from Paul at Aradian who'd found us a new, pressurised twin-engine Beech aircraft, I was back at a much more familiar helm and on the fly again.

Memories: Christina's 5th birthday, the day she got her first bike.

Memories: the time Christina went to a party dressed as Little Red Riding Hood.

Catherine (on the left) and Caz at their graduation a couple of years after we went to Menorca together.

It was the June of 2007 when we went to collect the new Beechcraft.

Chapter Ten
The Bitter-sweet Years

2007 to 2009 were bitter-sweet years for us. Shortly after the arrival of the new pressurised Beechcraft Paul had found for us, Christina received the news she'd been hoping for from Preston: she'd passed her BA with Honours in Journalism and was as thrilled as she was relieved.

In anticipation of the good news, we'd already booked the best hotel we could find at short notice and had flown out to Sharm El Sheikh for a two-week break.

Egypt in June was hot. Seriously hot. Down by the pool, baking bodies in a range of shades from boiled lobster to cremated beef lined up on plastic loungers that had been parked so close to each other that there was barely enough room between them for a bottle of suntan lotion.

It wasn't a place I wanted to be but for the first couple of days, all the girls wanted to do was join the basting bodies and bake in the scorching sun. Christina and Catherine had each brought an armful of books and seemed content to oil up and turn brown. Marie was happy to join them.

I can't say I've ever been one for sunbathing. If I go brown, I go brown; if I don't, I don't. I'm not a perfect tan-seeker and the curse of tan lines that sun-seekers get all wound-up about has never really concerned me. The body beautiful is for Baywatch babes. Mine just gets me around. I've always seen myself as more of a Ford truck than a Lamborghini. Besides, after an hour parked up on a sun-lounger, terminal boredom sets in and I have to find something interesting to do.

At the other side of the pool was a dive centre. That looked interesting. Outside on the pavement was an A-frame festooned with advertisements for different activities: beginner courses; speciality courses for more experienced divers; snorkelling trips to Ras Mohammed National Park; boat trips and reef dives.

On the other side, there were pictures taken during a wreck dive on the Dunraven, a British steam ship that hit a reef and capsized in 1876 on its way back from India; and alongside were several beguiling images of the famous SS Thistlegorm.

Bombed and sunk in 1941 and discovered by one of my boyhood heroes, Jacques Cousteau and his team on the dive-boat Calypso in 1955, Thistlegorm was a name I knew. I'd seen Jacques Cousteau's film and had watched, spellbound as he rang the ship's bell with his diving knife, then scratched away at the coral to reveal the name beneath a decade-and-a-half of encrustation.

I remembered holding my breath as he pulled open the door to the bridge for the first time and swam inside, a massive three-pack of tanks on his back. The Thistlegorm sounded fascinating; an irresistible opportunity. I'd dived wrecks and reefs in the Caribbean, the Indian Ocean and on several occasions while we were on holiday in other far-flung places but I'd never dived in the Red Sea.

Eagerly, I collected as much information as I could and headed back to the baking bodies by the pool side.

Back at the pool, the girls had started to change colour and were already covering various bits of themselves with towels. They had their own wetsuits in their rooms and we'd all brought our BCDs, regulators, fins and masks just in case they decided to go for an official diver certification but they wanted a few more 40-degree 'chill' days before contemplating any serious activity.

Marie was happy to relax with them so I headed back to the dive shop to see what entertainment I could arrange. A dive to the Thistlegorm meant a 5am start at the quayside but how could I not take the opportunity to visit a wreck Jacques Cousteau had discovered before I was even born?

I have to say, diving the Thistlegorm with another 20-something boatfuls of curious pleasure divers all eager to take the plunge wasn't the enjoyable experience I'd hoped it would be. As I entered the water, I could see dozens of divers below, some already finning around the wreck, others clinging like mussels to a rope as they decompressed on their way back to the surface.

It was a spectacularly-beautiful wreck, of that there was no doubt and on that particular day, in the crystal-clear waters of the Red Sea, the visibility was incredible. The dive started at the deepest point, the stern but it was the front section that fascinated me most. It was lying upright on the sea bed and had remained pretty much untouched by the bombs that had landed amidships.

The holds were still full of Second World War motorcycles, Bedford trucks, tracked military vehicles, aircraft parts, tyres and ammunition. To the port side some way from the hull lay the remains of a locomotive, its smoke-box door wide open at the front and its buffers, wheels and coupling rods still clearly visible above the sea bed.

Looking back from the bows of the ship, it was possible to see most of the front section and on the deck, much of the equipment... winches, chains and davits were still visible. Even on Nitrox, bottom time was too limited to take everything in on one dive.

As I ascended the stairs on the port side and made my way back towards the winch and the shot line that anchored the dive boat, I couldn't help thinking how the crew of the Calypso would have disapproved.

Years of over-diving – and little or no respect for where shackles had been attached to secure the myriad of dive boats that visited every day – had taken a serious toll on the metalwork. It was tragic to see scores of lines attached to anything that looked as if it might provide an anchor point for the dive boats above.

Rather than treating the wreck with the reverence a war-grave deserves, recreation divers had unwittingly but callously desecrated what should have been preserved and venerated, transforming Jacques Cousteau's Thistlegorm into a giant money-earning fly in the middle of a web of lines and ropes.

I took a camera on the dive but returned to the surface without taking a single picture.

A few days later, Christina and Catherine both qualified as Open Water Divers. More for fun and to accompany them than to satisfy any real need, I took an underwater photography course.

I have a feeling the instructor probably learned more from me than I gained from the *get close and don't put your finger in front of the lens before you press the button* tuition but it was good to see the girls having some fun.

My picture of a shoal of Glassfish circumnavigating a giant Brain coral turned out well and I managed to get a nice close-up of a Clownfish defending his sea anemone...just before he bit me.

Before every dive, the instructor had told us to watch out for turtles. There had been several reports of sightings and Christina, especially, wanted to see one. I think it was the last dive we did that she wasn't feeling particularly well and decided to sit it out on the boat with Marie and a book while Catherine and I went down.

She was more than disappointed when we returned. We had close-up photographs of a three-metre shark that had been eyeing us with some curiosity and we'd spent the last ten minutes of the dive playing around with a turtle on the top of the reef in three or four metres of water. A proper little poser he'd been, too. The photographs were very good.

I'd rather naïvely expected there would be photography in Sharm El Sheikh to rival the souks and medinas of Tunisia and Morocco but the old town wasn't that old. It had been made to look old for the more intrepid tourists who strayed beyond the bright lights of the heaving Naama Bay area.

Stuffed with clubs, restaurants, tourist traps and guides who'd try to accost us every few minutes and take us to one or other backstreet perfume shop, Naama Bay reminded me of a mini Las Vegas with Shishas and hustlers.

We did take a Desert-at-Night tour that provided some really excellent photo opportunities. The barbecue was tasty, the entertainment was colourful and the guide seemed to know every constellation and every star in the sky, though he had no answer when I asked him why it was that the three great pyramids on the Gisa Plateau lined up exactly with the three stars in Orion's belt.

He'd clearly never read Erich von Däniken.

It wasn't long after we returned from Egypt that Christina started work. She'd found her first job as a radio broadcaster with Lowestoft's Beach FM and she was back in her old room. It was good to have her home again.

Every evening after she'd readied herself for the night, I'd sit on the end of her bed and we'd chat about the day's events, the ideas she was working on, the people she'd met. I knew nothing about broadcast journalism so to me it was all fascinating.

She loved her job and gave it her all. She was an inexhaustible reader of everything from books to newspapers, an enthusiastic interviewer who'd dig deep into a story to come up with an inspired angle, a capable and talented writer. In radio she'd found an outlet for her passion.

But one topic that came up time and time again in our conversations wasn't related to work and it seemed to be pointing towards some quite unusual abilities that went well beyond anything Marie or I had ever experienced.

Mother had readily accepted everything Christina told her since the first time she'd confided in her as a small child. They seemed to have an understanding that ran much deeper than just a grandma-granddaughter connection and a very genuine affection and warmth existed between them. They shared an innate ability to know when the other was troubled by something. If Mother was worried, Christina often felt it and called her.

While we were concerned about some of the things Christina talked about, Mother regarded them as perfectly normal, as if everybody was the same. She seemed to know intuitively what was going through Christina's mind and remained steadfastly empathetic.

The rest of us tried to play it down, or make light of it. Catherine, especially, was deeply sceptical.

Vividly, I remember Christina recounting awful nightmares when she was only in her teens. One repeated every night for a week or more. She couldn't give much detail but she said something dreadful was going to happen and it was something to do with flying. Every time she closed her eyes, she felt panic. She was distressed, shaken, emotional. People were going to die, she said and she could see flames.

I called Mother the morning after her first nightmare. The good morning greeting had hardly escaped my lips when she asked if Christina was all right. *You're not flying this week, are you?* she asked, without pausing to hear the reply.

Catherine took this shot of Christina and me shortly after the girls qualified as Open Water Divers in Egypt.

Catherine on her qualifying dive.

Catherine and I spent the last ten minutes of the dive playing around with a turtle on the top of the reef.

Christina, 2007: Bachelor of Arts (Honours) in Journalism.

Catherine, 2009: Bachelor of Arts (Honours) in Hospitality Management.

A few days later, I went into the office to find several members of staff gathered around a computer screen. They were watching aeroplanes crashing into sky scrapers in America. It was September 11th, 2001.

After that, Christina's nightmare never returned.

One evening, just before I headed upstairs, she launched into a lengthy account of some of the things she'd found herself facing. They were beginning to trouble her deeply and it was something she'd been coping with pretty much on her own for a long while. Only Mother had taken her at her word and seemed to understand. It set me thinking about some of the things that had happened over the years and the superficial responses she'd received from all of us from time to time.

What do you say when, at not much more than five or six years of age, on hearing someone had died at the age of 40, your child turns to you and says, *I won't live that long?*

What do you do when before reaching the age of ten, she asks if she can visit a particular place in France *to see where she was buried during the French Revolution?*

How do you respond when she confesses to being frightened of dogs and sleeps with the light on because *in a previous life she and her family had fled to the forest to escape attack and every night, her father would leave a fire on in the tepee because she was scared by the howling of the wolves?*

And how do you react when she describes a First World War soldier in great detail and asks if you know who he is – *because he's stood at the end of the bed just behind you?*

Do you smile and put it down to a fertile imagination?

Do you take it seriously?

How should you react?

At first, we were dismissive. *Don't be silly*, Marie told her. *You won't die before the age of 40. You're going to have a long and happy life.*

Have you been reading about Marie Antoinette? I asked, somewhat glibly, when she recounted having her hands tied in front of her and being left to die in a pit during the French Revolution.

Then Marie reminded me, she never liked to lay on her back when she was a baby but on the occasions when she did, she would always lay with her hands together at the wrists, fingers apart. It seemed curious, unnatural but we never read anything into it when she was only a few months old.

I think it was nine or ten years after she'd first told us about her previous life in France that Jean-Paul sent me a cutting from a newspaper: foundations were being laid for a leisure centre in the park Christina had taken us to see and digging had been stopped when pits had been found. Archaeologists had dated the skeletal remains in the pits to the time of the French Revolution.

Was it pure coincidence?

Some months into her radio career, she was going through a collection of photographs with my mother – Christina and Mother loved combing through relics from the past together – when a small, hand-coloured print fell from between the pages of an old album. Mother had no idea who it might be. Most of the photographs had been inscribed on the back to identify who was in the picture. Some had been dated.

There was no name on this one and no date but it matched Christina's description of the First World War soldier she'd professed to see standing at the end of the bed in her bedroom a week or so earlier: the polished brown boots, the badge on his peaked cap, the brown belt, the polished buttons and the crown and three stripes around the cuffs of his khaki jacket.

Everything matched her description.

Could she have seen the photograph when it had been in an album at the bottom of a box that had been in the loft and forgotten about long before she was born?

I'd brought the box down mistakenly along with some other things Mother had wanted to look through only the day before the photograph was discovered. It was still taped up. They'd opened it together and found the album beneath a collection of artefacts that seemed to date from the time of my grandfather.

Mother had no recollection of whose album it might be. She knew none of the people in the photographs and refuted ever having seen it before.

Then there were the nightmares before 9/11. How can those be explained?

On several occasions, we tried to put her to the test without her knowledge. On one occasion during her university years, Marie and I had driven up to Preston to see her and having arrived much earlier than expected, we decided to stop off at Samlesbury Hall. It was not far from the restaurant where we'd arranged to meet and on arrival, a tour was just starting so we joined it.

It was fascinating to learn about the history of the hall but one thing in particular caught my attention: the story of a young man who, as far as I can recall, had been forbidden to marry and consumed by grief at the death of his equally-devastated beloved, he'd killed himself in an archway.

After lunch, without telling her anything of the history lesson, we took Christina to the hall. It was enjoyable to look around and for half an hour or so we pottered about but as we approached the archway, she stopped. *I'm not going over there,* she said in a matter-of-fact voice. *There's a dead bloke in the archway.*

It wasn't written anywhere. She'd never been to Samlesbury before. She didn't know she would be going to Samlesbury that afternoon. The tours had all finished so she couldn't have overheard anything. How could she know that?

I always switched my phone off before a flight because it interfered with the radios in the Puddle-Jumper. Well do I remember it vibrating in my pocket just as Marie and I were about to taxi out. It was lucky I'd forgotten. *You're not flying today, are you?* Christina asked. We'd already started up and asked Air Traffic Control for permission to taxi to the holding point. *Don't. Not today.*

She was quite insistent, so I called the controller on the radio, told him there was a problem and we needed to shut down. With the aircraft back in the hangar, we headed home and thought no more about it.

On the news that evening was a report about an aircraft that had crashed not very far from the place we'd have been carrying out pre-flight engine checks.

Sitting at the end of her bed one evening, we'd gone through the day's events and I was just about to head upstairs when she announced completely out of the blue that she needed help. It wasn't like Christina to ask for help. She was very independent and always knew exactly how to deal with any issue that came her way. If there was a problem, more often than not I'd get to know about it after it had been resolved.

Flattered she'd seen fit to involve me and keen to assist, I asked what I could do. The answer was not something I could ever have anticipated, not at all.

She needed help to shut out all the people who wanted to communicate through her, she said – the ones who kept her awake at night. I was dumbfounded. What could I do? I had no knowledge or experience of anything like that.

It's happening all the time. I'm going to see a psychic, Dad. If he's any good, I need to work with him, find out how to stop this. Will you come with me?

Thinking back, the number of times she'd come out with seemingly bizarre tales we'd later discover were irrefutable – and the inexplicably accurate intuition she'd demonstrated on many occasions – should have been evidence enough to convince anyone this was not just fantasy, fiction or the product of an unusually fertile imagination.

But it was so off the wall, so impossible, so outside my sphere of comprehension or anything I'd ever experienced, that I needed to know more. I'm not sure I needed to be convinced it was palpable but I did need to understand what was happening to her, what was happening around us, in our own house.

If a visit to a psychic would prove that conclusively one way or the other or provide the help she needed, then I had to go with her.

I had no idea what to expect when we arrived at the village hall where the Evening of Clairvoyance had been arranged. It was a scruffy little place, in need of a good paint and it smelled of damp. A couple of dozen old tables had been set out with chairs around an area that had been left open.

We sat down at one of the tables near the front and waited. A dozen or so other folk were already seated and waiting in silence and more were heading through the door. If they knew each other it wasn't apparent. I couldn't help thinking how much like a dentist's waiting room it felt.

Christina smiled. *He's on form tonight,* she whispered. *You'll see.*

She'd never met him, he hadn't appeared yet but already she seemed to know.

If I'd expected theatre, drama, a spectacle of smoke, spells, spooks and hocus-pocus, there weren't any. Our psychic arrived, announced who he was and quietly told everyone that sometimes spirits would come through to him, sometimes they wouldn't. It was just the luck of the draw. He needed a moment to link in and then we'd see if there was anyone waiting to make contact.

You could have heard a pin drop as he closed his eyes.

Almost immediately, he announced there was another clairvoyant in the room. She was well-known by a lot of people but not for her psychic powers. She was very talented, very creative – an artist maybe? A musician? An actress? A writer? He was getting a very clear sign. *Did that mean anything to anyone?*

He'd already clocked that his subject was a she and there were several ladies in the room but nobody responded. Christina didn't even look in his direction.

Someone wants to talk to this person from the other side, to reassure her that everything will be OK. He ventured a few names but none seemed familiar.

Slowly, he edged towards our table, his eyes still closed and a hand tentatively outstretched. *I'm getting a very strong feeling from the table here.*

I'm being told you shouldn't worry. You will get over what's troubling you. You're destined for great things. A lot of people will admire you.

His focus was completely on Christina to the exclusion of all others in the room and he was speaking directly to her, his eyes now wide open.

You love your job, don't you?

It wasn't so much a question, more of a statement and as far as I could see, a pretty accurate one.

You won't be long in it, though. You'll move away soon. I can see you with a lot of people around you. You'll travel a lot.

At the end of the session, he asked if he'd been accurate. Christina smiled and nodded. It seemed they'd both hit their targets.

Some weeks later, she teamed up with a lady who was also a psychic. Christina reckoned she was very good – she certainly helped her overcome the night-time telephone exchange, as she called it – but when Christina persuaded me to go for a reading, I was less than impressed with what came out of it.

Her mentor seemed unable to get much of my background, or what I did. The reading seemed to be mostly guesswork, pretty inaccurate guesswork at that.

She could see me on the back of a boat. I was relaxed. She couldn't describe it. *Did that mean anything to me?*

It didn't. Boats weren't really my thing.

Several spirits had messages for me, she said, but when I asked what the messages were, one by one they vanished without revealing anything.

I put it down to my interview style.

At least she'd managed to help Christina.

While we'd been in Egypt, Christina had turned 21. She didn't want a party when she returned. Instead, she wanted to wait and have a proper celebration to mark the occasion. When the day came, Catherine and I were drafted in to help with the catering.

I've changed a bit now but I was never a big fan of parties when I was a kid. I remember with some horror the white-bread-and-banana-sandwiches, pass-the-parcel and the obligatory dancing I used to try and sit out in the loo until the music stopped.

I hated dancing.

Banana sandwiches didn't rate much better.

As for pass-the-parcel, I couldn't see much point in wrapping a twopenny whistle in three week's worth of grubby newspapers.

Only the out-of-tune renditions of the 'Happy Birthday dear whoever-you-are' song nobody really wanted to sing – and 'The Bumps' that the lads I never wanted to associate with administered with great delight when the birthday boy got back to school – scored lower in my book.

But Christina's idea of a party was a bit different: there was music, there was food, there was alcohol and from the moment she started in radio, there were celebrities. Lots of them. In the sun room, in the lounge, in the dining room, in the garden, by the fish pond, on the bridge, feet dangling over the waterfall – at her 21st, they were everywhere.

I lost count of the number of times I served drinks to someone, only to be told moments later, *That's so-and-so, Dad. You know...from the BBC...from ITV something-or-other...from Sky TV... from...*

So, who's the chap in the corner by himself? I remember asking.

Oh, he's a policeman.

From Crimewatch?

Sarcasm doesn't suit you, Dad. He's married to the girl over there. You know her. She presents the news for...!

If I'd have been 30 years younger, I'd probably have rolled my eyes.

The only bit Christina didn't get about parties was the budget. She wanted nibbles and dips for about 60 guests: maybe a few pizzas and things like that; a curry or two with rice and naan breads – *but not too hot, Dad*; a chilli con carne people could dip into; a few desserts and cakes; perhaps a bar with gins, Campari and stuff like that to start with; some Champagne and Prosecco to get the party started; white wines, red wines to go with the food; maybe a Cognac and some liqueurs, *if you have some spare, Dad. You know – a party!*

Neither Catherine nor I were terribly surprised when she offered us 15 quid in small change *to cover the cost* and waved us off to Tesco with that radiating smile she used to charm everyone so easily. It always worked on me.

Those were the highlights of 2007.

After the summer, the subprime mortgage crisis kicked off a financial atom bomb in the USA that quickly ricocheted into our back pockets. The little pot we were hoping to bring back to the UK from the sale of aeroplanes with Janos evaporated at much the same time as the bottom fell out of Lehman Brothers.

We thought we'd found a buyer for the company and we were hopeful of clinching a seven-figure deal. Proposed changes to Entrepreneurs' Relief had provided us with a target date to complete the transaction in early 2008, without which we'd have faced a huge tax bill on the sale. It was looking promising.

Then Gordon Brown did a u-turn and the focus was lost. With the economy drifting steadily into recession, our potential company sale drifted away with it.

At much the same time, the house we'd just extended and restored at huge cost crashed in value as the UK property market slid into the dust of a worldwide economic recession, the like of which hadn't been seen for the best part of a century.

Things were no better in Poland. A large chunk of the spare cash our Polish company had built up had been siphoned-off by the guy we'd entrusted its management to and he'd disappeared along with it.

It became impossible to administer from the UK and with everything that was going on back home, there was no real prospect of us recruiting and training a new manager, so we paid all our suppliers, shut down the titles, closed the Polish operation and shipped all the equipment back to the UK.

The combined effect sent our early-retirement plan straight down the pan.

A couple of months later, Marie hit me with the ultimate weapon of mass destruction: she demanded a divorce.

That's what you want, she told me.

It surely wasn't. I thought I was married for life. It was like being hit between the eyes, on the back of the neck and in the nuts all at once.

Marie had been my rock, my anchor, my raison d'être and my constant companion for 33 years. We'd been through everything together, the ups and the downs. Everything we'd built, everything we'd done, we'd done together.

One thing was certain: there was no persuading her to change her mind. I'd got the chop on top of everything else that was going wrong. It took me a week of coaxing before Christina would even speak to her after that.

I suppose I am a pretty full-on guy and not the easiest to live with – probably the combination of Yorkshire and Scorpio. Then there's the creative element to contend with. It's a pretty lethal cocktail however you look at it.

But the truth is, I don't know whether it was that, whether she'd just had enough of everything and I was part of it or whether she knew her condition was worsening and she felt she was holding me back in some way.

If it was the latter, I can only admire her the more for that.

Whatever it was, I lost a wife but gained a little sister.

I still get a hug when we meet. She comes around for dinners and lunches occasionally. We work together constantly, though most of the time it's remotely through emails and phone calls.

We still own half the company each.

She knows if she has a problem she can call me and I'll be there immediately… just like I always was.

We have stayed friends. That's important to me. You can't wipe out more than three decades together and forget it ever happened. There were too many good times, too many shared moments to sweep everything away in some fake tsunami of dejection and hostility.

That's for soap operas. It wasn't for us.

If there is an upside to divorce, ours was probably the cheapest separation in history. It cost £340 in court fees. Everything else we agreed on.

I suppose if I'd been of a disposition to hit the bottle, this would probably have been the time to do it. I'd certainly been knocked sideways by the number and ferocity of the broadsides that had come our way.

And that last one had been a real belter.

Altogether they'd done a great job in taking us from the euphoria of success to the edge of the abyss in just a few short months.

As the weeks and months passed and the recession started to take its toll on the industry, sales across all the magazines began to drop as advertisers pulled in their horns. Readers started falling off the mailing lists. Scores of magazines were being returned to the mailing house, their recipients no longer in business. The whole industry was in pain.

Disquiet and dissatisfaction among staff had become rife. As the recession deepened and problems that should have been left at home turned into distractions at work, the disparate bunch we'd brought together and welded into a team steadily shifted away from collaboration and co-operation and started splitting apart at the seams.

Egotism rose through the ranks and with it came inflexibility, indolence and intransigence.

No one seemed to care whether they did a good job any more. Some didn't even care whether they turned up for work so long as their salary went in the bank at the end of each month.

With everyone focussed on self-interest, petty squabbles started breaking out. Nothing was right for anyone. The atmosphere had turned toxic.

In just a few short months, I'd ceased to be the provider of employment, the catalyst who made good ideas work and the facilitator who kept everyone on course.

I'd become the unsympathetic boss who said no to raising salaries; the one who asked for co-operation to get everyone through difficult times together but didn't deserve it; the one who had to haul people over the coals for taking liberties with sick days and making minimal effort when everyone needed to be pulling their weight and redoubling their efforts.

That Marie and I were also the ones subsidising the salaries of everyone from our own savings while not taking one ourselves counted for nothing.

We'd become the enemy.

It was a salutary, if sobering lesson to learn about human behaviour in a time of crisis.

But at the back of my mind was a phrase my grandfather used to wheel out when things weren't going well: *when the going gets tough,* he'd say, *the tough get going.* It was his way of saying don't quit, think positive and get back in the saddle.

I reckoned that if we could keep everybody, not lose any staff, keep paying salaries – even if it took us below our comfort line – we'd be well-placed to hit the ground running when the recession was over. When the money started flowing again, motivation would be easier to rekindle.

How wrong I was.

I didn't bargain on the world being quite such a different place when, finally, the economy started moving and demand returned for advertising.

Chapter Eleven
The Renaissance

Control over my own destiny is something I've always felt the need for. 30 feet above ground on a ski-lift I'm approaching the edge of my comfort zone. 30,000 feet up in an aeroplane with the controls in my hand, I'm fine.

It's not that I'm a control-freak because if I have a good co-pilot, nobody is happier than me to hand over the reins, sit back and admire the view from the window.

I'll never fight anyone for the wheel on a car journey if I have confidence in the driver.

But when the brown stuff hits the fan, I'm not of the disposition to roll over, lay there like a spatchcock chicken and wait for the paprika to fall.

I'm genetically-programmed to do something, correct the yaw, regain control, restore straight and level.

Remedying the problems at work proved much more difficult than I could ever have imagined. There was no short-term fix. If I'd been more ruthless, more narcissistic – maybe more 'businesslike' – I'd have done what most company bosses would have done and either pushed redundancy notices out to everyone to cut overheads at the earliest opportunity or closed the company and started afresh.

It would have been painful, ruthless but efficient and swift and Marie and I would have saved a lot of cash in the long run.

I'm not one to shy away from taking difficult decisions but I wasn't born to be mercenary when the livelihoods of families are at stake. Leaping out of a stricken plane and watching from my parachute as others plummeted to earth just wasn't in me. Besides, there was plenty that was good about the magazines and it was a solid business if only I could re-engage the staff.

What it needed was time. What I needed was time – a pause, a step back from the coalface; time to think lucidly, find the wood among the trees and come up with a workable solution and a new direction. Respite was long overdue.

The ferocity of six months of brown stuff hitting fans that all seemed to be pointing in my direction at once had become overwhelming. There had been no let-up. Inability to exert any positive influence over the direction in which things had progressed had eaten into what little reserves I had and it had left me exasperated.

At work, I was on a short fuse. At home, I was finding it difficult to keep a lid on my emotions. Christina knew it. Marie knew it. Everybody felt it. At times, it must have been like having a fire-breathing dragon around.

Perhaps realising that only time out would provide clarity, somebody, somewhere – call it my 'guardian angel' if you like – must have decided to take things in hand. Out of the blue, a distraction arrived that obliged me to think about something else.

Never in a thousand years could I have imagined myself with anyone but Marie at my side but a month or two earlier, she'd dropped the axe on the back of my neck for no reason I could figure and called time on 33 years of fidelity. I'd gone through the whole package of self-recriminations and come out the other side just as perplexed as I went in. It had changed nothing.

When someone else arrived on the scene, I didn't know whether it was guilt, surprise, flattery or elation I felt most.

She was bright, bubbly, fun to be with.

I could lose the troubles of the day when I was with her.

In a matter of a few short weeks, she managed to turn my life upside down, inside out and shake it 'til the dust fell out.

At first, she was my escape, my distraction but as time went on, we became closer. She was different, though we enjoyed many of the same things.

When we were together, it felt good. When we weren't, little things would happen that would make me wonder whether we were really in tune. I guess that's normal but after three decades with the same partner, I was a bit out of the swing with new liaisons.

I can't say it was an easy relationship. Sometimes it would blow hot, sometimes cold. She was enigmatic, private and often preoccupied with things that were seldom revealed.

Although we only found time to meet once or twice a week, things could pop up at short notice that would prevent us being together or dates would be cut short for some mysterious event that would mushroom out of nowhere.

There wasn't the openness between us that I'd always enjoyed with Marie.

I missed that.

There was a time I thought we might end up together – we certainly discussed it on occasions – but it never happened. One day she returned from a trip and even more suddenly than it had started, it finished.

I was a bachelor again.

But in that 12 months, being away from the coalface more often and not driving so hard had been worthwhile. We'd lost one or two staff along the way and there had been some improvement at the office. Sales had stabilised. They weren't where they had been before but at least the company seemed to be returning to a more even keel.

When an opportunity emerged from an unexpected source that was too good to miss, I took a chance and grabbed it. I was back in the saddle again.

It might seem like an odd thing for a publisher to consider but I'd been approached by one of the guys who worked at the local carwash I used with a business idea.

He'd grown sick of being number two to someone who didn't appreciate him, he said, and wanted to move on, establish his own business. He'd set everything up for his boss and knew the operations side well.

What he didn't have was the financial where-with-all or the knowledge of how things worked in Britain to establish his own company, set up a lease and deal with planning departments, highways officials, work contracts, accounts, payroll and the administration side.

When he proposed we should look for premises together, I was lukewarm to start with but the more we talked it through, the more it sounded like an idea worth exploring. If we could find a site, he said, he'd run it if I financed the equipment and the cash-flow and dealt with the official stuff.

It sounded like a reasonable proposition and the potential was there to make good money without me being involved full-time, so we started our hunt.

Finding office premises would have been easy. They were everywhere. Finding a garage site to convert that wasn't already occupied in an area where there were opportunities proved to be much more of a challenge.

With the local area saturated, we started looking further afield – Yorkshire, Lancashire, even up as far as Newcastle, Carlisle and Scotland. Nothing seemed to work. If the site had potential, the area didn't. If the area looked promising, the sites had already been taken.

We'd pretty much exhausted everything on our hit-list when, on the way back from a lengthy hunting trip, we chanced to stop off for lunch and stumbled over a garage with a *To Let* sign in the window.

We'd found our first carwash site and the renaissance had begun.

April 27th, 2009 was the day the decree nisi became absolute and Marie got her wish.

In the summer, Catherine graduated and started looking for work.

It was the year Christina decided to head off for the bright lights and explore opportunities as a freelance journalist in London.

A new business venture had popped up out of nowhere and I'd secured the lease with a new business partner.

And in the autumn, absolutely by chance, I met Olena, the lady who would eventually become my second wife.

It was the beginning of a new era for all of us.

Over the months that followed, we commissioned an architect to remodel the garage site. The planning authorities, the utilities and the highways agency all had their say to ensure everything complied with local regulations. Then the builders arrived to pull down walls, fill pits, fit roller-doors, modify the access points and paint markings on the road to direct traffic. Finally, decorated throughout and fully equipped, we opened in early 2010.

It wasn't long after that Olena and I arranged our first date.

Olena was Ukrainian and lived in Chernihiv. She was like a breath of fresh air: no hang-ups, no enigmas, nothing clandestine, just big blue eyes, a captivating smile and an easy-going personality. The fact she was tall, slim, clever and gorgeous were inescapable bonuses.

When she told me she was a consultant endocrinologist, I had to Google endocrinology to find out what it was. I can't say I'm much the wiser now but at least I can pronounce it so it looks like I know what I'm talking about.

Between the September of 2009 when we first met and the March of 2010 when we arranged our first date, we wrote scores of letters – hundreds – to each other. I always knew when she'd had a quiet night-shift at the hospital where she worked. The following day, a long letter would be waiting for me.

Eagerly, I'd open my email to reveal the topic of the day. There seemed to be no limit to her interests and nothing we couldn't discuss. Best of all, she enjoyed photography, art, travel – we even had similar cameras.

When she asked if I'd like to meet up for a proper date, it felt like all my Christmases had arrived at once. She was going to India for a medical conference in the February. *Could we meet there?*

India in February... that <u>did</u> sound nice. I'd never been to India. But February was the worst possible time for me. It was production time for the March edition of Furniture Journal. Until the very end of the month when the magazine went to print, I'd be nailed to my desk, writing furiously, putting everything together, proofing.

Tentatively, I suggested March. *How about Kiev?* came the reply. So, Kiev it was.

I remember well the frantic emails from India: *Help! What can I eat? Everything is so hot!*

She and her medical travelling companions had been out for a meal after leaving the hospital and ordered something that wasn't too spicy. I knew from my student days working with Parvez and Chef Hassan that 'not too spicy' by local standards wasn't quite the same as 'not too spicy' by western standards.

The chicken dish they'd chosen turned out to be seriously hot. No one could eat it, so they returned it requesting something with less chilli.

I couldn't help laughing when I read the waiter had brought the chicken back and declared it would be much better now. He'd washed it!

By the time we met in the March of 2010, we'd already got to know each other quite well. It didn't stop us chatting non-stop all the way from the airport to the hotel in the centre of the city. It didn't stop us chatting when we found a café that evening. In fact, we were so absorbed in conversation that by the time we were ready for our second coffee, the café and every shop around it had closed.

We'd sat down just after seven but the hours had flown by. Midnight had arrived and we hadn't noticed.

The following day was intensely cold, double digits below freezing. Snow had been falling gently all morning as we walked arm in arm along the old streets of Kiev, dipping in and out of shops and occasionally stopping for coffee – and an opportunity to thaw.

Dressed for English winter and wearing normal shoes and a smart, black Crombie, I was totally unprepared for serious weather. In the underpasses lined with flower sellers, I was fine but trying to keep upright as we walked along Khreschatyk Street was impossible. More than once I was grateful for Olena's high boots as she anchored her heels in the ice and I slid hopelessly around her in every direction.

It was all part of the fun of the moment and looking back, it seems we laughed and smiled non-stop all day.

That evening, we decided to venture out for dinner but in the time it had taken to shower and change, the gently-falling snow had turned into a blizzard of epic proportions. With only an umbrella for protection, the hotel restaurant seemed the better option.

Aside from the Georgian wine, which we both agreed had more probably been distilled from the antifreeze of an ageing Volga than anything resembling a bunch of grapes, the meal was pleasant, if a bit bland.

Payment had to be made in the bar – one card machine for food, another for drink – so, leaving the wine for the waitress, I excused myself and went to settle the account.

It was dark in the bar area, almost too dark to make out the numbers on the hand-written bill but at least those on the card machine were illuminated. Impatiently, I poked away and hit the OK. Glancing back towards the table, Olena had already left. Presuming she'd gone to the ladies' room, I headed into the foyer.

Just beyond the bar in the entrance to the foyer was a gleaming black grand piano. The lid was open, though I hadn't heard anyone playing while we were dining. We'd passed the ladies' room on the way into the restaurant so I presumed Olena would see me easily enough on her return if I went for a closer look. Intrigued, I sauntered over.

You know how it is when you walk past a baker's shop and there, sitting amid row upon row of tantalising cakes is a bun that takes your eye.

It fixes your gaze.

You stare.

It stares back, cream oozing seductively from a neatly-hewn crevice topped with a bright red cherry.

It's got your name on it.

It smiles.

You smile back.

It wants you.

You want it.

And before you can resist, you're reaching for your wallet.

A fine instrument can have the same effect on a musician – even a musician who is well out of practice – and this one had captured my attention.

Quietly, not wishing to be noticed, I opened the lid.

The keys were pristine. I could almost imagine the huge, sonorous tones rising from its strings, the richness, the softness, the power. Just the gentlest touch would reveal how good it was. It was tempting. But it was late. There was no one in the bar. Perhaps no one would notice if I gave it a try.

Good evening! a voice penetrated the gloom from some feet away.

I hadn't seen anyone.

But it was not at all a commanding voice, a reprimanding voice. Quite the opposite. It was a feminine voice, a soft voice with a discernibly Russian accent. It was quite unlike Olena's.

Tearing myself away from the piano, I turned towards the voice, anticipating some waif-like creature would drift into view in a receptionist's uniform. To my surprise, perched on a tub chair under a discreet spotlight was a small, slightly dumpy figure with long blonde hair and a skirt that seemed far too short for the legs it made no attempt to cover.

Her resemblance to Miss Piggy from the Muppets was uncanny.

Do you play? she asked, throwing her mane back over a naked shoulder to reveal a short, stubby neck.

Kermit the Frog was nowhere in sight, so she had to be addressing me.

It had been some time but yes, I played.

I glanced towards the ladies' room, hoping Olena would emerge but she didn't.

Are you here on business?

It was the piano I wanted to see but she seemed determined to engage in conversation.

No, a meeting with a friend, I replied, more out of politeness than any wish to communicate. *And you?*

It didn't really matter whether she answered.

Oh, I work here.

I remember mentally scanning through the hotels I'd been to: the ultra-professional Radissons; the Hiltons; the country house hotels. Even downstairs in reception, the staff wore uniforms, smart ones. They all seemed to have jobs, too – jobs that kept them busy, not draped on tub chairs under a spotlight in a second-floor foyer.

What do you do? I asked, seating myself at the piano and lifting the lid again, this time more determined.

Gold letters shone out from a sea of unblemished black gloss on the underside of the lid. It was a Bösendorfer, a big German grand. It was begging to be played.

The cherry and the cream oozing from the crevice got the better of me.

Stroking the keys softly, a pianissimo arpeggio sprang forth, then another, then a flourish with sevenths and ninths. Jazz chords were glorious. The bass had a depth and richness that was unmistakably German. This was an instrument to savour.

Suitably wowed, I paused momentarily without lifting the sustain pedal to enjoy the diminishing overtones that coloured the final chord.

I make friends with lonely men.

The voice from beneath the spotlight interrupted my moment of pleasure. I'd quite forgotten the question I'd asked. In fact, I'd completely forgotten she was there.

Are you a lonely man?

The cream soured almost as quickly as my foot relinquished the sustain pedal. There was definitely no cherry in sight as I closed the lid.

Moments later, a hand came to rest on my shoulder. It was Olena. *Did you not see me?* she asked. It was dark in the bar that connected the restaurant with the foyer. I thought she was in the ladies' room. *You walked straight past me and started to play. It was beautiful but I thought you didn't want to sit with me! Don't stop. Play more. I like it!*

Suddenly, there was something – someone – much more special in need of my attention than a big, black Bösendorfer.

The following day, the snow storms and the blizzards abated and the sun came out. It was a perfect sight-seeing day and in Kiev there was a lot to explore.

Our first stop was the Golden Gate, a 20th century reconstruction of the 11th century gateway to the city.

Next came St Sophia's cathedral. The Golden Gate was fascinating but in the morning sun, St Sophia's eclipsed it. The golden domes of the cathedral contrasted sharply with the deep blue of a pristine spring sky, providing the perfect backdrop for some memorable pictures.

Enthusiastically, we shot away – sometimes the cathedral, mostly each other.

Olena was an easy model to photograph in her long, dark fur coat and the fur hat she had perched on her head at a jaunty angle made for some beautiful portraits. She was natural in front of a camera and seemed to know instinctively what to do.

I was just as impressed with her skills as a photographer.

From time to time, I'd stand back and watch as she experimented to find the perfect angle from which to take her picture. The shot taken, she'd return to show me how she'd framed the subject with the branches of a tree so it echoed the shape, or how she'd used a low angle to include something that had caught her eye in the foreground.

Then we'd compare notes: how to make this more striking; how to make that stand out; how to defocus the background more without losing depth of field on the subject.

She certainly knew her way around a camera.

About ten minutes walk down the hill from St Sophia's was Independence Square, our next stop on the sight-seeing tour but after the snowstorms the day before, the pavements had become encrusted in a thick carpet of compounded snow and ice. It was treacherous.

I'd managed to remain more or less upright all morning but the first hint of a slope defeated me. Time and time again, Olena would haul me back to my feet.

As I slithered my way down Sofivs'ka Street, she stopped to point out a figure on a plaque. I never did find out who it was. I must have been ten feet past her and clinging to a door by the time she'd finished explaining his significance.

I'm not normally one to visit shopping malls without a reason and generally, it has to be a good one – like the seam in my last pair of jeans has split from ear to ear – but after the torturous ski slope between St Sophia and Independence Square, the Globus Mall under the square provided a welcome sanctuary.

At last I could stand up without falling over.

Just down the steps was a restaurant, an Azerbaijani restaurant. Neither of us had been to an Azerbaijani restaurant before. It sounded exotic, unusual, exciting.

Inside the door was a different world, a Middle Eastern world with hints of Turkey, Iran and the eastern Mediterranean. Richly-woven tapestries in reds and earth tones enclosed sumptuously furnished private dining areas around the edge of a discreetly-lit dance floor.

Hourglass-shaped Darbukka drums had been pushed to one side, as if a performance had recently finished. We later learned we'd narrowly missed a belly-dance.

In one of the private areas, a small group of half a dozen diners was being served with plov, kebabs, minced lamb in vine leaves and savoury pancakes from a huge platter. It looked wonderful. The fragrances were enticing. Eagerly, we took our seats.

If the meal was divine, the company surpassed it.

Dishes arrived, wine arrived and as we shared them, dipping in and out of each other's choices, the conversation flowed effortlessly between us. We must have been there three, maybe four hours because when we left it was dark outside.

Colourful lights lined Khreshchatyk Street as we made our way back to the hotel, arm in arm. Every now and then, we'd pause to window shop. It was March but in the snow, the lights and the window dressings made it feel more like Christmas.

With the hotel coming into view a few hundred yards ahead of us, quite unexpectedly Olena took a right turn. It seemed to be entirely the wrong direction. The street was much narrower and under the canopy of a department store that had closed its doors to shoppers for the day, there were no lights.

It proved to be a defining moment in our relationship.

Back at the hotel, the cityscape from the window of the upstairs foyer was spectacular, all the more so because we had found each other. The snow had started to fall again. We'd just made it back in time.

On the street below, footprints were filling rapidly and in the few short minutes we'd been watching, the road had joined the pavement in a seamless flow of white. The stillness and the silence added to the perfection of the moment.

It was as romantic as any Christmas.

We had only been together three days but when I returned home, the exchange of emails between us intensified and every now and then we'd punctuate letters with a phone call.

Olena wanted to know more about England and what it was like where I lived. She'd never contemplated living anywhere other than the Ukraine but now it seemed like a possibility we might end up together, she wanted to know whether it really did rain every day and whether it was true the English only ate fish and chips.

Well do I remember the dismay in her voice when I told her I lived in a village.

Mum wants to know if you have a cow, she said.

Over the phone, I couldn't tell if she was being serious.

I had hundreds of horses on each wing of my aeroplane but no, I didn't have a cow.

It wasn't until I returned to the Ukraine and experienced village life for the first time that I realised why she had been so taken aback by the prospect of exchanging city life in the Ukraine for village life in England.

It was April when I returned. The weather was just as inclement as it had been in March and when we arrived in the village where her mother and father lived, the taxi bogged down in foot-deep mud and snow the instant its wheels stopped turning. Ramming it into reverse and revving hard until the clutch smouldered and the tyres found grip did the trick.

I must have looked a picture as I walked through the door to their house for the first time, spattered from head-to-toe in thick dollops of mud.

Neither of Olena's parents spoke English. I knew no Ukrainian at all and my Russian was limited to yes, no and thank you but it didn't seem to matter. The welcome was warm and genuine.

Almost immediately, glasses arrived and a toast of home-made Samagonka was poured. Then, while her Father, Mykola, sampled his first pint of Yorkshire's finest Old Peculier, Nadia and Olena brought a banquet fit for a king from the kitchen: home-reared turkey, duck and chicken; sausages, bread, soup; buckwheat, home-grown vegetables; preserved tomatoes and cucumbers; mountains of potato from the garden – and salo [pure, solid, white animal fat, generally eaten raw and served with a liberal sprinking of salt].

Dish after dish appeared until the entire table sagged under the weight.

We'd only arrived an hour earlier but tucking into the feast while Olena translated the conversation, it felt like I'd been part of the family for years.

Ukrainian village life isn't like English village life. People don't make their money in the city and move out to the country for a better lifestyle. It's harder, much harder in the villages.

At the same time, there is a wholesomeness in growing your own food, rearing your own animals, picking apricots, walnuts and mulberries from your own trees, being able to see the stars at night and hear the wind rustling in the trees through open windows.

Yes, that's the romantic image, I know.

In reality, it's a simple life with few creature comforts and even fewer luxuries and it's not a life many youngsters favour. For the most part, the younger generation has fled to the cities to find work, leaving the older generation to toil unaided.

It's hard to make ends meet when all you get is a monthly pension equivalent in value to 20 litres of petrol in the UK.

Me, I've never been a city creature. I can admire a cityscape, visit a few sights, enjoy the restaurants, do the touristy thing for a while – but then I want out. I need fields, forests, lakes, space.

If the word *countryphile* existed, I'd be one.

Olena's third floor flat in the city was nice enough but it was intensely hot from the communal heating system that served the whole building. There might have been lethal six-metre icicles hanging from the guttering outside but inside, the temperature was sweltering.

Through the walls, floors and ceilings, the conversations of neighbours could be heard constantly. It was insufferable when they rowed. Squabbles always seemed to break out late in the evening or in the middle of the night.

Passers-by would stop and converse loudly below the window at all hours, sometimes shouting to friends several floors up. The over-riding hum of traffic noise and the blaring of car horns made sleep difficult.

And yes, I know, that's the *unromantic* image.

A *cityphile* would see it very differently, I'm sure.

Beautiful churches with golden domes, open parks with trees, ramparts with canons, unbelievably good restaurants that served tasty dishes, plentiful markets just a stone's throw away, a river with a beach, history, fresh fruit like we never get in the UK – the city of Chernihiv had them all.

But for all its simplicity, in the village there was air to breathe, there was peace and there was nature.

There, I felt instantly at home.

Going to fetch water from the well and waking up at five in the morning to find ducklings in my shoes was immeasurably more pleasurable than breathing fumes and listening to bickering through the wall.

Olena's parents were the icing on the cake. They were genuine, open, warm, accepting – just like mine.

It was on this trip that I met Olena's daughter, Yuliya. She was nine years old at the time and to say she was shy might just be the understatement of the year. Every time I spoke to her, she'd run to Olena and hide behind her. But she was a bright little button and one of the first things that struck me about her was her artistic eye.

The three of us had gone to the park one morning. Yuliya had taken Olena's camera and with the setting on automatic mode, she fired away enthusiastically. The way she handled it, the subjects she chose, the way she experimented with angles, shot into puddles to capture reflections, framed subjects – instinctively she seemed to know what made an interesting composition.

They were not the photographs I'd have expected from a nine-year-old.

I could imagine my father turning some of them into carpet designs, curtains or wallpaper quite easily.

On the way back, we passed a kiosk at the edge of the park. It was full of souvenirs – stuffed animals, pottery characters, plastic balls in nets, everything I'd normally avoid. A small metal crocodile no more than six or seven centimetres long caught Yuliya's eye. She seemed mesmerised by the way its metal vertebrae articulated and kept taking it out of the basket, playing with it, then putting it back.

It can't have been more than a few Hryvna, so I bought it.

Crocodile! she exclaimed excitedly as I handed it to her.

Olena smiled.

I'd learned the name of my first animal in Russian.

Now I could say *da, niet, spasiba* and *crocodile* fluently.

In the days that followed, Yuliya taught me the names of all the animals in her plastic zoo: *dog, cat, squirrel, cow, bird, magpie, spider, owl, pig, duck, chicken, hare, rabbit, fish…*even *dinosaur*.

By the time I returned to England, my conversational Russian hadn't advanced one iota but I was fully conversant with Russian zoology.

That summer, I invited Olena to the UK. She had a week's holiday due to her, so we planned several excursions. Along with a visit to Cambridge, days out near the sea and a taste of English village life – that was essential – I booked a hotel on my favourite British island, Guernsey.

I'd told her plenty about Guernsey – the little chapel that was only just big enough to stand up in, the Freesia Centre, Fort Grey in the sunset, the beautiful seascapes and beaches, the harbour at St Peterport and the lovely restaurant Steve and Jayne had introduced me to where they served lobster overlooking the harbour. I watched her eyes light up as I painted colourful descriptions of them all.

With good weather forecast, we could fly at 3,000 feet so she would see more of England en route.

I didn't have a cow she could tell her mother about but at least she'd be able to tell her about the hundreds of horses on each wing when she returned.

Landing at Guernsey Airport, we were immediately directed to taxi to the western apron. It's usefully close to the tower, within easy reach of the main road and there was short-stay parking close by so we could easily wheel our cases to the hire car I'd arranged.

I always loved it in Guernsey. It's one of the most aviation-friendly and welcoming airports I've ever flown into. The controllers are always helpful and efficient, the ground staff make everything easy and the landing and parking charges are

In the autumn of 2009 I met Olena, the lady who would eventually become my second wife.

I was impressed with Olena's skills as a photographer.

Nadia, Olena's mother.

It was on my second trip to the Ukraine that I met Olena's daughter, Yuliya.

Olena's father, Mykola with Yuliya and me.

reasonable. Oh, and the refuellers... I never needed to call them. They'd always pull up in front of the aircraft just as we shut down the engines.

We taxied in, parked up, shut down and right on cue, the fuel truck arrived.

Guernsey prices are without VAT so the fuel guys always know they'll have a customer whenever a plane comes in from the mainland. With a thirsty Beechcraft, they could be sure we'd want a fill and this bird could take £800 as an apertif.

The moment I gave the thumbs up for full tanks, the refueller connected the earthing-wire, removed the filler caps on both wings and began pumping. I set about the task of getting things out of the baggage hold.

Going diving? he called over the noise of the pump on the bowser as I hauled out a wetsuit and threw it on the grass by the port side prop. *There are some dangerous waters around here!*

I smiled.

I didn't normally keep a wetsuit in the plane.

Diving wasn't in the plan.

The suit had moved during the flight and was blocking access to our bags so it had to come out first.

Olena emerged down the air stair just in time to see the cap going on the last tank. I forget what she said exactly but it was something to do with the dinner suit that had slipped off the wing. Still on its hanger with my white shirt and bow tie beneath, it had dumped itself unceremoniously on the grass but appeared to be none the worse for its adventure.

Suddenly, I was aware the refueller was smiling – smirking – as he climbed into the cab and started to fill out the paperwork.

Are you paying by card or by carnet? he asked, returning to seriousness. *Card, please,* I replied, handing him my Visa.

Dutifully, he noted down the numbers from the front and the expiry date.

Then he turned the card over to check the security code and spontaneously burst out laughing.

Olena looked puzzled.

What is the problem? she asked, surprised by his reaction.

Are you serious? spluttered the refueller on hearing her accent.

Is this a 'You've Been Framed' joke?

I could only shake my head and shrug.

We'd just landed an aeroplane with a registration number that ended with the letters RJ – Romeo-Juliet in the phonetic alphabet.

I'd taken a wet suit out of the forward hold.

A tall, slender, good-looking woman with a Russian-sounding accent had disembarked.

A dinner suit had slipped off the wing.

And the security code on the back of the card was 007.

I bet to this day he's still trading on the story with his drinking buddies.

We enjoyed a fantastic time in Guernsey. The weather stayed warm and sunny for us and we met up with Steve and Jayne as well as visiting Fort Grey, Saumarez Park and the Little Chapel I'd told Olena so much about. We enjoyed the candle factory and the Freesia centre, strolled along Vazon beach, took in the views at Fermain bay and shot dozens of pictures around Castle Cornet when the evening lights came on.

We even managed to fit in a boat trip to Sark, a walk around the entire island and a lobster thermidor. It had been a glorious few days.

I was so pleased when Olena told me she had enjoyed my happy place as much as I had.

The following autumn, we announced our engagement and set about exploring where we should live. The options seemed pretty straightforward: either the Ukraine, where Olena had climbed the medical ladder and had a daughter and elderly parents; or the UK, where I had two companies, two daughters and elderly parents.

We'd already visited some nice properties in the Ukraine on a previous trip and compared with England, they represented good value for money. We'd found quite a large house overlooking a lake with woodland views and its own boat-house that was very affordable. For a cash sale in dollars, the builder had offered to drop the price even further.

It was very tempting.

The biggest obstacle for me was the language. When you need to ask someone for help to find the biscuits in a supermarket, it doesn't get you far reciting the names of animals.

Olena spoke excellent English but the obstacle for her was a whole raft of English tests and medical exams to prove her medical qualifications were genuine so she could practise in the UK.

We decided on a compromise: start in England and consider other options if she and Yuliya didn't settle.

If Olena and Yuliya had been from anywhere in the EC, they could have moved to Britain the next day but they were Ukrainian. Ukraine might be a European country but it isn't an EC member state. Ergo, Olena needed a visa – and not just a visitor visa or a business visa like she'd had before. This time, she needed a fiancée visa.

Neither of us could ever have imagined how harrowing or how difficult it would be to get one.

For a country that prides itself on its openness and seems to grant asylum to

En route to Guernsey: Olena takes control of Romeo-Juliet.

Olena with Romeo-Juliet after refuelling in Guernsey.

some of the most unlikely candidates, you would think the UK's Border Agency would welcome a highly-qualified medical consultant with open arms, maybe even fast-track her entry.

They didn't.

They turned us down.

Not a genuine couple, they said.

Not enough proof.

I'd printed out and bundled up 600 letters that we'd written to each other during the previous year, collated over 400 photographs of us together, collected photocopies of airline tickets and passport stamps to prove we'd made umpteen visits to see each other.

I'd collected bank statements and investment documentation to prove more than adequate income, savings and investments and packaged the whole lot together with the application forms and everything else that was demanded of us.

I don't know whether I was more confounded or more furious when the application was rejected as a 'marriage of convenience'.

Who were these bureaucrats to declare it was a marriage of convenience without having met either of us?

How dare they proclaim we couldn't get married and start a new life together in Britain?

I was British.

This was my country; the place I was born; the place my ancestors had put down roots more than eight centuries ago; the place where I'd lived, worked and paid taxes all my life.

It was outrageous.

We could have gone to any other EC country, married and returned to Britain to live together under Surinder Singh rules but because we'd chosen to make a formal application – and subject ourselves to ridiculously intrusive scrutiny, insufferable bureaucracy and shed loads of inconvenience and cost – we had been penalised. It was unreal.

Olena was upset.

Her parents were disappointed.

My parents couldn't understand it.

I was beyond livid. Volcanic wouldn't have described it adequately.

I must have spent the whole of the Christmas break collating more paperwork, copying, scanning, dotting and crossing everything for a second time. We'd been given a finite number of days to make an appeal and no allowance had been made for Christmas Day, Boxing Day, or New Year's Day – and it was less than a week before

Britain shut down for the festivities when the notification had arrived. But we made it. The appeal went in straight after New Year and it arrived on time.

While the Border Agency officials deliberated, I arranged another trip to the Ukraine.

After the stressfulness of the news and the midnight oil we'd both burned over the Christmas break, the thing we needed more than anything else was to spend some chill time together.

We'd stayed at the Bakkara hotel almost every time Olena and I had met up in Kiev. Overlooking the river, it was always relaxing. Booking was generally easy but this time it wasn't.

First my computer froze and wouldn't restart without a battle. It probably felt the same way as I did about Border agency bureaucrats - that or I'd thumped the keys too vehemently over Christmas.

Then the hotel website reported an error.

In the end, I phoned. A couple of misdials later, reservations took the call and everything was sorted. Of course, the price had gone up because I wasn't booking through the website but we agreed on river views and because we'd stayed there before, the receptionist confirmed a discount and promised to send confirmation by email.

Efficient as always, the email arrived and with it came the confirmation. But it wasn't the usual confirmation. At the very bottom it read in big, bold letters:

WE HAVE MOVED. PLEASE NOTE OUR NEW ADDRESS.

They'd upped anchor since our last visit to Kiev and sailed the hotel across the river to moorings adjacent to Venice Island.

It was a bit of an adventure getting there. The taxi driver didn't seem capable of changing gear without catapulting us from the back of the cab to the front and despite Olena telling him clearly that he should be looking for a boat and heading over the bridge to Venice Island, he insisted on driving away from the river and into the city where the traffic was at its heaviest.

It racked up a good fare but eventually we made it, checked in and booked a table in the restaurant.

Most of the diners had already finished eating and were on the cigarette course by the time we arrived. It was late and the few guests that had lingered in the dining room didn't seem to care that every table had a no-smoking sign. The room was thick with acrid smoke.

Hastily, we stuffed down a small dish of Verenyky and left.

We awoke late the following morning. On deck, the air was damp and a light mist hung low over the Dnipro river, shrouding the myriad of tall buildings that overlooked its banks.

Each time we'd stayed on the Bakkara it had been moored at the quay on the city side of the river. This time, it sat quietly at its new moorings on the opposite side, quite some distance from the city. It was certainly more tranquil but there was no quayside on which to disembark and no easy access to taxis and the metro.

The snow that had fallen in the days and weeks before had started to melt into giant mudslides around a car park that was still in the making. A steep aluminium gangway, still decked with Christmas garlands, hung precariously between the boat and the bank. It was our only route to land – and the car park.

Olena looked wonderful that morning. She always looks wonderful but we'd planned to go to the ballet in the evening and after our taxi experience the previous day, we'd taken the decision to dress smart-casual so we could have a late lunch without needing to return and change.

She had chosen a silky, above-the-knee black skirt and a black and white top to go with the tall white boots I'd bought her as a birthday present. To keep out the cold, she'd brought a fur coat and a cute hat that sat low over her ears.

She looked a million dollars as we made our way gingerly up the gangway and headed for the taxi rank, steering carefully away from wreaths and sodden, trailing ribbons that adorned the railings on either side.

The hotel had kindly organised the taxi for us and sure enough, just as we arrived at the end of the gangway, a muddy-shoed doorman signalled its imminent arrival.

Most of the taxis in Kiev were saloon cars. They were not generally large saloons and most tended to be a bit scruffy but they usually did the job.

It says on the paper that we should look for a white Fiat Doblo, Olena translated. *Do you know what a Fiat Doblo looks like?*

I didn't.

But no sooner had the words left her lips than an elderly white Fiat bumped its way around the corner and slid to a halt in front of the doorman. Olena turned to me: *Is this a Fiat Doblo?* she asked, fearing the mud-smeared van might be our chariot.

It was.

Moments later, the driver's window cranked down awkwardly and a well-tanned face with an untamed beard beamed out.

Was that headdress a Ghutrah I saw perched above jet-black eyes and greying eyebrows?

Maybe not. But it was similar.

And was that tunic a Thobe our driver was wearing beneath an old, grey anorak?

It seemed curious garb for Kiev.

Words were exchanged between the driver and the doorman, whose sweeping gestures implied our boarding was to be expedited with haste.

Picking my way through the mud, I opened the sliding door as far as it would go to allow Olena access, carefully holding the hem of her fur coat away from the muddy door sills as she climbed aboard.

Inside, the floor seemed to be a continuation of the car park and the seats weren't much better. Scruffy cream curtains festooned the side windows and dangled irregularly from home-made wires that had been pinned into the plastic window surrounds with tacks.

I was glad not to be turning up to Bizet's Carmen in it.

As the door slid noisily to a close the Doblo lurched into life. Bangles and beads clattered noisily, swinging back and forth across the windscreen. It was difficult to see out of the windows but Kiev didn't seem to be in the direction we were heading. Instead, we were making our way down a narrow track towards a forest.

The back seats of the Doblo provided a high vantage point with a view over the driver and the multitude of souvenirs that were gathering dust on the dashboard. Ahead was a narrow, winding track between the trees. It was muddy – very muddy – and the well-worn ruts made progress difficult.

A shallow dip lay ahead and immediately after it was an incline.

In preparation, the driver accelerated down the slope but still lost traction in the climb. Keeping a straight line had become a battle but it wasn't one he seemed to be winning.

Moments later we slid backwards into the dip and without the momentum to climb, slowly but surely, the Doblo sank into the deepest part of the mire.

For some time, we rocked back and forth, the rear wheels spinning furiously as the driver inched us gradually back in the direction from which we'd come. Bangles and beads jangled over the clatter of well-worn suspension but slowly – ridiculously slowly – we regained some traction and progressed up the last incline.

The rest of the journey was comparatively uneventful, except for the occasional stretched black Mercedes that blew an irritated warning as we meandered without signals from one lane to the next through busy Kiev traffic.

There seemed to be a lot of stretched black Mercedes out that day.

It was hard to tell when we had arrived at our destination. What the curtains didn't obscure, mud on the windows from our off-roading adventure surely did. Even the driver was far from certain of the precise drop-off point.

Olena fired some instructions in Russian before turning to me. *It's over there,* she translated, watching anxiously as the drop-off point appeared momentarily, then disappeared behind a curtain.

Why is he going this way?

First one opportunity to turn was missed, then another.

Finally, he found a turning point and swung the mud-spattered Doblo across several lanes of fast-moving traffic. With horns blaring from all directions, we jolted to a halt facing the traffic flow head on.

We'd arrived.

The driver seemed completely unruffled by the whole event as he turned, grinned a black-toothed grin and handed Olena two business cards in exchange for the fare I'd given her to pass on.

He wants to know if he should wait?

I shook my head.

On the card, there were two telephone numbers to one side of a picture of the driver leering over the roof of a much smarter, much whiter taxi than we'd just arrived in. In the photograph, he wore full Arab headdress and sported a menacing smile – and in his hand was a Kalashnikov rifle that pointed skywards at an angle. At the top of the card, three words stood out in big, bold capitals:

TAXI BEN LADANA.

They seemed to sum up the experience very adequately.

We enjoyed the opera. Olena loves dancing and the performance was very skilful... but nothing seemed to go quite to plan after that.

The Pirogovo open-air folk museum we'd spent many enjoyable hours looking around in early summer was closed. I had hoped to get some winter shots of the characterful cottages and the beautiful old windmills against a bleached winter sky just before the sun went down but it was not to be.

There was no white snow to soften the slopes and the sky remained shrouded in characterless low-level stratus. We'd picked the wrong day to buy tickets. It was January and not long after Russian New Year's Day. Everything was still closed.

There were some spectacular cityscapes to photograph along the river and a nice park from which to photograph them, so we headed there instead. There were also some beautiful views from the top of the hill, Olena told me as she took my hand and pulled me in the direction of the entrance to the funicular.

I hoped we weren't going to take it but that was clearly her plan.

As we headed for the ticket office, shades of Chamonix came flooding back: dangling from a rope in a biscuit tin suspended between mountains; the views I couldn't enjoy because the wretched thing had lurched to a halt over a gorge and there were no wings and no engines; waving goodbye to the girls as they disappeared in cloud 3,000 feet up a mountain; no control.

How I hated those things.

The funicular didn't have wings, engines or any controls I knew how to work but at least it had rails. It was attached to the ground. I assumed it had brakes, though

I didn't notice if there was a driver to apply them. Still, there was that wretched string to be relied upon and as far as I could see it was responsible for pulling us up the hill and preventing us from bolting back down again.

I'd already paid for the tickets and climbed aboard before Olena told me there was a walking route. But we survived the 230-metre trip.

I think it was the following evening, just before my flight back to the UK, that we returned to the Azerbaijani restaurant we'd discovered by accident on our first date and on this occasion, we were in time to catch the belly-dance.

We'd enjoyed Bizet's Carmen immensely but here, with the dance floor just a few feet away, it was more intimate, more personal. As the lights dimmed and the Darbukka beat started, it felt like we were almost part of the performance.

The lighting was spectacular and the dancers performed with energy, whirling around in their brightly coloured bedlahs. Neither of us could resist the opportunity to get our cameras out.

As Olena shot away from different angles, I set my camera up on the table. I wanted something different out of my photographs, something abstract that emphasised the atmosphere and the colour and captured the energy and excitement of the moment.

Choosing a slow shutter speed allowed the movement in the dance to blur. A soft blend of colours emerged on the screen as first one dancer, then another moved into the spotlight.

The results provided an interesting starting point.

Zooming out during a long exposure produced some interesting images, too but again, it didn't create the effect I wanted.

It wasn't until I started shooting double exposures – the first at an action-stopping speed, the second at a slow speed to create blur and fill the shadows with soft colour – that the camera started to pick up on the atmosphere. It must have taken 20 or 30 shots but finally, I got the one I wanted.

Flavoured by an unexpected photo opportunity and some album-worthy raw files to play with back home, the meal tasted even better than before. It had been a fitting grand finale to our January break and at last, we'd relaxed a bit and consigned the anxieties of the festive season to the shadows for a while.

We both hoped and expected the appeal would result in a visa being granted. There was nothing more we could have done. We'd provided masses of proof, reams of information, gone above and beyond what they'd asked us to send.

A few weeks after I returned to the UK, a letter arrived.

It hadn't made a scrap of difference.

They'd refused us again.

That would have been enough to put many people off, make them change their plans. Maybe that was the intention. I don't know. If it was, it was short-sighted.

Olena was a doctor.

The NHS was short of doctors.

She wanted to work and she had a lot to offer – 16 years of clinical experience, much of it working with rare and unusual endocrinology cases that had developed through the generations since the Chernobyl disaster. She was also something of an expert in alternative therapies and had used them to good effect many times when more conventional allopathic treatments had failed to bring results for her patients.

She had a lot to bring to the party.

Whatever the reason we'd failed to get through on appeal, the refusal only strengthened our resolve. It was no longer a visa application, a polite request for permission for the woman I wanted to be with to join me in the UK. Now it was a battle and the battle lines had been drawn.

The gauntlet had been thrown. What we needed was some big guns on our side; the artillery.

The Conservative constituency office was three doors down from our company's offices. The Conservative Club was two doors the other way. If I couldn't find the armaments I needed in one or other, Britain would be losing a tax-payer and the Ukraine would be gaining one. Of that, there was little doubt.

Determined to take this as far as it needed to go, I picked up the phone, called the constituency office and made an appointment to see my MP.

I'd never met an MP before. To me, MPs were just pictures on a poster, faces on The News that only ever emerged from their lairs at election time when they wanted something.

For the most part, whenever it came to elections, they'd hit the trail, take one look at the house, see two big Mercedes in the driveway and decide it wasn't necessary to call.

The Reds gave up at the gate. I could see the look of resignation written into their body language from 100 feet away.

The Yellows never made it to the village. The whole area was off limits for them.

The Blues assumed we were blue and walked straight past.

The Purples hadn't got their act together by then but I'd have chased them off faster than a seller of religion if they'd stepped on the doormat.

Apart from that, they were just names and now was the time to see if they were names with teeth. I needed one with serious bite and I wanted his incisors in the ass of the bureaucrat who had denied our appeal.

The constituency office was a bland building with an empty entrance hall protected from the rest of the world by a coded entry-system. It wasn't at all like our plush offices.

Once inside, a lady greeted me. She announced herself as the PA to the MP. She must have had a name but I never found out what it was. At least she was personable.

With a smile, she showed me to the inner chamber – a featureless, sparsely-furnished room with an old school desk, two school chairs to one side and a rickety swivel-chair on which was sat a stooped figure.

I'd barely made it through the door when the stooped figure launched himself towards me from behind the desk sending the swivel chair hurtling backwards. Lunging for my hand, he began to shake it vigorously in an exaggerated show of forthrightness.

Skinny, quite tall, probably mid 50s and with a mass of black, curly hair and low set eyebrows, I couldn't help thinking he would easily pass for a village vicar.

Do you mind if my PA sits in on the meeting? he asked, raising a bushy eyebrow and nodding his head as if to encourage a positive reaction to his own question.

I had no objection.

To say he was a public figure, someone used to being in the company of others, he seemed very uneasy and not at all relaxed.

As I took a seat, he nodded his head continuously.

I couldn't help wondering if it was the influence of Churchill – the bulldog one sees nodding through the back window of cars, rather than the politician.

Now, er, er...erm... he started, searching for a name that wasn't forthcoming. *I understand you have a problem with...er...er...*

An immigration matter, his PA continued, as if trying to get him started.

Yes, yes, yes! And you'd like me to er... support you with...er, um, a letter to er...

The embassy in Kiev. She'd finished his sentence again.

He nodded deeply, pursing his lips thoughtfully and scratching the black curly mass that had fallen casually over his forehead in a mop. The nodding, the handshake, the ums, ers and mild grimacing seemed to be masking the fact he hadn't read the notes his PA had placed on the desk before him. It didn't feel like we were off to a great start.

Now, er...Mr er..., he faltered, wringing his hands. He'd lost my name as well. *Perhaps you can tell me about the um...er...problem.*

Starting with our first meeting in September 2009, I launched into an abridged version of the events of the last year and a half: how we'd met; the letters we'd written to each other; the time we'd spent together; the deliberations we'd been through before deciding where to live; the huge wrench it would be for Olena to move to the UK because of her job; and what a major coup her defection to the National Health Service would be.

Oh, a coup! Yes, yes. A veritable coup! he exclaimed excitedly.

I'd never read any Charles Dickens but it seemed like a phrase with its roots in a dusty novel.

As I started to list the paperwork we'd submitted, the proof we'd provided, the supporting documentation we'd sent, the nodding head lowered progressively towards the desk. There was a hint of interest when the pictures came out. The first was Olena leaning back against the bonnet of the Mercedes with the plane towering over it in the background.

Oh, oh, I can see you are indeed a man of means! he blurted.

The nodding had moved up a gear but the black mop quickly sank to the desk again as we skimmed through various shots of Olena and me together, pictures with Yuliya, pictures with Yuliya, me and her grandparents, pictures with my parents, more pictures of us together, different locations...

Oh, absolutely, yes, absolutely... he interrupted, pausing for further nods. *Most definitely we will support you and er...your, er, your...*

Fiancée. His PA finished the sentence again.

It was not hard to see who was most likely to be doing any supporting that might come our way.

Handing his PA a copy of the letter I'd sent to the appeals tribunal, I explained that in it was all the information about what had been sent, a month-by-month resumé of our meetings and all the case numbers for the application and the appeal.

Is there, erm, anyone else of meritous standing whose support you might be able to counsel? he asked, nodding as if to confirm the answer himself.

Only you.

Oh... oh, quite. Yes, quite so!

His PA had been scribbling furiously in shorthand on a notepad throughout our conversation. She seemed very switched on.

I... er... I have no, er, hesitation whatsoever in lending our support to your case.

Turning in her direction, he nodded deeply as if to suggest she should note his comment but she was already ahead of him and awaiting the next.

I can see you have a most genuine relationship – and I can see it would indeed be most devastating to you both that such an occurrence should have, er...

Occurred. She finished his sentence again.

Yes, yes, yes! My PA will write a letter with all haste, won't you, my dear? In the next week or so...

*The first picture the MP saw was Olena leaning back against the
bonnet of the Mercedes with Romeo-Juliet in the background.*

Of course, came the reply. *I will have it ready for your signature tomorrow morning. It will be positive,* she added, turning to me with a smile. *You need not worry further.*

Towards the end of April 2011, another letter arrived on the doormat.

This time Olena had been granted her Fiancée visa.

At last, she could start to make arrangements, hand in her notice at work, make preparations for her move to the UK. But nothing about the application had been straightforward and there was certainly no good reason to relax now.

We hadn't been granted the full six months to rearrange our lives, starting from the date of the letter that had just arrived. They'd used the date of the appeal as the starting point, so now there were only three months in which to organise everything.

We'd been given until the end of July to uproot, reorganise, find somewhere to live, move, arrange our wedding, find a venue and tie the knot – without which Olena's visa would expire and she'd become just another illegal immigrant.

At the same time, I had the July edition of Furniture Journal to write.

The war was far from over but at least we'd won the battle – for now.

Chapter Twelve
A New Life

Olena and Yuliya arrived at Gatwick airport early in the June of 2011 and we moved into a rented house that we'd furnished together by sending photographs back and forth across the internet. It was a nice place, large and airy. It had the big windows Olena wanted, plenty of light and space, substantial gardens, a sauna, a swimming pool and a tennis court to keep Yuliya occupied.

I set up an office in one of the bedrooms so I could work from home and in the limited time we had, we found a registrar who could perform the ceremony and arranged the wedding and reception.

After the events of the previous months, the moment we became man and wife felt as much like a triumph over adversity as it did a happy occasion. Beethoven's Fifth might have been more appropriate than whatever the music was that came from the antique cassette recorder in the corner as we took our places at the front of the ceremony room.

The sun streamed through the windows and the registrar did her thing while Olena and I smiled at each other continuously.

The moment had finally come and I don't think either of us could really believe it was happening.

But the very second the ring slipped on Olena's finger, the Border Agency's clock started ticking again. She was no longer my fiancée. She was my wife.

Within a few short weeks she would need a Spouse Visa to stay in Britain. That, we were reasonably assured, would be granted – for another fee – so at least we could relax for a while, enjoy time with our guests and take some time out to visit Olena's parents.

We didn't take a honeymoon. Instead, we went to the Ukraine for a family celebration with Olena's mother and father. It was nice to see them again. It was always nice to see them but especially now we were all family.

We'd printed some of the wedding photographs my Russian friend, Dmitry, had taken on the day and while Olena's mother and aunt purred over them, her father and I chatted away over a beer.

Not that it was ever a proper conversation, at least not in a conventional sense.

We'd been given three months to uproot, reorganise our lives, find somewhere to live, move, arrange our wedding, find a venue and tie the knot.

Between visa applications we took time out whenever we could.

Mykola didn't speak English, I didn't speak Russian but after a couple of Samagonkas and an Old Peculier, we always understood each other perfectly.

After a while, with the girls heavily embroiled in animated conversation and oblivious to the pair of us in the corner, we headed out into the garden and left them to it.

There were tomatoes to pick, there was a chain-saw that needed mending and there was a small mountain of wood to cut for the winter. While I set about sorting the chain-saw, Mykola went to wring the neck of some poor unsuspecting bird that hadn't realised its destiny lay in the cooking pot that evening.

Fresh, farm-reared meat might taste better than supermarket meat but if you make its acquaintance and it clucks at you under a fence or moos at you over a gate, it reveals its personality. That levitates it immediately to pet status in my book. Knowing I could no more kill the bird than eat it if we met face-to-face, I made a point of staying in the woodshed with the chain-saw until the deed was done.

I might be a *countryphile* at heart but I'd never make a livestock farmer.

Those two weeks were the longest time we'd ever spent together in the Ukraine. They passed far too quickly.

Yuliya spent a few days with her father, we squeezed in the odd lunch and dinner with some of Olena's friends and colleagues from the hospital where she used to work, we visited the market and bought a few cooking pots to take back home but all too quickly it was time to head back to the UK for the next battle in the never-ending visa war.

This time the battleground was in Croydon.

In readiness for visa day, we packed everything meticulously – passports, divorce papers, marriage certificate, birth certificate for Yuliya, bank statements, letters from accountants and investment banks, the essential certificate to prove Olena's fluency in English and the application form. Everything was prepared, put in order and sealed in an envelope ready for presentation. Unlike the last time we'd applied for a visa, this time we were confident.

The UK Border Agency office in Croydon was a scruffy place. Dreary, unkempt, uninteresting, it didn't inspire optimism.

At the door stood a very short gentleman. Like the building, his uniform had seen better days but the UKBA epaulettes on each shoulder suggested he had official status. The swagger as he walked towards us confirmed it.

Whatever it was he said as he made his way in our direction, I completely missed. The accent made it impossible to catch.

He repeated.

I missed it again.

By the third attempt, he was getting agitated.

From the far corner of the entrance foyer, a security guard approached.

Problem, sir? he asked.

I could understand him perfectly.

I explained.

He nodded, raising an eyebrow in a gesture of comprehension.

He would like to know what time your appointment is, sir.

It was 1.30pm but we had been asked to report 30 minutes before and it was already one o'clock.

The official pointed to his watch excitedly and uttered a few more incomprehensible words, gesturing towards the door we'd just come through.

He would like you to come back in ten minutes, translated the security guard.

If we do, we will be late, I explained, *and we don't want to miss our appointment because we've come a long way.*

Begrudgingly, the short official waved us through to a crude waiting-area lined with 1970s plastic chairs. Other people were already gathering. Whatever it was he said as we passed him I still didn't understand but his gestures needed no translation. We sat down.

A minute or two passed before a door opened and almost immediately a queue started to form. Another official arrived at the head of the queue with a large plastic tray. In his hand was a belt.

Put here belt, watch, all what metal thing, go scanner, he shouted as the first row pushed past him.

Is that a Polish accent you have? I asked as we waited for Olena's handbag to chug through on the belt.

Tak, tak came the reply.

I wished him good day in Polish but he was another one too agitated for polite conversation.

We moved on.

No sooner were we through the scanner than a petite lady, I guessed of West Indian descent, approached us.

Have ya got de form for ya visas out? she called. She was much more cheerful and had a lovely complexion and the whitest of white teeth. She was the first person we'd seen with a smile on her face. *Ya must bring it over dis way.*

We'd packed it. It was neatly encased in an envelope, sandwiched between other documents, all ready for the official meeting we were expecting at 1.30. I fished it out of my attaché case and handed it over.

As a family, we enjoy photography and art. To me, a camera is a technical paintbrush and no subject inspires the artist in me more than nature and landscapes.

People make fascinating subjects and I enjoy shooting on location and street photography every bit as much as studio work.

Ben, my salvation from work.

Ya dun well! she proclaimed, scanning through the pages quickly. *Nice writin' – but it is de wrong form!*

We'd printed the form from the website the week before but there had been a price hike since. A new version had replaced it the day before our appointment but we didn't know. The only change was to the price – and that was on the first page.

Could we change the numbers on our form to save filling everything in again?

Oh, no.

Could we take the first page from a new form and attach it to the one we'd so meticulously filled in?

Definitely not.

We had to fill in new forms – two sets, each around 40 pages, beginning to end.

Thrilled, we found an unoccupied counter and set about the task as everyone who'd arrived after us filed past.

Half an hour or so later, with the new forms completed, we joined the next queue. As we waited patiently for our turn, occasionally making polite conversation with the petite lady, the time for our appointment ticked by.

It turned out she was from Barbados. She was thrilled when I told her I'd been to Saint Lucy where she'd lived as a child and I knew it was the birthplace of Errol Barrow, the first Prime Minister of Barbados. She didn't seem at all like the others we'd met on the way in.

I couldn't help wondering why anyone from such a beautiful Caribbean island might choose to work in such a dreary place.

At each counter ahead of us, an argument was taking place. First one applicant, then another left the room, either furious or in tears. Finally, our turn came.

The three of us stood side by side at the counter. Yuliya could only just see over the top.

Good morning! I ventured, pushing the forms through the gap under the bullet-proof glass. There was no response. This one didn't smile.

Without looking up, he groped for the forms and muttered something inaudible as he perused the opening pages.

Sorry, I didn't catch that, I said, leaning towards the glass so he'd hear me. Déjà vu was already setting in.

He muttered again. I caught something garbled in a dialect I didn't recognise but the raised voices from all directions around us stifled any possibility of making out the words.

Could you speak a bit louder, please?

The third try was no better.

He looked up, clearly angry. His big, brown eyes narrowed to vindictive slits the moment they contacted mine. *Do you speak English?* he yelled loudly, springing off his chair towards the glass that separated us and thumping the counter top.

Dammit! If there's one thing guaranteed to make me see red, it's some pipsqueak with an oddball accent at the other side of a bullet-proof glass screen yelling dumb questions about my ability to speak my own language. I'm from Yorkshire. It's Queen's English from God's own county that comes from my lips. The thump on the counter had sealed his fate.

Remember Lou Ferrigno in the 1970s TV series 'Incredible Hulk'? First the eyes glaze over as the blood morphs the capillaries. The teeth clench involuntarily. Blood pressure hits the red zone. Seams rip as muscles bulge. Skin turns green. Another impeccably-tailored Tyrwhitt shirt meets a grim end.

I can feel it all happening.

I'm willing myself not to respond.

I can feel Olena's hand reaching for mine and squeezing. This was her visa at stake and Yuliya's. A sideways glance said it all. She'd seen the angry Yorkie that was about to launch through the glass and was sending calming glances.

I was just climbing down from the ceiling when, with another thump on the desk, he yelled at me again: *I asked you, do you speak English?*

This time, restraint was just not going to happen.

Yes! I yelled back, not sparing glass from the blast. *I am English! I speak English! If you spoke English, you'd know that! My family has lived in England for over eight centuries. But I can't hear you if you mutter behind the glass! Speak up, man!*

Suddenly the slits widened to reveal shock and he fell back on his seat.

All around us, the arguments and fights seemed to have stopped. Heads turned in our direction. I must have ramped up the volume more than I thought.

Any more questions? I yelled, intentionally maintaining the momentum I'd built up.

The big brown eyes hit the papers on his desk.

Do you have passport? he muttered in broken English, a little louder than last time.

Vehemently, I shoved all three under the glass.

With the battles either side of us on hold I could hear him better.

Where is married certificate with names?

That went under the glass with equal force.

Where is divorce paper?

One after another, he went through everything we'd brought, scarcely lifting his eyes above the level of the countertop.

Finally, everything checked, he pushed the whole lot back under the glass in a messy heap and without a further word or an upward glance from behind the glass, waved us off for the next stage in the process like some lord impatiently dismissing a serf.

Upstairs in the UKBA offices, it was less dingy. The petite lady from Barbados had also moved to the next floor and with a huge smile, she directed us to a queue that was waiting to pay. The two oriental ladies taking payments were much more smiley than the surly Rottweilers downstairs.

Almost apologetically, they took my Visa card from under the glass screen and another four-figure sum made its way to UKBA.

Released with a number on a piece of paper, we took our seats in the inner sanctum. Like downstairs, the waiting area was insipid and characterless: a bit like the departure gate in a third-world airport with rows of plastic seats bolted to the floor facing yet more glass screens and partitions behind which only one person seemed to be working.

If this was the way all applicants were treated, I could quite imagine why the seats were fastened down.

We were way past our appointment time when our number came up on the screen and the girls were called through for biometrics to be taken.

Hello! came a voice from behind the curtain. As they sat down in turn and had fingerprints taken, I picked up on another accent.

That's an interesting accent you have. Where are you from? I asked.

Where you think I from? came the response in broken English.

Hungary, maybe? The Czech Republic?

No, I from Kaunas, he smiled. *You know where is the Kaunas?*

Taip. Sveiki! Koks tavo vardas? I'd remembered enough Lithuanian to say yes, hello and enquire after his name. It might not have been perfect but it worked.

Hey, you speaks pretty good Lithuanian! Me? I'm Kęstutis. You been in the Lithuania?

Sure. Many times. I know Kaunas. Nice city.

I can't recount the rest of the conversation. It switched to Russian when the girls got involved.

Biometrics taken, we perched ourselves back on the plastic chairs and watched as the clock counted the hours and minutes after our appointment time. It was getting late. The place had all but emptied when our moment arrived.

The papers that were once meticulously ordered were in a dishevelled heap in my case but at least the official at the other side of the glass screen seemed a little more patient than his colleagues downstairs.

Silently, he flicked through everything we'd brought, comparing details, checking passports, the marriage certificate, birth certificates, statements and investments. Occasionally he'd disappear and return with a pale photocopy of one or other of the documents to add to the collection.

With little else to pass the time, I found myself wondering what his accent might be. He didn't look as if he was of Far Eastern or Asian descent. There was no hint of Africa or the Caribbean in his looks. The former Soviet states could have been a possibility. No one from Germany, France or Italy would want to work in the UK Border Agency and he wasn't blonde so I ruled Scandinavia out.

Where do you think this one is from? I whispered to Olena.

She was well past caring. We hadn't eaten since the early hours.

Slowly and purposefully, he leaned towards the screen and pushed the passports and some of the other documents through the gap. Two more envelopes followed.

These are your visa confirmations, Madam, he said, looking directly at Olena. *Your biometric visas will arrive in the post in a few weeks.*

I was stunned.

Apart from the petite lady from Barbados and the security guard on the main door who'd translated for us when we first arrived, he was the first official we'd met at the UK Border Agency that day who might have had a sporting chance of passing the English exam Olena had been obliged to sit to prove she was fit to live here.

Two years later, both Olena and Yuliya had to apply for Leave to Remain. With each visa application, each level, the fees mounted and the documentation and the bureaucracy became more intense. Then came the 'Life in the UK' test.

That was a pointless waste of time.

Would it make her any more British to know which British cyclist had just won the Tour de France, which year England last won the World Cup or what the ethnic demographic of various UK cities was?

Unlike our then Prime Minister, who fluffed the question on prime time American TV, Olena *did* know what the Magna Carta was. No one stopped him from returning to the UK because of it.

It was a huge relief when they both became eligible to apply for citizenship and finally had British passports in their hands. I could never have imagined back then that a few years later we might all find ourselves facing restrictions and rubber stamp bureaucracy just to travel between Britain and the EC.

It can't have been long after Olena received her spouse visa that a very curious thing happened. It was well after midnight and we were fast asleep when the mobile phone I keep on my bedside cabinet started ringing. I always put it there as a precaution in case Mother or Father ever needed anything.

They had my number at the top of the pad on their telephone table so it was easy to find and whenever I'd been to see them, the last thing I would say before I left was always *Call me if you need anything.*

Anyway, you know how it is when you wake up suddenly. Nothing functions properly for a few seconds. Dazed, not quite with it, I groped in the general direction of the noise. I awoke instantly when I caught sight of the number on the screen.

If there was one number I didn't want to see in the middle of the night it was that one.

Is everything OK, Mum? I asked.

It's not your Mum, it's your Dad, came the answer. *And no, something is wrong.*

It certainly was.

Father was stone deaf.

He hadn't been able to use a phone – any phone – for years.

Since the onset of his dementia a few years before, figuring out where to find phone numbers on the note pad wasn't something he could do without someone prompting him.

Suddenly, it seemed he could not only remember where the number was and how to dial my number, he could hear perfectly. He'd heard my question the first time and this was the first conversation we'd had without voices being raised above normal speaking volume for decades.

I'm worried about my Mother, he continued. *She's been out walking on the moors. I haven't heard from her for a while and I think she's lost. Can you call the police for me?*

Father's mother, the grandmother with the glass eye, had passed away a good 25 years before but if there was one thing I'd learned about his condition, it was to accept whatever he said as if everything was normal and play along.

She's fine, Dad. Stop worrying. The police brought her here.

When she's finished her cuppa, I'll take her home. Just go back to bed and stop worrying. I'll take you to see her in the morning.

Relieved, he thanked me and put the phone down.

The following morning, I arrived on the doorstep early, half expecting to see Father with his coat on and ready to go. Mother was puzzled. *This is a surprise,* she said. *What brings you here at this time in the morning?*

She hadn't heard him get up in the night. I'd had a perfectly coherent conversation with him about an entirely fictitious topic in the early hours but he had no recollection of calling me either. To this day, I can't understand how his hearing came back.

Dementia is an awful affliction. It's distressing for those who suffer from it and it's just as distressing for those who have no option but to watch on powerless, knowing it will only ever get worse.

There were times when Father didn't recognise Mother. *There is a strange woman in the house,* he'd say. *Get rid of her!*

Mother always knew the real Dennis, her Dennis, the Dennis she'd been married to and lived happily with for almost 67 years didn't mean that. He'd never have spoken to her in that way.

I can't begin to imagine the torment she must have been going through to see him so confused and upset. It was distressing for all of us but for her it can have been nothing short of agony. She never complained. She was always the epitome of patience. *He'll come back to me,* she'd say. *We just have to wait.*

There were moments of lucidity. Sometimes he'd paint or draw but the beautiful flowers he used to paint for Mother had become distorted, gnarled, twisted as if he was trying to tell everyone through his art about the conflict and the torture that was going on inside his head.

The subtle watercolour washes he was so good at had been replaced with raw, Fauvist colours that came straight from the tube and he'd scratch away with an ink pen over the top, adding contorted detail that cut deep into the surface of the paper.

It wasn't difficult to feel the torment that was ravaging him.

Strangely, he never forgot who I was. He'd forget Mother, Marie, the girls, Olena and Yuliya but he always recognised me and remembered my name.

Whenever I could, I'd go around after work to give Mother some respite. Sometimes, Father would offer to make a cup of tea. *You scrounging basket,* he'd say with a cheeky smile on his face. *You've only come here for a cuppa.*

More often than not, I'd get hot water or a cup of cold milk with a tea bag in it but it didn't matter. It was helping him to do normal, everyday things and that was keeping his brain active, putting off the day when he'd probably lose us all.

Mother was always grateful for the break and would sit at his side, holding his hand, happy he was getting some enjoyment out of the moment. It was good for her to have company, too. Father had carers who came to see him several times a day but it had become a very empty life for her.

On evenings when he felt like conversation, we'd talk about the things he did when he was in the RAF or the moment he first met Mother on Morecambe promenade. He could still remember much of his Malay, Singalese and the other languages he'd picked up while he was in the Far East.

Occasionally, he would wheel out the odd phrase to confound us. It was good to see him laugh when we didn't understand. That was the real Dennis, the mischievous Dennis and it was wonderful when he shone through the mist of confusion.

Quite often, he'd talk about his mother. He never really got on that well with her – nobody did – but as his dementia progressed, he remembered her with increasing fondness.

His favourite tale was from when he was a boy. He'd been entertaining some friends and decided to raid his pot piggy-bank to buy them all an ice cream. It was typical of Father. He was always generous. He'd give his last penny to anyone he thought might need it more than him.

Anyway, on returning home to find the broken piggy bank, his mother was shocked and wanted to know how he'd got into it.

A huge smile would always crease his face at this point. *I smashed it with a brick,* he'd tell me, gleefully.

His mother was mortified. She'd been saving pennies in there too.

As time went on, the episodes became more frequent and from time to time, Father would go walkabout. He'd get up at crazy times of the night and toddle off. Mother would be beside herself with worry but she was always reluctant to call.

For a long time, she refused to have carers but now Father was facing the prospect of having to go into a special home, a secure home, she was afraid he would be taken away and there would be nothing any of us could do. No one liked that idea, so we all fought it.

He'll be fine, she'd say. *I'll look after him. For better or for worse is what we said when we got married. Your father would have looked after me, so I want to look after him. We belong together.*

When he didn't return from one of his midnight walkabouts, Mother became really anxious. Already in her early 90s, there was no way she could follow him to coax him back. Her eyesight wasn't good enough to see in the dark and in recent years she'd broken several bones falling over booby traps Father had inadvertently left strewn across the floor.

When she called me in the early hours of the morning to say he'd disappeared, I phoned the police immediately. They responded instantly to the call and set about scouring the lanes and fields while paramedics attended to Mother.

It took me the best part of 45 minutes to get there from where we lived but by the time I pulled up behind the Police car, Catherine was there and they'd already found him barricaded in the sun-house at the bottom of the garden.

Not wishing to be disturbed as he hunted for the oil pastels he'd left there some time earlier, he'd told the policeman he would shoot him if he tried to open the door.

Understandably, the officer had backed off, anxious about Father's state of mind and worried he might have a gun stashed somewhere.

One of the paramedics had made a pot of tea for Mother, so we hastily poured one for Father and took it down to him.

He took one look at familiar faces, smiled and handed over the sawn-off plastic hosepipe he'd been wielding without a struggle.

No arrest was made.

The sun-house episode took a heavy toll on Mother. She wanted to look after him but it was beyond her and now she could see that. She was wearing out herself.

With much reluctance, she agreed to one day a week respite care. Father would attend a secure day-centre for people with dementia where he would be cared for by trained staff who knew how to look after him while she took much-needed time out for herself.

The first couple of weeks went well. Father seemed to enjoy his new surroundings and had taken it upon himself to teach everyone new languages. Mother certainly enjoyed a break from endless routine of sitting on the settee with Father as he reminisced over his wartime adventures. She knew them all and could recite them by heart.

I think it was the fourth week when she received a call from the day centre to say he'd gone missing. Immediately, she called me.

I don't know what to do. They've called the police but they can't find him.

Various calls to the day centre and the police resulted in a confusing assortment of conflicting messages:

He's been found safe and well.

The police won't release him.

He's back at the day centre.

He's with a neighbour.

The Police Event Number is 118 – quote if you have a problem.

Finally, the day-centre manager called. *He's back,* she reported. *He's fine and he's enjoyed his little adventure!*

That's good news. But how could he escape?

We don't know. There are members of staff present all the time, there are CCTV cameras inside, outside and on the door and the door can only be opened with a six-figure security code that's changed daily.

It was surreal.

Father, an 89-year-old dementia-sufferer who had severe memory problems, restricted mobility and walked slowly with the aid of a frame, had escaped the eagle eyes of several members of staff in a secure day-centre dedicated to dementia patients.

He'd evaded closed-circuit television cameras inside the building.

He'd made it unchallenged to the locked exit door.

Unaided, and with a million possible combinations to choose from, he'd apparently cracked the six-digit code and opened the door.

He'd deftly dodged the security cameras outside and crossed a busy road.

And although he was very hard of hearing, he'd managed to scrounge a cup of tea from someone he'd never met before.

It had indeed been quite a feat – one that was even more impressive than the early morning phone call when his hearing came back. I was proud of him!

If she hadn't been at her wit's end, Mother would also have been quite amused to learn of the adventures of her errant Houdini at the day-centre.

Mother and Father always enjoyed meeting people from different parts of the globe and Father, in particular, loved the opportunity to wheel out his languages whenever we gathered all our friends together from different countries. International parties, we called them and they were a lot of fun.

We usually organised an event for the first day – sometimes a boat trip around the Broads, a flight over the Marrams in north Norfolk or a lunch with some sight-seeing in a characterful old town – then we'd all cook dinner together the following day.

Alejandro always had to be in London around the time of the Book Fair, so with the dates of the exhibition cast in stone, we usually tried to arrange our get-togethers so they coincided with his visit.

That year – 2012 – was the first international party Mother and Father couldn't attend and everyone felt their absence.

Jean-Paul, Luc and Josette came over from France. Hinrich flew in from Germany. Dmitry, who hailed from Nizhny Novgorod in Russia, had already been with us for a few days. So had Alla, Olena's friend from the Ukraine. Alejandro diverted from London and various other friends arrived from different parts of the UK.

It was a cosier event with fewer people than we'd entertained on previous occasions when the girls were at home but it was the first Olena and I had hosted as a couple. It was nice to see everyone together again, mingling, chatting easily among themselves in whichever language worked for them at the time.

On the last day, we all cooked together and as always, Jean-Paul officiated as Maitre de Vin.

It was as Olena and I were preparing the dessert course that we became aware of excited chatter from the far corner of the lounge. The volume had increased. The intonation denoted surprise, delight, and it seemed to be emanating from a small group that had gathered around Jean-Paul.

He'd opened the dessert wine.

A glass had been poured.

It had been passed around.

Noses had got to work on the bouquet.

Heads were nodding in appreciation.

The cork, still on the cork screw, was circulating.

Melvyn, you are zee most incredible 'ost! Jean-Paul proclaimed enthusiastically as Olena and I arrived with dessert trays.

I am?

Bah, oui! Incroyable! echoed Josette.

Always zare are zee surprise but zis… zis eez… Incroyable!

Absolument incroyable! Luc agreed.

It was a nice dessert wine – we knew that because we'd brought a few bottles back from the Crimea and opened one a few months before – and it was even nicer to be appreciated but I couldn't quite see what might be deserving of such an accolade.

Jean-Paul was in raptures: *Never 'as we tasted a wine so special.*

Non, non! Never! agreed Luc. *Jamais! Très spécial!*

Before we were married, Olena and I had taken a flight from Kiev to the Crimean Peninsula as a short break to a part of the world I'd never visited before. She knew the Yalta region quite well and hadn't exaggerated when she told me the scenery was spectacular.

Beautiful waterfalls cascaded from sheer cliffs, there were little pathways through forests, mountains, lovely gardens and wonderful views over the Black Sea. We visited the famous Swallows Nest, a miniature Gothic castle in Gaspra that was perched precariously on the edge of a steep drop overlooking the sea but when she suggested we might try a wine-tasting at Massandra, one of the region's best-known wineries, that felt much more intrepid.

With some horror, I remembered the awful Georgian wine we'd ordered on our first date in Kiev.

We've had some pleasant ones since but that was as rough as a newly gritted road and about as drinkable as the tar they pour on it.

French wines, Spanish wines, Italian wines, German and Austrian wines, Australian and South American wines I know my way around moderately well and usually manage to find one I like. I've even got American wines in my collection. But I'd never tried a wine from Crimea before.

I could almost hear the feint ringing of alarm bells in the distance as my taste buds braced for another tongue-stripping experience.

The young reds weren't very special but when the more mature reds and the dessert wines came out, they were much more interesting – indeed, some were really excellent. We never got to try the White Muscat Livadia or the Livadia Red Port that we were told sells at prices north of £4,000 for a bottle but we brought a few bottles of Muscat home along with a Pinot Gris.

It was one of the white Muscats, a 1983 vintage, that Jean-Paul had opened.

He handed me a glass, then, with accentuated reverence, the cork followed it. Everyone was watching.

If a pin had dropped, we'd all have heard it.

Mille huit cent quatre-vingt-quatorze, he whispered, shaking his head in disbelief. *Mille huit cent quatre-vingt-quatorze. Melvyn… eet is incroyable!*

In the hush that followed, the penny dropped.

He'd taken 1894, the date on the cork, as the year the wine had been made and convinced everyone of its age.

We didn't have the heart to tell him 1894 was the year Tsar Nicolas II founded the winery.

It wasn't long after that an invitation arrived from one of Olena's friends to a different kind of party: a murder mystery. Olena leapt at the chance. I cringed.

Too late – she'd already accepted.

I've never been into parties with games – I developed an early dislike of pass the parcel, banana sandwiches and over-diluted orange squash when I was a kid – but this one, she told me, would be different. There was a brief and we'd all been allocated roles.

Olena was to play the part of a maid. I was to play the part of a newly-ordained Irish Catholic priest who'd been sent to a far-flung corner of the diocese after striking up an affair with the aforementioned maid. Uniforms were obligatory.

We can buy our outfits on line, Olena assured me and as the party wasn't for a couple of weeks, there was no rush to learn my lines.

Oh, deep joy. *Learn my lines.*

There was no pass-the-parcel at this party but acting had become the new banana sandwich.

I wasn't sure which I hated most.

I'd just sat down in my office and had started work on an article for the next edition of Furniture Journal when the phone rang. It was our hostess. Hastily, I concluded the morning pleasantries and passed the handset to Olena. The conversation switched to Russian and I tuned out.

Some time passed and the enthusiastic chattering ceased.

All OK, dear? I questioned, not really looking up from the article that was taking shape on my screen. I was already heavily into the benefits of polyurethane hot-melt adhesive when compared with ethylene-vinyl acetate for edge-banding bathroom furniture panels and didn't really want to lose the thread.

Dear, came the response, *when is a ninth?*

She had a cute way of mixing up 'a' and 'the' sometimes.

The ninth of what, dear?

A ninth of this month.

Tomorrow. Why?

A long pause followed. I'd finished the introduction long ago and was well into the meat of the article before I realised there hadn't been an answer.

Why did you want to know about the date, dear? I repeated, pausing for a moment to glance over my reading glasses.

Olena was looking unusually sheepish.

She didn't do sheepish.

Something was going on.

We have to get uniforms. A party is tomorrow.

Tomorrow? You only mentioned it this morning. How are we supposed to find a cassock, surplice, dog collar and cross for me and a maid outfit and feather duster for you by tomorrow?

Suddenly, I could see my morning's work vanishing in a whirlwind of frenzied distraction.

And so it was.

Everything had to be abandoned as we went in search of an old, white shirt to turn into a pinny; a frill to stitch around the edge; a feather duster from the hardware store; false eyelashes and nails – not for me; stiff, white material from which to craft a dog collar; wood to make a cross that would be painted with fast-drying gold acrylic and hung around my neck from the only lanyard I had, courtesy of Lufthansa.

And while the glue dried on the cross, I finished my article on adhesives.

As acrylic-gilded ecclesiastical accessories go, this one looked the business but with no possibility of knocking a cassock and surplice together before the party, Father O'Flat-hat would have no option but to go in his day gear. The black suit, black socks and black shoes were hastily pressed and polished. And, thank God, Tyrwhitt did a black shirt.

Do priests wear double cuffs and crisp cutaway collars with their dog collars?

The collar clash might have looked a bit of a dog's breakfast but the options were limited.

One thing I was certain of: Dave Allen would have chuckled as we dressed for the party. As I donned my all-black outfit and Olena put the final touches to her maid's uniform, batted her half inch-long eyelashes and mounted her high heels, I got to work on the Irish accent.

To anyone who hails from the Emerald Isle, it probably sounded about as Irish as Theakston's Old Peculier but it was the nearest I was likely to get for a role play.

International party: Luc, Josette and Jean-Paul (below) with the 1894 wine.

As for learning lines, there really wasn't much chance of that. I resigned myself to reading from the pulpit on the night.

But Father O'Flat-hat and his acrylic-painted cross certainly got a few waves from passers-by as we sped down the lanes to the party in a stretched black S-Class Mercedes.

A bad lad I might have been with the maid but at least I didn't turn out to be the murderer – even if I had the perfect gangster car.

Father O'Flat-hat and the maid.

Chapter Thirteen
The End of an Era

2013 and 2014 weren't good years for the family. As fast as my father's condition was deteriorating, so, too, things at the carwash were heading downhill. In the four years I was a director, it did well but I can't say it was ever a business I was particularly comfortable with.

The original plan was to expand into half a dozen sites and we'd investigated several that had shown potential but I wasn't happy with the way things were being run at base camp and hesitated when the opportunity came to invest in more.

That didn't sit well with my fellow director.

He wanted progress.

He wanted more sites.

He wanted them now.

I was the investor.

Why wasn't I doing something?

Staff turnover was ridiculously high and that didn't fill me with confidence. Each time I visited the carwash there would be new people. Others had been fired. They seemed OK to me but if they smiled at customers the wrong way or failed to live up to expectations in a ridiculously short timeframe, they'd be gone the next time I went up. It's the Lithuanian way, I'd be told.

It certainly wasn't mine.

I couldn't see how we could manage more sites, especially not sites that were hundreds of miles apart, when we had such poor staff retention at the first.

When the opportunity presented itself, I sold my shares, pocketed the profits and never looked back.

It was May 26th 2013 that I took the controls of the aeroplane for the very last time.

Some friends of ours, Lara and Jim, had travelled down from Scotland to spend a few days with us and Lara, who hailed from the same city as Olena, had always wanted to fly in a private aircraft. The two of them had pretty much organised the time and the date between themselves, so it was more by good luck than good management that they'd chosen a bright, sunny day with few clouds and a light breeze.

With the aircraft out and fuelled, it just remained for me to book out with a time slot and we could get airborne.

Hey, is that Mr Earle? came a booming voice from the other side of the clubhouse as I jotted down the departure and return times on the booking-out form. I didn't know too many Americans. It had to be Tom, the flying instructor who had shepherded me through my FAA instrument rating and was now the chief examiner for the Federal Aviation Administration in Europe. We hadn't seen each other for years.

Are ya goin' flyin'? he called.

That was the plan.

You cain't be too far off your check ride. When's it due?

I had a couple of months to run but then I'd need to arrange a date for a flight test.

I'm free if you can manage an extra passenger.

It was a rare moment to see Tom on home turf and even more rare that he should be available. It usually took weeks to catch up with him and when I did, he could be anywhere in Europe.

The opportunity to get the flight test out of the way was too good to miss – but we'd have passengers, first time flyers. We'd have to go a bit steady, not throw them around too much.

Oh, sure! We can do that! Tom assured. *Let's go!*

Lara and Jim were already admiring the aircraft with Olena and Yuliya as Tom and I walked across the apron. *Mr Beech sure did build a fine airplane when he built these!* Tom said, patting the starboard engine with obvious affection for the brand.

I was busy with the pre-flight checklist.

Lara looked puzzled.

Tom is my flight examiner, I explained, realising I'd forgotten the introductions. *We've known each other for years. He's going to put me through my paces while you and Jim enjoy the scenery. You'll have two pilots on board.*

Suddenly, Jim looked worried.

Put me through my paces probably wasn't the most tactful phrase to use.

Maybe it wasn't a particularly encouraging sign to hand out sick bags as I made my way through the cabin either but it was a habit I'd adopted many years earlier after a seasoned flyer had redecorated my first aircraft on a short hop to see a client.

As we taxied out, engine run-ups complete, Tom launched a volley of questions at me: *What's your blue line speed? What's your Vx speed? What's your VLO? Tell me about Class A airspace…*

True to form, we'd no sooner got airborne than he pulled an engine. So much for not throwing my passengers around.

I think we were about half an hour into the flight when, after a series of steep turns, the unmistakable scent of unhappy passengers drifted into the flight deck. In the cabin, Lara and Jim were both face down in a bag.

I think we'll call that a pass, Tom chuckled.

Two or three weeks later, I was putting my contact lenses in when I noticed what I thought was a greasy smear on the right lens. Cleaning the lens didn't shift it. Alarmingly, without the lens in, I looked right, the smear moved left; I looked left, it moved right.

A visit to my optometrist confirmed the lens was not the problem.

It wasn't especially serious and didn't affect my acuity but the moment I told my aviation medical examiner, without offering an appointment to check for himself, he grounded me.

All it had taken was a two-minute phone call to finish my flying career.

I suppose I could have contested it, gone to an ophthalmology consultant, fought for my licence – and if I'd been younger I'd have challenged it vigorously – but the convenience of having our own aeroplane had long since evaporated with the growth in low-cost airlines.

Fuel prices had soared since we bought the first aircraft. Landing and airport parking fees had gone off-the-scale crazy and European legislation from EASA was intentionally making it difficult for anyone with an American-registered aircraft to keep it in the UK.

The cost of ownership seriously outweighed the benefits and the plane had outlived its usefulness.

With some regret, we put it on the market through Aradian, Paul sold it for us and I hung up my flying gloves.

Another chapter had closed.

Not long after that, Father took a turn for the worse.

He hadn't been able to swallow solid food for some time but things went from bad to worse when he lost the ability to take liquids. He needed to be on a drip to stay hydrated but the staff at the home he was in couldn't get him to cooperate. Every time they put it in, he'd pull it out.

In the end, no one could persuade him, not even me.

With Catherine and me at his side, he faded away quietly in the early hours of 18th July 2013 through simple lack of water.

Fifty-seven years he'd been at the head of our small family. The chasm he left behind in all our hearts was an impossible one to fill but he'd had a long, happy, fruitful, fun-filled life. And he'd lived it to the full.

What more can any of us ask?

Almost exactly a year later, on July 22nd 2014, Mother followed him. They'd been married 67 years and that last year without him had been agony for her. With no reason to continue, she gave up. The only thing she wanted was to be with her Dennis.

Quietly, with Catherine, Olena, Marie and me at her bedside, she drifted off to be at his side again.

It was the end of an era.

In the years leading up to 2014, the magazines had continued but as staff had left or retired, we hadn't replaced them. Staff numbers were dwindling. By the summer, I was going into the office to find a handful of people in different parts of the building and wondering why we were still paying to heat and light offices that once housed almost 30.

At the same time, a couple of key clients had subtly hinted that Furniture Journal wasn't the magazine it used to be. It was still making money but it looked dated, tired, in need of TLC and it was in danger of dropping behind some of its competitors.

My attention had been on other things and I hadn't spent enough time on it. A shake-up – a proper one – was well overdue and it needed setting on a new course. That would necessitate some changes at the company.

Over the next few months, Marie and I grasped the nettle, negotiated a couple of redundancies, put Kitchen Journal and Bathroom Journal together as one title with Catherine as editor and I took Furniture Journal back under my control.

Just before two of the biggest exhibitions in the biennial calendar, my publication manager on Furniture Journal announced his retirement, so I inherited the job of selling advertising as well as writing articles, designing pages and preparing each edition for print.

I was right back where I started in 1993.

You might think that was a bad thing and I suppose to anyone preoccupied with growth, acquisition and empire-building, it probably was.

I didn't see it that way.

At last I could have some fun from a creative outlet I'd invented a couple of decades earlier. I'd put employment issues, back-biting and petty staff squabbles behind me and with the review edition, Furniture Journal's recovery was firmly under way.

By Christmas, we'd sold the building the company had occupied since 1994 and put a good dollop of cash in the corporate pot and with every edition that followed,

I pushed the envelope further. In little more than a year, Furniture Journal had a new look, new services, a fresh new offer for its advertisers and sales that more than doubled its revenue.

At last, it had the attention it deserved, it was growing in reputation and the big name, global blue-chip brands were with us again.

Mother, Father and me in 2009 – the last photograph we ever had taken together.

April 8th 2017: the best picture of Christina and me together that we'd ever had taken.

What Christina and Oli had found was beyond special.

Chapter Fourteen
Christina

With Catherine employed as editor of Kitchen and Bathroom Journal and well-established as the proprietor of CSJ-PR (her own burgeoning PR company), Christina working full-time for the newspaper she'd lauded since her university years and the publishing company back on the road it should never have departed from, life seemed to be getting back on track again.

We'd had a tough few years but the future was looking bright.

All it needed to ice the cake was a *Proud Dad* moment – and that arrived with an invitation to London at the end of December 2016.

Christina had announced she was getting married a few months earlier. While she and Oli, her husband-to-be, were on holiday in Canada, she'd sent me a picture of the engagement ring he had bought her.

She had found her Mr Right and she was over the moon.

Now it was time to choose a wedding dress.

She'd decided on the bridal stylist she wanted to work with and had already booked an appointment in the OXO Tower when she called me. There was no mistaking the excitement in her voice. There were several dresses she liked and she'd set aside 30th December to try them.

They're not cheap, Dad, she assured me. *Catherine and I were just wondering if you might like to help me choose the dress?*

I couldn't help smiling. I had a pretty good idea what that meant.

What father could resist?

December 30th arrived. It was a dank, grey day and a thick mist hung over the Thames as we made our way along the side of the river from the underground. The buildings that lined the opposite side were just about visible but Blackfriars Bridge was little more than a vanishing smudge on an off-white canvas.

Not that it mattered. Christina was on top of the world.

As we picked our way through the crowds from the tube station, there was a discernible spring in her step and she wore the kind of infectious smile that compelled total strangers to smile back.

It was often that way when she and Catherine got together – they could both turn heads and knew how to enjoy the moment – but on this particular day, the sparkle was brighter than any New Year's Eve firework display on Victoria Embankment. Everyone on Southbank was being carried along by the euphoria of *her* moment, or so it seemed.

I always enjoyed shopping with the girls when they were younger, though I confess, when it came to clothes shopping for me, it was generally one of those chores that had to be done rather than something I'd do with much enthusiasm. Buying trousers in job lots of half a dozen when I found some I liked hadn't equipped me well for wedding dress shopping.

Three-quarter sleeves I understood. Much beyond *36, long-fitting in black* pushed my knowledge of haute couture.

As the girls purred over a couple of dresses that had taken Christina's eye, the stylist switched to a foreign language:

Do you like the chiffon? This is a lovely organza. Batiste is very good for a summer wedding. Would you prefer off-the-shoulder or bateau neckline? This filigree is lovely, don't you think? Or do you prefer Guipure? We can offer tiered lace. That's a lovely A-line. We also have it in Dotted Swiss...

The girls seemed to be keeping pace with the idiom but it wasn't until Christina emerged from the fitting-room and twirled in one of the dresses she liked the most that any of it made much sense to me.

If the first dress took me by surprise, the second she appeared in knocked me sideways.

This was my daughter; my little girl.

She was all grown-up and getting married.

She looked amazing, stunning, fabulous; a picture from the front cover of a bridal magazine.

Suddenly A-line meant something. Tiered lace...wow! Bateau neckline – I was getting there.

What do you think of the tulle, Dad? Better with or without?

Definitely with!

It could be dyed so I could use it as a cocktail dress after the wedding.

Nice idea.

It's expensive.

Do you like it?

Of course!

Do you want it?

Um...

Then go for it!

OK. If you insist!

It was a *Proud Dad* moment par excellence when the decisions had all been made and the time came to reach for my wallet.

With both girls heavily committed to work and me embroiled in exhibitions, reviews and factory visits, there hadn't been time to get everyone together to mark my 60th birthday but Christina and Catherine had hatched a plan and proposed a belated celebration at a snazzy Michelin star restaurant Christina had found.

She'd managed to free herself from work commitments for an afternoon, so on 8th April – almost six months after my 60th – Catherine and I drove down to London for a long overdue get-together.

The meal was everything Christina had said it would be. The girls had even thought to have a birthday cake delivered to the table. But it was not the meal nor the finishing touch I remember most. It was the special moment we spent together; the chance to spend time with them both; the chance to chat and laugh together like we used to do when they were at home.

I hadn't realised quite how much I'd missed that.

At the end of the evening, Catherine took the best picture of Christina and me together that we'd ever had taken.

I will treasure that picture – and the memory – always.

It was the last evening we ever spent together as a threesome.

Christina and Oli had hoped to marry on Mother's birthday but either the registry office or the venue they'd chosen for the reception – the Chelsea Physic Garden – wasn't available, so they settled for 8th July.

They couldn't have picked a better day.

The clouds parted, the sun shone and as the bride and groom made their way down the steps from the registry office to take their first walk together as man and wife, the world seemed to be smiling with them.

They both had successful careers, they had their house in the west of London, they had plans, they had a bright future and now they had each other.

I don't think I ever saw Christina happier than on that day.

As she and Oli looked into each other's eyes and smiled for a formal photograph among the midsummer scents and the greenery, there was no mistaking what they felt for each other.

What they'd found was beyond special. It was beautiful.

I could only stand back and admire, content that in some small way I might have played a part in helping set the scene.

If anyone would have told me that in fewer than eight months from the day she was married, my beautiful, amazing, talented, irreplaceable elder daughter's life would come to an abrupt end, I would never have accepted it but on 2nd March 2018, in the most tragic and unlikely circumstances, Christina died.

She was just 31 years old.

After an evening out in London with Lorraine, her friend from university years, Christina slipped getting into a taxi and sprained her knee. It didn't sound good but a sprained knee is just a sprained knee, right? Nobody ever dies from a sprained knee.

A little over a week later, she texted me from hospital. I knew she was relieved. It was the longest text conversation we'd had in years:

Seen physio this morning and the best news ever is I don't need surgery! Physio said to damage my knee like I have done but not need surgery is amazing really – like a 1pc chance. I'm so relieved. Unlucky yet so lucky at the same time. Yet to see the consultant but happy days! Physio has spoken to the consultant beforehand and seen my MRI, so all should be good. Hope to be back on my feet without crutches in the next month.

Shortly after leaving the physiotherapist, while still in the hospital, she turned to Oli and said she didn't feel well. Minutes later, my amazing, wonderful, beautiful elder daughter was fighting for her life. A pulmonary embolism was taking her from us.

She was just 31 years old and her own childhood prophecy had come true.

Anyone who didn't know Christina and doesn't know me might expect emotive and passionate writing at this point: pain described with lurid adjectives, despondency in spades. Depression.

I'm not Jade.

We're not a family that belongs in a soap opera.

Besides, it wasn't like that.

On the face of it, that may sound a heartless, unfeeling thing to say but that's not me either. I felt it, of course I did and in the beginning, I reacted like any other father who's lost his daughter.

It's had an effect on me, a profound one but maybe not entirely in the way anyone might expect.

There are no adequate words to describe the pain of losing a child. It's not the way things are supposed to be. Kids are supposed to outlive their parents. It turns your whole world inside out, head-butts everything you think you understand about life and makes you question the reason for your own existence.

In that respect, I was no different to anybody else.

Of course, I went through the whole self-interrogation thing: Why her? She had so much to live for, so much more she could have achieved. Why not me? I'd had a life, made it to 61 and had a good time getting there. It didn't seem fair.

I remember after everyone had left the funeral, I stood there in the empty hall with both hands on her coffin, staring at her picture on the top and crying my eyes out. I'd have swapped places with her in a millisecond if I'd have been given half a chance.

I'd always been around to put things right, mend things when they went wrong.

For the first time ever, this was something Dad couldn't mend.

I'd failed her, failed as a parent.

The sadness, the grief, the sorrow, everything I was feeling in that moment… it was unbearable, beyond pain.

But none of the emotions that were running out of control inside me were about Christina. Everything I was going through, it was all about me – *my* sadness, *my* grief, *my* sorrow.

It was pure unadulterated selfishness.

Nothing needed mending because nothing had been broken.

Yes, her life among us had ended but I was feeling the pain of her loss, not what I should have been feeling for her because she'd lived and I'd helped to give her some of what she needed while she was with us.

It's a choice we all make: I could shed tears over her loss or smile through the sadness and the grief because she was still my daughter and I'd been lucky enough to have played a part in her life.

In that moment, like many of the scores of admirers, colleagues and friends who came to her funeral, I chose tears.

She had achieved her task, perhaps quicker than any of us might have liked and she'd moved on in typical Christina record time. That was something I needed to be proud of, to celebrate with her, not to go into despair over.

Maybe that was something she was already telling me in the empty hall: *Come on, Dad. Get a handle on this. It won't get you anywhere. Nothing will change. What's happened has happened. Now you need to be happy for me. You helped me get where I am and that's where I need to be.*

Perhaps this shocks you? It isn't mean to.

Perhaps I'm not explaining very well. Let me try starting from a different position.

Death is not what most people think it is.

It's not the end.

It has to be seen in context.

Of course, when Christina died, I shed tears. I felt the loss and the pain. It affected me deeply. I'm not without heart. But the only way I could deal with the trauma without the pain searing deep into my inner core and scarring it beyond recognition was to admit she was right all along and that I was wrong ever to have doubted her.

You see, Christina was adamant that she had been here many times before – and she convinced me of it time and time again, both while she was alive and in the months after her death.

We're not a religious family, not in the slightest, so don't expect the whole God and the Angels thing to follow.

Ben, our Border Collie, was the only one who greeted the Jehovahs enthusiastically. They never came back after he sank his teeth into the cuff of the lead evangelist for trying to recover a copy of The Watchtower that had been pushed under the doormat.

Decades earlier, my stint as a church organist had already quashed any prospect of me becoming religious in any recognisable format. After catching the vicar and the head chorister performing together in the vestry, I had graphic proof the clergy were just as capable of hypocrisy as the rest of the non-ecclesiastic world.

From the way some of them behaved, it was clear they believed even less in what they were preaching to their congregations than the old badgers on the back pews who lapped up their duplicity *for insurance*...in case there really was a Heaven to go to.

But when your own daughter starts recounting past lives in some detail and hours, days, weeks, or even years later, you find yourself staring at what seems like cast-iron proof that what she's told you isn't fiction or the invention of a fertile imagination, it certainly makes you think about what's in store and how this life fits into the grand scheme we're not allowed to know about yet.

It makes you realise death is not the end of the book.

It's just the end of one chapter and that one chapter has a specific purpose, sitting as it does amid other chapters that, taken as a whole, make up the real biography.

Christina's chapter with us had been written. The world had read it. She needed to move on, start the next.

She appeared to have no doubt about why she was here.

She'd chosen us as her parents because she needed certain experiences to grow. *It's what we all do,* she said. She was very matter-of-fact about it. It seemed as if she knew beyond doubt.

But this is my last time here, she told me once. *I don't need to come back.*

It was a little over a year after her death that I went to see a psychic – the one Christina and I had been to see years before. If you caught him on a day when he hadn't been on the bottle he was good, she always said. And early that Sunday morning, the morning of Christina's 32nd birthday, he was on form.

You're psychic, aren't you? he announced as I relaxed in the chair opposite his, my digital recorder running at the side of me so I didn't miss anything.

There had been tinges but I'd never really thought about it with any seriousness. We had our psychic in the family and there was no need for another.

There's an aura around you. It's very clear.

You'd make a good copper. You know instantly whether you like someone or whether you don't and your instincts aren't often wrong.

You don't tolerate fools gladly. Please or offend you'll tell people what you think.

Out of choice, you don't have many friends but you'll do anything for the ones you have and they'll always be your friends, whatever happens in life.

He'd got off to a good start. That was me to a tee.

As the session progressed, he revealed plenty of things about my mother and father. All were accurate.

But what about Christina? That's who I really wanted to hear from. Did he not see anybody else?

Your mother and father are hogging the show. All three of them are together, I know that but no one else is coming through. Maybe she is not ready. Maybe she knows you are not ready. All I see is a very bright, white light; a pure spirit; someone who has been here many times before.

Someone who has been here many times before.

How often had I heard that?

That could only be Christina.

She'd made it.

She'd achieved everything she needed to achieve here and she'd arrived. She'd won her place.

She'd won her place.

Some years earlier, shortly after the death of my father in 2013, I called Christina and at one point during the conversation, asked if she'd seen anything of him. *Yes,* came the reply. She'd been out with a friend to a restaurant and had seen him sitting at one of the tables. *He said to tell you this is your phone call, Dad. Does it mean anything to you?*

I spent the rest of our conversation fighting back tears.

Every time Father went away, even if it was only a day out to the coast with Mother, he'd call to say they'd arrived safely, or they'd returned safely. It was always short and to the point: *We're back,* he'd say or *we've arrived. This is your phone call.* And that would be it.

Father only ever called me, no one else. Christina had relayed his exact words. He was OK, and that's all I needed to know.

With such evidence that this life is just a phase in which we learn what we need to progress to the next, I cannot dwell on the sorrow I still feel because she's no longer among us.

I am sad that I will not see her for a while.

In that respect, I'm no different to any other father who loves his daughter but when I've figured out what I'm supposed to learn from this life, when I've collated the skills and the experiences I'm here to assimilate; when I've achieved what I'm meant to achieve and my turn comes, I know what's already inside me, *the real me* that tasks this body, will move silently on to collect instructions for the next chapter in its development.

And one day, maybe I will get a chance to tell her properly just how proud I am of her and congratulate her on all the achievements she kept largely under her hat.

Despite all her accomplishments, Christina seldom told me in much detail about her work after she moved to London. I knew she'd had to fight for her place among the ranks of seasoned professionals. I knew she'd been published in a good many magazines and was still broadcasting on radio. She mentioned it almost as an aside when The Sun took her on.

She'd always wanted to work for The Sun. Not many people get the chance, she told me while she was still at university. She admired the way the newspaper communicated with its readership but when she became its Health Features Editor, I found out almost by osmosis.

Sometimes, she would tell me about the features she was working on. On the odd occasion, she'd call me to ask for help or to see if I had the contacts she needed but for the most part I wasn't of much use to her.

Several times, usually through Catherine or Marie, I found out her stories had made the front page and I'd text her: *Proud Dad! Well done!*

Texts always had to be short and to the point. We seldom got to speak.

She was at work and it was intense; a relentless cycle of short deadlines and copy dates that made mine on Furniture Journal seem like a writer's holiday.

When she came up with the idea for The Sun's 'Who Cares Wins Awards', I knew it was to honour the unsung heroes of the NHS but its significance to a newspaper that I'd always thought of as being more scandal and sensationalism than soul completely missed me.

It was only after her death that I learned much about her work in London and just how well-regarded she had become.

When she was posthumously recognised as Health Editor of the Year 2018 by the British Medical Journalists Association – and then, within minutes, the announcement came that she'd won the coveted Outstanding Contribution to Health or Medical Journalism Award – it was all too much to take in.

This was my daughter – my little girl – they were applauding: *the Best of the Best* they called her. *Outstanding. An incredible talent. A formidable journalist.*

I was as stunned as I was proud.

Through her journalism she saved lives, they wrote...on the front page of <u>her</u> paper, The Sun.

Christina had somehow penetrated the hard shell of tabloid journalism and had genuinely affected the lives of her closest colleagues as much as those whose stories she told in her pages – and in her own inimitable way, she'd influenced the very nature of the paper.

She was amazing, absolutely amazing her colleagues said in a unique 15-page tribute in The Sun On-line and they unashamedly bared their souls to prove it.

Senior columnist Lynsey Hope wrote: *Christina was regularly first in to The Sun's offices and last to leave – because for her, the job was not work but a crusade. Her mission was to save and improve the lives of you, our readers and to champion the work of those who dedicate their own lives to healing others.*

It is thanks to her that last summer we launched our first Who Cares Wins health awards celebrating the NHS and its staff.

It is thanks to her that our Smiles at Christmas campaign last December raised more than £130,000 for kids with cancer with CLIC Sargent.

She also worked to raise awareness of everything from brain cancer, mental health and dementia to breast, ovarian and prostate cancer.

Truly knowledgeable about her field, she also made her colleagues healthier — once clocking that an asthmatic writer was using his inhaler incorrectly. He had been getting it wrong for decades.

She also went above and beyond when interviewing people for stories, on one occasion cleaning the house for parents who were struggling with a poorly baby.

Many of those whose concerns were reflected in the articles she wrote queued up to pay tribute. In *Proud Dad* mode, I reprint them in awe:

NHS England chief executive Simon Stevens said: *Christina was a talented, knowledgeable and dedicated journalist whose compassion and verve shone through her work. From The Sun's fantastic and moving Who Cares Wins Health Awards to her campaigning coverage of organ donation, Christina's stories jumped off the page because she put people front and centre.*

A specialist at Great Ormond Street Hospital for Children, said: *Christina told the stories of patients and their families with great sensitivity, helping to raise awareness of complex conditions. She was passionate about healthcare and that really showed in her work on Who Cares Wins.*

Sun columnist, Lorraine Kelly wrote: *Christina was such a lovely, kind-hearted woman with real compassion, who was brilliant at her job.*

I was lucky enough to work with her when she was fundamental in setting up the Who Cares Wins health awards. I know she was already looking forward and had so many plans to make it even bigger and better.

Hugh Adams, of the charity Brain Tumour Research added: *Christina became aware of our work through her friend and fellow Sun journalist Nicki Waterman, who ultimately lost her brain tumour battle.*

She wrote about the devastation of a brain tumour diagnosis and the need for more research funding. She asked questions and worked so hard to make sure her story was the best it could be. I will miss a kind, compassionate friend who made a difference.

The actress and former Liberty X singer, Michelle Heaton recalled: *I've known Christina for years, we really connected. We worked together again before Christmas when my panto cast in Newcastle visited the city's Royal Infirmary to see the children on the cancer ward. When Christina asked you to help, you didn't say no. She was warm and funny and beautiful.*

NHS Blood and Transplant, which manages organ donations for those who need them, said: *Christina was very passionate about organ donation and she always wrote sensitively about it. She worked hard in spearheading a campaign at The Sun in 2016 which saw every reader given a donor card. We are very grateful for all her work.*

Caroline Harding, of Jeans for Genes and Genetic Disorders UK commented: *Many of the 500,000 children with genetic disorders in the UK do not have a public voice. Christina's compassionate interviewing and incisive writing explained the impact of rare, complex conditions and gave these forgotten children that voice.*

By telling their stories simply and powerfully she galvanised thousands of generous Sun readers to take part in Jeans for Genes Day and to donate.

It is the mark of a life well lived that you leave the world a better place. Christina certainly achieved that.

Justin Coghlan, co-founder of men's health movement the Movember Foundation, said: *Christina was instrumental in helping us reach the millions of men across the UK, unearthing the story and telling of men going through their health journeys to educating men on early detection and the importance of staying connected.*

She had a genuine passion and dedicated an amazing amount of time. She always went above and beyond, and through her writing, she truly changed and saved the course of so many lives. The world lost an amazing, young, talented journalist. We will miss her dearly.

Photographer Stewart Williams, who went with Christina to Kenya in 2015 to see Sense International's work with deaf and blind children, remembers: *She asked me to come with her for the charming reason that, 'If I'm going to be hot, sweaty and irritable there's only one person I want to be squashed next to in the back of a car'. Still my best shoot ever.*

Kris Hellenga, Sun columnist and founder of breast-cancer awareness charity CoppaFeel! said Christina was a huge support with her column: *She had very innovative ideas and she questioned everything. I liked that about her. Above all she cared, offering kindness and compassion through some of the darker times of writing my columns. She put humans before work and because of that she helped us save lives. I only hope she was aware of the huge impact she made on many people's lives.*

Sun nutritionist, Amanda Ursell recalls Christina's impact on her daughter: *Mummy, said my little girl Coco, her eyes growing bigger by the second when she first met Christina. Is – that – Snow White?*

Funny, clever and brilliant, Christina was a dream to work for. The phone would ring pretty much day or night. 'Hello lovely. Are you busy?' would come her singing, sunny voice. 'You are? OK. Well anyway, I need a spread on ready meals. Best, worst, you know. By 4pm. Thanks. Chat later'.

She knew you wouldn't let her down. She made you believe in fairytales...and impossible deadlines.

In 2017, Christina was among a group who pedalled 187 miles across India in a week in memory of The Sun's fitness expert Nicki Waterman, who died aged 53 from a rare brain tumour in 2016. The trip raised more than £50,000 for brain tumour research.

Of this toughest of challenges, Christina said simply: *It was Nicki's wish to help others with brain tumours, something I promised her I would do.*

Sue Baker OBE, of mental health anti-stigma campaign Time To Change said: *Her work has helped to shine a light on an issue that affects millions of people. She went above and beyond to support our first ever Time to Talk Day over five years ago, when she encouraged The Sun readers to talk more about mental health and in her words, 'shatter the deafening silence surrounding mental health issues'.*

We know her articles sparked many conversations, helping those of us living with mental health problems to feel less isolated and ashamed. Christina wanted to get people talking about mental health in order to break the taboo.

I can still remember her phoning me to ask if I thought Father would mind if she mentioned him as an example in one of her articles. He was always one to put others first and if he could help anyone, whatever the circumstances, he wouldn't hesitate, so Father got his place in The Sun as well.

After her death, The Sun set up an award (in her married name) at the 'Who Cares Wins Awards' she'd masterminded. There must have been 300 people inside the British Medical Association in London that evening, maybe more. I don't think I've ever seen so many celebrities and famous faces in one place.

Prime Minister, Theresa May, opened the ceremony and Lorraine Kelly hosted the presentations. It was the ultimate *Proud Dad* moment. Christina always noticed the *Proud Dad* look. I just hope she saw it then too. I really do.

I think what took me most by surprise wasn't her achievement. I always knew she could achieve whatever she set her mind to, just like her sister. I used to tell them both *Reach for the stars because if you only reach for the moon, you'll never get off the ground.*

Christina hadn't just reached for the stars, she'd become a star.

What had side-swiped me was the fact that with stardom comes a spotlight and that's something she would have deflected to someone else immediately, without hesitation.

She even demanded her sister remove a post on Facebook wishing her a happy 30th birthday because she didn't want to draw attention to herself.

Yet, as I see it, her contribution since she joined the paper in 2011 marked a turning point in The Sun's history. At her pen, it had successfully transitioned into a newspaper with a real soul that had a worthy crusade at its core. That deserved all the recognition she got and it extended beyond her own paper.

The journalist's trade magazine Press Gazette ran a long tribute written by columnist Freddie Mayhew, in which she was described as the perfect journalist and a perfect colleague.

The perfect journalist. A perfect colleague.

My tough, professional daughter would have blushed.

The article quoted The Sun's head of features, Colin Robertson: *Christina was the perfect journalist. She really knew her stuff and could clearly and expertly explain what would often be a highly-complicated medical story. She was deeply passionate about her patch. Anyone who was at The Sun's incredibly moving Who Cares Wins awards could not have failed to have heard glowing tributes from the many brilliant nominees. She cared about each and every one of them and was desperate to have their stories told and given proper credit. Most of all, Christina was a perfect colleague and friend to so many of us on The Sun. She was smart, she was kind, she was funny and she was always there to offer a helping hand.*

The Sun's assistant editor, Sean Hamilton, said Christina's work ethic and attention to detail was remarkable. *She was always so organised and on top of things. She was able to handle anything – whether it was a weekly eight-page health pullout, a Christmas campaign requiring daily content or a one-off complicated feature.*

She often juggled all of those things at the same time. Christina constantly amazed me.

I still can't comprehend how she managed to distribute hundreds of thousands of toys to kids in December 2016...or how she raised £125,000 for kids with cancer at Christmas 2017.

The Sun's former health editor, Lynsey Hope said: *Christina made it her business to save lives, and so I feel so incredibly sad that hers has come to an end prematurely.*

Christina was incredibly invested in everything she did, her friendships, her work and her marriage. She was an incredible support to me when I went on maternity leave, looking after the health section single-handedly.

The Sun's editor-in-chief, Tony Gallagher said: *The heartfelt tributes paid to Christina by those that knew her best show just how dearly she will be missed.*

Her energy and passion for the job were evident in everything she did and she fought tirelessly for the people whose stories she told. She was a credit to the newspaper and to her profession. It is a tragedy to lose her so young.

Her ability to explain complex medical stories with utter clarity made her a formidable journalist. She brought all this to bear in masterminding The Sun's Who Cares Wins awards for NHS staff last year.

A large number of the nominees had formed strong bonds with Christina as she told their stories and they were glowing in her praise.

It came as no surprise when Fabulous magazine named Christina as one of the Women of the Year 2018 on the opening spread of the story.

Prime Minister, Boris Johnson ended the 2019 'Who Cares Wins Awards' by paying tribute to Christina for having launched the awards in 2017. I couldn't be there to hear it but it was another *Proud Dad* moment when I found out.

Me, Catherine, Marie, Lorraine (Christina's best friend) and Oli (Christina's husband) arriving at The Sun's 2018 Who Cares Wins Awards.

Theresa May asked to meet the family at the Awards ceremony in 2018.

Chapter Fifteen

The Next Chapter

If there was one thing more than anything else that got me through 2018, it was work: Furniture Journal.

Two days after Christina's death, I had to be at an exhibition in Birmingham. It started on the Sunday. People were expecting me to be there and I couldn't let them down. I had appointments and there was no one else to fall back on so I did what I always do: I focused.

I pushed everything else to one side as best I could; I set off at the crack of dawn and drove myself through a full day of stand visits, discovered a bunch of interesting new products and produced a 20-page review for the May edition from one day's work.

It was hard to keep a lid on my emotions, mask the pain in front of customers, get the job done. Very hard. There were more than a couple of awkward moments when one or other asked if I was OK.

Then on the Monday, I caught a red-eye, same-day return flight to Ireland for a factory visit to conduct an interview and take photographs for a two-page feature.

A couple of days after Christina's funeral, Olena and I drove to Nuremberg for three intensive days at the Holz-Handwerk show and in that same May edition we produced a second 20-page review.

Another trip to Ireland followed for Furniture Journal's July Silver Jubilee edition and no sooner was I back home than I was heading out again for another three-day stint at the Xylexpo exhibition in Milan – and another 20-page review.

The deadlines I'd so often cursed for taking me away from time with family had turned into my salvation and with each edition I pushed the target further and further beyond anything the magazine had achieved before.

Page numbers increased dramatically.

We cranked the print quality up to a standard only seen in the best fine-art publications.

We launched an interactive app edition so we could show videos of the machines featured in the printed edition and made it available free worldwide.

Sales figures shot up exponentially with major international advertisers booking two years ahead instead of edition-by-edition.

The magazine started winning accolades from major clients in Italy, in Germany, in Austria and beyond.

Articles and photographs I'd taken for Furniture Journal were being reprinted in other magazines around the world, some as far away as South Africa and New Zealand.

One after another, editions broke all-time company records.

Furniture Journal had ceased to be a job. It had become a one-man crusade with me as writer, editor, photographer and salesman.

But by the Christmas, with little or no time out and the pace unrelenting, I was beyond knackered.

The only thing I remember about Christmas 2018 was that I'd hit another all-time company record the week before the holiday started.

That and the absences around the Christmas dinner table.

It would have taken a good deal more than a record edition to put any of us in the festive spirit that year.

As much as work had been my distraction from the events of 2018, Ben became my salvation from work.

It was September 2017 when Ben arrived. I never wanted a dog. I'd had a Siamese cat as a pet from the age of three and adored her but the day she arrived I started sneezing and it didn't stop until the day she died at the grand old age of 15. The possibility of a repeat – however remote the chances – wasn't something I wanted to contemplate.

Besides, when the girls were younger, we'd take precious holidays a few days at a time between deadlines and head off to far flung places. If we'd had a dog, I reasoned, we wouldn't be able to go away without leaving it in kennels. That didn't seem fair. So, while the girls were growing up, we never had a pet.

All that changed after a visit from a local electrician.

Have you heard there have been more burglaries in the village? he asked, his job on the electrics finished. *It's up to seven now.*

The latest break-in was just across the field from us but I wasn't too concerned we'd be a front-line target. We had an alarm, security lights at the back, sides and front and a fancy new eight-camera CCTV system that had been installed only a couple of months earlier. It would alert us the moment anyone entered the grounds, wherever we were.

That won't do you much good, he said. *Five minutes is all it would take to get into this place.*

His explanation of how easy it would be to get past all of the systems we'd bought wasn't something any of the security experts we'd invited to supply them had thought to mention.

Now, Olena was concerned. It was a big place. She was often alone with Yuliya when I went on trips. It was a quiet village. There were no street lights and only open fields behind the house.

What could we do?

I got a dog, came the answer. *An Alsatian. Nobody will get past <u>him</u>.*

From the looks that shot between Olena and Yuliya, I had a pretty good idea what was coming next.

A couple of days later, we arrived at the Dogs' Trust in Snetterton. The girls had found two Border Collies on the internet, both about two years old, both in need of good homes.

Not that one, the rehoming specialist told us after a half-hour inquisition that covered everything from the house and garden to the time we could devote to training and our experience of collies – or lack of it. *She's a fighter and she doesn't get on with other girl dogs but Ben might be good for you. He's about two. He came from Eire. He was very underweight when we picked him up as a stray. He only arrived this week. Would you like to meet him?*

I'll never forget that first meeting when she brought Ben out to us. He came straight to me as I sat on the floor and immediately laid down and put his head on my leg. The instant he looked at me with his beautiful, big brown eyes, all my reservations melted.

He knew darned well he'd found his forever home.

For anyone who's never had a dog before, starting with a Border Collie is a bit like jumping in a Ferrari the day after you've passed your driving test. They're high-speed, high-mileage dogs, very intelligent, need to be on the go and have an innate sense of timing that's as accurate as any Swiss timepiece. And they need a job to ward off boredom.

Ben was no exception.

Long before the alarm went off in a morning, he'd bring his ball and nag until he got his first five miles of the day. Come lunchtime, a nose would push my arm repeatedly away from my keyboard so I couldn't type. That was his way of saying *Come on, it's my time now!*

Half an hour before the end of the day, he'd start again, nosing my arm until I quit work.

It wasn't always me who took him out but I was usually his starting point. He knew I'd nag for him.

Throughout 2019, Olena attended a medical conference that took her down to

London for the last weekend in every month. With Yuliya at university from the autumn, Ben and I could enjoy a boys' weekend. It didn't matter what the weather was like. It could be raining sideways, he didn't care. Some weekends we covered 50 miles or more.

It was his job to chase the ball, catch the ball, chew the ball. It was mine to find it after he'd put it down and run off to watch from a suitable vantage point. That was his way of making sure my attention stayed on him. Any lapse in concentration and another ball would be left in the long grass for the foxes and the rabbits to play with.

In an evening, we'd play games in front of the fire until one or other of us was declared the winner. It was always Ben. Then he'd roll over and sprawl out on his favourite red rug, occasionally yawning and stretching, momentarily opening a watchful eye to make sure the 'flock' that had retired to the sofa wasn't straying.

In front of the inglenook, lit only by firelight from a huge wood-burner and a couple of discreet floor lights, it was impossible not to smile.

Since his arrival, Ben had changed our lives completely.

We've found doggy restaurants so we can dine together and swapped five-star hotels for weekends away in places where he can stay with us. Gone are the days of the long-haul flights we used to book to far-flung places. Now we head for the Lake District, the Cotswolds, the moors, open countryside, fields, forests and quiet beaches.

Ben has travelled the length and breadth of Britain and is quite happy curled up on his cream leather seat behind me. Long journeys and new experiences don't faze him. He's been to France, sailed to St Martin, enjoyed fish suppers on the back of Jean-Paul's yacht and spent the night with me under the stars while Olena and Yuliya bunked down in the forward cabin.

He'd have been visiting Spain and Portugal with us this year if it hadn't been for lockdown.

The distraction he has provided from work has been more necessary than I could ever have imaged. I am as grateful to him for obliging me to take long walks in places that inspire and refresh (and for distracting me with playtime) as he probably is for having a place to call his own and the chance to enjoy home-cooked game pie and the other special doggy meals I've become adept at creating for him.

Yes, I know he's a Border Collie. But he's *my* Border Collie and he deserves the best. It's Ben I have to thank for reminding me there is more to life than just work.

Despite Ben's distraction, by the early part of 2020 I was still setting new sales records for the magazine when Covid-19 arrived in Britain – and with it came lockdown.

Suddenly, there were no factories open to visits. Planned meetings that had taken months to arrange were put on ice. Product development in the market we served all but ceased. One after another, exhibitions were cancelled or rescheduled, only to be cancelled again in the weeks that followed.

The May edition that should have contained substantial reviews of major exhibitions in Birmingham, Nuremberg and Milan slimmed down to 60 pages with the loss of both overseas shows but with the printer furloughing staff three weeks before our scheduled handover date, it was a straight choice between producing a slim edition or not publishing at all.

Not publishing was unthinkable. Production had to be brought forward and that meant burning the midnight oil again.

As always, Furniture Journal was published on time.

But in the weeks and months that followed, while the UK endured the horrors of another man-made crisis and tens of thousands suffered, we stayed at home, battened down the hatches and crossed our fingers Coronavirus wouldn't turn up on our doorstep.

I can't begin to imagine how hideous it must have been for all those on lockdown who lived umpteen floors up in a small flat, especially those who had small children. It must have been very difficult and beyond claustrophobic; a truly dreadful time. My heart goes out to all of them as much as those who suffered loss.

My good friend David, who I'd known for more than 45 years, didn't make it through the crisis. *I can't die now*, he once told me, laughing off dozens of arrhythmic attacks in his own inimitable way. *I've been fitted with a defibrillator that restarts me every time I keel over*.

It didn't stop him getting Covid-19.

We'd known each other since we were at the School of Music together and in our late teens. I couldn't even go to his funeral. Lockdown restrictions forbade it.

Olena, Yuliya and I were among the lucky ones. We lived in the country and had air to breathe. We had a big garden. And in a year that was already on track to be one of the warmest on record, we had the freedom to wander freely within the confines of our own boundaries.

And we had Ben. With him, we could walk for miles and never meet another soul.

For the first time in 30 years, lockdown meant I had no targets and no deadlines on the horizon. I could almost begin to imagine what retirement might be like.

I know it's not for everyone but that's not a prospect that fills me with dread.

I enjoy my job, I enjoy the industry I work in and I enjoy spending time with the people I've met along the way; I enjoy finding new products, photographing them and coming up with novel ways to stimulate interest in them.

There is no greater thrill for me than seeing my work in print and learning in the days and weeks after its publication that it's had a positive effect for the people and the companies I've written about. And it brings a warm glow when those with whom I work voice their appreciation.

I have been co-operating with Furniture Journal for a number of years – and co-operation it is, writes Gabriele De Col, Managing Director of the global Italian woodworking machinery giant SCM's UK company. *The quality of the finished product is always impeccable.*

Attention to detail is first class, writes Malcolm Cuthbertson, Managing Director of Weinig UK, the UK arm of a global woodworking machinery manufacturer with its manufacturing base in Germany. *Without doubt the most effective publication we use.*

The photography is imaginative and playful, writes Edward Quant, Sales Director for David Clouting, the UK distributor of Korean giant LG's decorative surfacing products. *Furniture Journal is both informative and, more importantly, an interesting and enjoyable read.*

Furniture Journal has been incredibly supportive and key in showcasing our company and new products, confirms Luke Thomson, Managing Director of Intelligent Fixings, a British company that's gone global since Furniture Journal first reported on its launch onto the world stage. *Customer feedback indicates that the magazine is an important and well-respected source for the woodworking world.*

I thank you from the bottom of my heart for the opportunity to share my fascination for the challenges of the future with you and the readers of Furniture Journal, writes Harald Klüh, a leading futurist and the effervescent Global Brand Manager at Austrian movement specialist Grass. *Our exchange was great fun...* It was. A lot of fun.

There are many more testimonials I could recount.

But the icing on the cake was when the Furniture Makers' Company, the leading light that judges and promotes quality in the furniture manufacturing sector, announced Furniture Journal's appointment as Official Media Partner for its Manufacturing Guild Mark in the autumn of 2020.

There are still ways I can be involved in all of those things, even if I take a back seat. But I've always said, if I can find someone else who can do my job better than me – someone who can take Furniture Journal to the next level – I'll happily step aside, let them take over and go find something else to do.

That doesn't mean I'm ready to be pensioned off.

I'd like the opportunity to travel more, work on my photography, put on more exhibitions and expand my coffee-table collections, maybe even put on a few photography courses for those who'd like to develop their skills. Perhaps I could be of help to Catherine with her PR work from time to time and keep my hand in, writing articles about some of the topics I've come to enjoy over the years. I've written this book during lockdown. Maybe there's another one in me. I'm not short of ideas.

But deep down inside, I've always felt there was something more important and vital that I needed to achieve: a mission; a task – something that's much more useful and worthy than the furrow I've been ploughing.

I've no idea what it is but it's a strong feeling I've had since I was quite young. Call it intuition if you like.

Maybe my destiny was to provide the supporting cast for Christina and Catherine, to provide the backdrop that enabled them to achieve great things. Christina was incredible. So is Catherine. In a few short years, she's grown her PR company to be the leading light in its sector, taken on the challenges of working with global blue-chip companies from around Europe and beyond, delivered hard-hitting marketing programmes for exhibitions, machinery, materials and components manufacturers and won the respect of an entire industry.

She's a chip of the old block – and just like me, she's done it her way.

Yes, I'm wearing my *Proud Dad* face again, I know.

Maybe whatever influence I might have had on Yuliya will see her with a Nobel prize for a great discovery in her field. It's not beyond the bounds of possibility. She's at university reading Bio Medicine, following in Olena's medical footsteps – and just like Catherine, she's ploughing her own furrow. There's been the odd *Proud Dad* moment with her, too.

But I don't think that's everything.

There's something else to follow.

Whatever it is, whatever awaits me, it's something wholesome, something worthwhile, something that will benefit others much more than me. That much I do know.

That's what I'm really looking forward to: the next chapter, wherever that takes me.